# Working Across Boundaries

Russell M. Linden

# Working Across Boundaries

## Making Collaboration Work in Government and Nonprofit Organizations

JOSSEY-BASS
A Wiley Imprint
www.josseybass.com

Published by Jossey-Bass
A Wiley Imprint
989 Market Street, San Francisco, CA 94103-1741    www.josseybass.com

Jossey-Bass books and products are available through most bookstores. To contact Jossey-Bass directly call our Customer Care Department within the U.S. at 800-956-7739, outside the U.S. at 317-572-3986 or fax 317-572-4002.

Jossey-Bass also publishes its books in a variety of electronic formats. Some content that appears in print may not be available in electronic books.

Credits are on pages 303–304.

**Library of Congress Cataloging-in-Publication Data**

Linden, Russell Matthew.
    Working across boundaries: making collaboration work in government and nonprofit organizations / Russell M. Linden.
        p. cm. —(The Jossey-Bass nonprofit and public management series)
Includes bibliographical references and index.
    ISBN 0-7879-6430-1 (alk. paper)
    1. Business networks.  2. Strategic alliances (Business)
3. Interorganizational relations.  4. Administrative agencies—Management.
5. Nonprofit organizations—Management. I. Title. II. Series.
    HD69.58 .L555   2002
    650.1'3—dc21                                               2002011933

Printed in the United States of America
FIRST EDITION
*HB Printing*   10 9 8 7 6 5

The Jossey-Bass
Nonprofit and Public Management Series

# Contents

## *Part III. Key Collaboration Issues and Tasks*

## *Resources*

# Tables, Figures, and Exhibits

## Tables

## Figures

xii    Tables, Figures, and Exhibits

## Exhibits

*To my brother, Jim. I truly value our wonderful lifelong partnership. Thanks for everything.*

# Preface

W hy do so many people find it difficult to work across boundaries? The question has intrigued me since the late 1970s. I
was director of a nonprofit agency serving the handicapped. One of
our programs provided teachers to work with parents of handicapped or at-risk infants. As the program grew, I began having conversations with other human services leaders whose agencies also
ran home-based services. Was there a way to pool our resources,
integrate our services, and greatly expand our effectiveness and
impact? Many of us thought there was. After all, the health department sent nurses into most of the homes our teachers visited. The
area's social services departments saw many of our clients. Some of
our families sent their preschoolers to Head Start. In all, more than
ten human services and educational agencies were seeing many of
the same families. It seemed obvious that we could pull together and
create an integrated program that included all relevant services.

Obvious, but not easy. We formed a steering committee and met
monthly for close to a year. Sadly, little came of the effort. Our organizations exchanged lots of information; we got to know one another
better, may have picked up some useful ideas for new funding
sources, but we found no way to do any meaningful collaboration.
Everyone seemed well-intentioned, there were no major concerns
about ego and turf, it just didn't happen. Why was that?

# The Collaboration Dilemma

I reflected on that experience several times over the next two decades, as my teaching and consulting brought me in contact with numerous managers and leaders who were trying to work across boundaries. Many of them came to the same frustrating conclusion I had reached: collaboration makes great sense in many situations, but it seems to be more the exception than the rule. It was a dilemma, one I was determined to understand and address. I call it the collaboration dilemma.

1. *The organizational environment surrounding government and nonprofit agencies today often requires collaboration.*

The challenges confronting our public and nonprofit agencies are today very complex: multiproblem families, urban sprawl and the loss of green space, drugs, low-performing schools, global warming, clogged transportation arteries, and now terrorism. These problems cut across agency and professional boundaries; addressing them requires joint effort from multiple disciplines, groups, and organizations. No single agency is formally in charge of these complex challenges, no single agency can fully address such problems by itself.

2. *Increasing numbers of public and nonprofit managers and leaders understand the need for collaboration today.*

I say this based on more than twenty years of experience leading management education programs for public agencies at the federal, state, and local levels, as well as programs for nonprofits. When I ask a class of experienced managers how many of them believe that collaboration is important to their agency's success today, 75 percent or more of the hands go up every time. And when I ask how many of them would have given the same answer five years ago, most of the hands go down. Today's enlightened leaders in both public and private sectors understand the value chains of which they are a part, and they know that most of their pressing problems can be solved by collaborative actions with others.

3. *Yet there is far more talk about collaboration than actual collaboration.*

That observation has been borne out through dozens of interviews with managers and leaders across government and in the private and nonprofit worlds as well. And that's the dilemma: the need for collaboration is clear; managers and leaders increasingly see that need; yet large numbers still work to achieve their goals by acting alone. It reminds me of the key point in a well-researched management book, *The Knowing-Doing Gap:* we have a great deal of knowledge about good management, but we don't translate that knowledge into action (Pfeffer and Sutton, 2000).

Why is that? Why are many capable, smart people not picking up on the collaboration option when most signs suggest that it would materially benefit them and their customers? That question captured my curiosity and stimulated me to start writing this book.

But that only got me started. The more I asked why many managers don't get it, the more I became inspired by those who do. Yes, it's important to understand what prevents good managers and leaders from using collaboration, because the hurdles and difficulties are real and must be anticipated. But it's more important to learn from the many who are succeeding. Their stories and lessons show the way to a powerful model of organizational performance and results. This book is about their stories, about the principles underlying their stories, and about the ways we can use those principles to transform our organizations and ourselves.

## Purpose of the Book

I wrote this book in the hope that it would inspire others to see the need for and the power of collaboration in their own context. More specifically, the purpose of this book is *to help practitioners address the hurdles to collaboration and adopt the strategies that lead to successful collaboration, in order to achieve better outcomes for their customers and communities.*

## Who Should Read the Book?

This book is primarily for practitioners. It will help the leaders and managers of our government and nonprofit organizations to appreciate collaboration's benefits, and it gives them a framework for getting started or getting unstuck. Many of these leaders would like to support collaboration because they see its potential, but they're not sure how to begin. How should they select potential partners? What kinds of projects lend themselves to collaboration, and what kinds don't? What are the most likely pitfalls, and how can they be prevented or addressed? Are there certain strategies that work consistently? This book provides answers to those and related questions.

This book is also for future managers and leaders, people now in the workforce looking to move up. As it turns out, collaboration is more common among frontline employees and their immediate supervisors than at the middle and upper management levels. That can be a major problem to the frontline professionals and technical people who do the real work in organizations. They often have to collaborate with people in other units and other organizations to get their work done, yet are frustrated when their managers don't see that need, or acknowledge the need but won't support it.

If you're in this category, I urge you to trust your instincts. You know that it is often necessary to cross boundaries in order to meet customers' needs. Collaboration *is* the smarter option much of the time, and young employees and students who will lead our organizations tomorrow need to know how to do it. If your efforts to collaborate are being stymied, don't let that diminish your desire to work across boundaries. Use the principles in this book to collaborate at your own level and demonstrate its potential. And if that's not possible, consider hiring yourself another boss.

This book is also for academics and their students. Many managers are going back to school for advanced degrees these days, and they hunger for practical courses that feature realistic problems and cases. These students aren't allergic to using theories; they're eager for practical theories that they can apply to their real-world settings. This book is written with their needs in mind. It includes a series of case studies about managers struggling to deal with familiar and difficult issues: customers with rising expectations, skeptical funding bodies that want evidence of positive results, complex challenges that no one agency can solve on its own, demands to use performance measures on outcomes that defy quantitative measurement. (The cases that formed much of the research for this book are described in Resource D.)

And academics should find the book thought provoking, because the cases reflect core issues: how to deal with multiple stakeholders who make conflicting claims on government and nonprofit agencies; how to develop a constituency for collaboration, when some stakeholders want their agency to go it alone; and how to create a norm or culture of collaboration in a political system founded on the concept of *separation*—separation of powers, of levels of government, of line and staff roles, of policymakers and policy implementers.

And to everyone who reads this book, an invitation: Make this book your own. Write in it, argue with it, note your own examples, add and delete as needed. Most important, apply the key principles and methods to your own situation, and customize it to suit yourself. In collaboration, as with so many areas, the real learning comes with doing.

## Organization of the Book

The book has three parts. The first is an overview of the topic. In Chapter One, I describe the reasons for the increasing interest in collaboration, and the many benefits that collaboration offers. I also offer a working definition of collaboration. Chapter Two includes a detailed case study of successful collaboration between a social services department and local police to deal with the victims and perpetrators of child sexual abuse. Chapter Three details the many hurdles to successful collaboration and gives examples of each. The hurdles are divided into four types: individual, organizational, societal, and systemic.

The book's second part describes a framework for making collaboration work. Chapter Four provides an overview of the framework, and illustrates the elements of that framework through a case study of information sharing in the criminal justice arena. Chapter Five describes the first level of the framework, which I call *the basics*. These are the prerequisite conditions necessary for collaboration to take root. The next four chapters describe the other key ingredients for collaborative efforts. Chapter Six is about the glue that holds most partnerships together: open and trusting relationships. Chapter Seven describes the factor most likely to overcome many of the hurdles to collaboration: high stakes. Chapter Eight offers some answers to a common question: What do we do when the other parties don't seem interested in collaborating? Those who have no formal authority to get others to the table need to use the art of influence and develop a constituency for collaboration. This chapter provides several strategies for doing so. Chapter Nine analyzes collaborative leadership. It turns out that collaborative leaders differ in some fundamental ways from traditional notions of effective leaders. This chapter includes a case study of collaboration in the human services field, then it describes four qualities that are common to most collaborative leaders, and offers some tips that leaders can use to improve their collaborative skills.

The book's third part addresses several leadership issues regarding collaboration. Chapter Ten discusses the question of timing: What are the most common phases in collaborative efforts, and what are the leadership tasks for each phase? In Chapter Eleven I describe several factors that can help collaboratives succeed, such as maintaining continuity among the principals, playing to each party's strengths, obtaining flexible resources, and using performance measures prudently. Chapter Twelve deals with the specific issues involved in collaborating within a single organization, describing the leadership skills and approaches required to foster collaboration across internal organizational boundaries. Finally, Chapter Thirteen addresses the question of scaling up collaborative operations and developing a culture of collaboration. It's possible to succeed in specific collaborative projects, and some persistent leaders know how to foster collaboration on their watch. But it takes additional effort to foster the conditions that invite and reward collaborative behavior on an ongoing basis, one that doesn't depend on strong, committed leaders. Only when we develop a collaborative culture in our organizations will we be able to reap the benefits of collaboration on a consistent and meaningful basis.

## Walls or Bridges? Why This Book Matters to Me

> Something there is that doesn't love a wall . . .

So wrote Robert Frost in his famous poem "Mending Wall" (Untermeyer, 1919, pp. 81–83). He doesn't see the need for the wall as his apple orchard isn't a threat to his neighbor's pine trees. He thinks the wall is an artificial thing, a useless barrier putting more distance between him and his neighbor.

> Before I built a wall I'd ask to know
> What I was walling in or walling out,
> And to whom I was like to give offense.

But no, his neighbor strongly disagrees, telling him:

> Good fences make good neighbors.

It's a phrase the neighbor learned from his father; he likes it so much that he repeats it at the end of the poem. But is that true? Do good fences, in fact, make for good neighbors?

Historians, philosophers, sociologists—as well as poets—have long noted mankind's predisposition to create walls. We build our power and sense of esteem by separating ourselves from others, by defining ourselves as different from and better than "the other." Nation states do this, as do religions, ethnic and racial groups, and social clubs. Our college campuses today are becoming balkanized;

it seems every group has its own eating area, study space, even its own housing. And, as we learned to our horror on September 11, 2001, some fanatics attract thousands of ardent followers by demonizing countries that follow principles different from their own.

We also practice this low art of division in our organizations. You can get a quick chuckle around most any office water fountain or copy machine by pointing out the latest "inane ruling" issued by the legal office, the timidity of senior management, or the micromanagement of the inspector general or auditor's office. We know all too well how to build walls, how to define those on the other side as inferior. Human beings seem predisposed to building walls and erecting fences.

Can we do as well at creating bridges? I believe that we not only can, we must. Why? Because the most pressing challenges facing our country—drugs and crime, disintegrating families, political gridlock, environmental threats, health care costs, ongoing racial tensions, can only be managed if multiple organizations and professions work collaboratively toward solutions. These problems are too huge, too complex, and much too important for any one agency to handle alone. Working across boundaries, many leaders are proving that collaborative solutions to these and other problems are both possible and powerful.

This book offers multiple examples of people using certain methods and principles to build bridges and work across boundaries to accomplish together what they can't achieve on their own. Their stories demonstrate that this is surely hard work. More important, they provide us with the framework, methods, and confidence to get on with the task. Their successes include stunning improvements in performance and results. And their voices reflect an enthusiasm, joy, and passion for their work. I hope this book will make their passion contagious.

*August 2002*                                    Russell M. Linden
                                              *Charlottesville, Virginia*
                                              *Russlinden@earthlink.net*

# Acknowledgments

While working on this book I've been blessed in receiving help, useful criticism, and wonderful insights and information from many people who have been extraordinarily generous in sharing time and ideas to help create this book. I'm very grateful for their stories, reactions to my ideas, and enthusiasm. My sincere appreciation goes to Gary Anderson, Shirley Arico, Saphira Baker, Ray Batvinis, Connie Bawcum, Bob Behn, Kay Bokowy, Debbie Brocht, Judy Brown, Donna Bryant, Jacqueline Bryant, Ray Bryant, Joyce Casey, Jim Chrisinger, Jim Cohen, Jay Coles, Rich Collins, Bennett Connelly, Elizabeth Conner, Robert "Buz" Cox, Connie Craig, Kris Debye, Myrna Deckert, Brian Demorrow, Tom Downs, Paul Fardink, Len Faulk, Nancy Fleetwood, Tom Forman, Otto Friesen, Matt Gallagher, Charles F. Gerhards, Barbara Glass, Barbara Gradet, Bill Gray, Dick Gregg, Allen Hard, Tom Henderson, Doug Henton, Con Hogan, Pat Hogan, Martin Horn, Scott Johnson, Susan Johnson, Debbie Johnston, Ed Jones, Cal Joyner, John Kirwan Keith, Tom Kennedy, Phil Lee, Bill Leighty, Leonard Lohman, Bill Lucy, Pam McAffee, Amalia Mendoza, Shelley Metzenbaum, Frank Miller, Kathy Miller, John Newell, Steve Nock, Dennis Owens, John Palensky, Jim Pipkin, Bill Potapchuk, Dave Radloff, Tim Reeves, Mark Reisler, Nick Ricciuti, Terry Roberts, Chuck Robinson, Jacqueline Rogers, Lorraine Rogstad, Linda Rosenberg, Terri Savidge, Lisa Schumacher, Everett Seastrum, Mary Beth Shaw,

Chuck Short, Donna Silverberg, Arianne Spaccarelli, Donnie Sparks, Gary Steinberg, Patti Stevens, Mark Thomas, Joe Thompson, Judy Tillman, Mark Vidor, Gordon Walker, Jim Webb, Joe Wienand, Marguerite Wilbur, Mich Wilkinson, Linda Winner, and Elder Witt.

My special thanks also goes to a group of colleagues who took the time to read and critique an earlier draft of this book, and whose reactions, criticisms, and suggestions challenged and helped me in innumerable ways. Their enthusiasm and tough questions continually stimulated me to think harder and learn more, and the book is far stronger for their efforts. My deep appreciation goes to Bebe Adolph, Frank Domurad, Scott Elliott, Peter A. Harkness, Alec Horniman, Mike Kaplan, Terry Newell, Bob O'Neill, David Osborne, Joey Rodger, John Schroll, and Steve Schwartz. And special thanks also goes to my editor, Dorothy Hearst, who has a delightful and effective way of offering astute observations while allowing the book to remain my own.

—R.M.L.

# The Author

*Russell M. Linden* is a management educator who specializes in organizational learning, performance, and change. He teaches at the Federal Executive Institute, the University of Virginia, the University of Maryland, and the Brookings Institution. His clients have included the National Geographic Society; the U.S. Departments of State, Treasury, and Education; the National Institutes of Health; various intelligence and military agencies; the government of the Cayman Islands; two state attorneys general; and more than five dozen nonprofit, state, and local government agencies. He has also managed in the human services field. He is the author of three other books—one of which, *Seamless Government,* was translated into Chinese. He lives in Charlottesville, Virginia, with his wife and two children.

# Working Across Boundaries

# Part I

## Working Across Boundaries

# 1

# Why Collaborate? And Why Now?

*We are just at the beginning of an era of essential
partnerships, alliances, and coalitions. We are learning
to build community beyond the walls of the organization, with the same kind of initiative and energy we
have used in building the organization within the walls.*
                                                    *Frances Hesselbein*

The future usually arrives before we notice it. If we pause and
reflect for a moment (which is certainly not the norm in this
multitasking, wired, 24/7 world of ours), one element of our organizations' futures comes into view: Managers, leaders, and frontline staff spend much of their time in groups made up of people from
other organizations. Those groups plan, operate, and evaluate joint
programs and projects. The groups have no one leader—but an
abundance of leadership. Their initiatives are managed by "goals
managers." The member organizations are held accountable *as a group*
by funders and other stakeholders. These groups have "relationship
managers" who are responsible for supporting and monitoring the
individual and organizational relationships involved. Some of the parties have dual appointments; they work for two or more member organizations of the coalition. External constituents help monitor and
measure results, and are informal members of the core group. Trust is
high, boundaries are fluid, there's a sense of excitement and passion.

## We're Changing the Focus of Organizational Change: From "Within" . . .

During the 1980s and much of the 1990s, leaders and managers around the country worked hard to make fundamental changes within their organizations. The key word in that sentence is *within*. Inspired by books like *In Search of Excellence* (Peters and Waterman, 1982), *Reinventing Government* (Osborne and Gaebler, 1992), *Reengineering the Corporation* (Hammer and Champy, 1993), and *Built to Last* (Collins and Porras, 1994), public and private sector leaders spent countless hours learning to reengineer processes, develop self-managing teams, adopt six sigma methods, flatten hierarchies, use just-in-time and lean manufacturing principles, empower workers, and adopt other changes to better serve their customers and communities. The efforts often led to major improvements in performance. The primary focus of change was internal, and that was an appropriate place for most organizations to deal with their radically changing environment.

## . . . to "Between"

In the first decade of the twenty-first century, the focus of many organizational change efforts is *between*—between organizations and their partners, be they suppliers and vendors, customers, or other organizations producing similar products and services. As the scenario at the start of this chapter suggests, we're living in a networked, organic world, and we're starting to understand the new skills, roles, and concepts needed to succeed on this different and dynamic playing field. There are signs of this shift all around us:

• On August 27, 2001, two huge competitors, the U.S. Postal Service and Federal Express, began a strategic alliance under which USPS delivers many FedEx packages to homes across the nation, and uses FedEx's air transportation network to move first class, Priority, and Express Mail around the world (Associated Press, 2001).

- In April 2000, then-Wisconsin Governor Tommy Thompson launched the Governor's Blue-Ribbon Commission on State-Local Partnerships for the Twenty-First Century. He charged the commission to come up with bold, even radical solutions to the problems and tensions that existed in Wisconsin's state-local relations. The commission responded with what it terms a strategy for innovative partnerships that could become a national model. One of its major recommendations: redistribute a percentage of state sales tax revenues to local governments that collaborate, and reduce funding to those that don't. You can follow this effort online, at http://www.lafollette.wisc.edu/reform.
- On January 25, 2001, about a hundred representatives from biotechnology firms in Maryland and nearby states met with military scientists to encourage research and development partnerships between industry and the army. It was sponsored by Tedco, a nonprofit organization formed to foster collaboration between state government labs and technology firms (Chea, 2001, p. E5).
- The majority of states are participating in the Streamlined Sales Tax Project, an effort to simplify and standardize sales tax administration, making it easier to manage for both vendors and states. Currently, each state has its own set of definitions, rebate procedures, and methods for handling bad debts. National vendors must learn fifty different state tax rates, processes, and rules. The Sales Tax Initiative is seeking voluntary compliance by all states rather than risk the possibility of federal legislation and regulation. For more, check the initiative's Web site, http://www.geocities.com/streamlined2000.

What's going on here? We're seeing a significant interest in efforts to collaborate across boundaries. In the natural resources area, federal, state, and local governments are collaborating to care for public lands that can only be managed effectively through an integrated effort. Growing numbers of nonprofit agencies are learning to collaborate with corporations, not in the traditional manner of seeking grants but rather by offering some of their social assets for the training, technology, and funds that companies are willing to spend in exchange for those assets. And CEOs of Detroit's Big Three automakers now meet regularly to share information and ideas. In the past, such sharing was tantamount to corporate treason. The same kind of sharing goes on in the high-tech industry, where companies like IBM and Apple fiercely compete in certain markets even as they collaborate on the designs of new products.

What's going on is that many public and nonprofit agencies are placing more emphasis on collaboration than they did in recent decades. Despite the many hurdles, managers and leaders are learning to work across boundaries to form successful alliances and coalitions. Their goal isn't collaboration for its own sake; this isn't some New Age management trend about to find its way into *Dilbert* cartoons. Rather, their goal lies at the heart of their organization's mission: they are *working across boundaries to deliver better service, value, and outcomes for customers, stakeholders, and communities*. That's the ultimate purpose of any worthwhile collaborative effort. And that is what this book is all about.

## Collaboration: A Definition

I've started to discuss the great interest in collaboration today. But the word itself needs to be defined. It turns out that *collaboration* means many different things to different people. Indeed, one of the challenges to effective collaboration comes from misunderstandings about its meaning. To some, it suggests polite cooperation. To others, it includes everything from shared data to joint operations. To a labor union representative, however, it means getting too cozy with management. And to a Holocaust survivor it conjures up horrific images of local citizens cooperating with the Nazis.

For me, the essence of collaboration is suggested by the word itself. Collaboration is about *co-labor*, about *joint effort and ownership*. The end result isn't mine or yours, it's ours. My working definition of collaboration (and I invite you to develop your own), is as follows:

> Collaboration occurs when people from different organizations (or units within one organization) produce something together through joint effort, resources, and decision making, and share ownership of the final product or service.

Notice that the focus is on producing (or implementing) something. A different type of collaboration occurs when various groups with different interests try to work together to formulate a policy or resolve an issue (such efforts often take place in the environmental, land use, and natural resources arenas). These are usually ad hoc initiatives, in which the parties try to use alternative dispute resolution methods (for more, see Snow, 1999).

## Why the Increasing Interest in Collaboration?

What's causing this high level of interest in collaboration? As with most social and organizational changes, there are several interconnected reasons. Exhibit 1.1 outlines the benefits to be gained.

Organizations often collaborate for the most pragmatic of reasons, to achieve cost savings through economies of scale. The Service First alliance between the Forest Service and Bureau of Land

**Exhibit 1.1. Collaboration Benefits.**

- Better use of scarce resources; cost savings
- Ability to create something that you can't create on your own
- Higher quality, more integrated product or service for the end users
- Potential for organizational and individual learning
- Better ability to achieve important outcomes

Management that began in the early 1990s is an excellent example. Today, people describe Service First in very lofty terms—synergistic, improved service to customers, enlightened stewardship of the land—and it is all of those things. But it began as an exercise in survival, when some managers in central Oregon and southern Colorado were struggling to meet increasing demands with dwindling budgets. They decided their only option was to share resources between the two agencies.

The second benefit is a fundamental principle for would-be collaborators. It makes sense to collaborate if it allows you to create something you can't make on your own. As veteran consultant Allen Hard puts it, "If you can do it on your own, don't collaborate! Collaborating is tough; if there's any other way to accomplish the task, do it yourself" (personal communication). Chapter Three will cover the many hurdles to successful collaboration. For now, suffice to say that collaboration isn't easy, but it does enable organizations to create products and services they can't produce independently.

Collaboration also tends to produce a more integrated service or product to the end user. When a social worker visits a family on Monday to discuss allegations of abuse, a health department nurse comes on Tuesday to discuss sexually transmitted diseases, a community action agency staffer shows up the next day to bring the parent to a job training center, and a school counselor calls by week's end to discuss one of the kids' truancy problem, that family is receiving many services. The question is, are those services integrated? If the well-intentioned human service workers don't collaborate, who deals with the entire family? Who ensures the family isn't receiving contradictory advice?

The fourth benefit has to do with organizational and individual learning, which is vital in today's environment. Charles Paulk, chief information officer of Accenture Consulting, says, "When one of our consultants shows up, the client should get the best of the firm, not just the best of that consultant" (Stewart, 1995, p. 209). Paulk is talking about customers' expectation of getting what they need quickly, easily, in one stop. They're not willing to be passed around from employee to employee, trying in vain to find one with a complete answer.

That's great for the customer, but how does the organization provide such seamless service? It requires continual learning by everyone in the organization, so that when one person gets smarter, everyone can get smarter. And continual learning occurs only in an organizational culture that encourages sharing, not hoarding, of information and knowledge. As Peter Drucker predicted in 1968, we are in an age of knowledge workers and knowledge work, and success in such times requires that we share knowledge easily.

Finally, collaboration is worthwhile only if it passes this critical test: Does it help the organization better achieve the outcomes (not outputs, *outcomes*) that it is in business to achieve: cleaner air, more kids ready to learn when they start school, roads in better condition? I'll describe many impressive examples that illustrate how collaboration often meets this challenge in such diverse areas as law enforcement, services for the aging, regional economic development and planning, highway maintenance, human services, university fundraising, environmental cleanup, financial services, and natural resources.

## And Why Now?

The many benefits of collaboration have always been there. Why are so many organizations interested in collaboration today? What's going on that is increasing the emphasis on working across boundaries? I believe the most important factors driving collaboration today are the complexity of the major challenges facing our society, the blurring of many organizational boundaries, the networked nature of our organizational world as it moves from mechanistic models to more organic ones, the increasing diffusion of authority over the major issues we face (a "nobody's-in-charge" world), the rapid advances in technology, and a public unwilling to accept—and fund—poor performance.

**Complexity of the Challenges**

Pick an important public issue or challenge, one that really concerns you. Education? Transportation? Terrorism? The environment and global warming? Health care? Each is important to tens of millions of citizens, and each is exceedingly complex. By *complex* I mean three things. First, we often lack a consensus on the goals. Take schools: some people want schools to prepare kids for work. Others believe the goal is to help them master certain core knowledge. Still others want schools to promote the society's mainstream values, or to prepare kids for a diverse society. The more goals we give to schools, the more complex their task.

Next, we frequently lack agreement on (or understanding of) the best means to our ends. In terms of transportation, say we could agree that an overriding goal is to help people get where they need to go, with minimal negative impact on the environment. How would you achieve that? Options include building more roads (though some communities have discarded that choice, believing that additional roads only *add* to the congestion problem). Or through mass transit. Or by designing urban and suburban areas differently, or changing lifestyles and driving less. In the late 1950s we had a consensus on the means for improving transportation: we built more freeways. Well, "build it and they will come" (to quote *Field of Dreams*). We built them, people and their vehicles came; today there's no consensus on the best means for improving transportation.

A third source adding to complexity is the growing number of specialists and active stakeholders of a given issue. Urban development is a prime example. In the 1950s, getting a new development approved was far less complex than it is today. Developers often brought their proposals and site plans to planning department staff, appeared at planning commission meetings, met with key officials, and got a decision in relatively short order. Today they must consult with the neighborhood residents who will be affected, the growing number of utility companies, neighboring governments (it's required to consult with them in some states) and different levels of government (state, federal), water quality and transportation experts, archeologists in some instances, landscape architects, and others. The need to touch base with so many entities is sometimes politically driven, sometimes required by regulation, and often driven by liability requirements. And, as with the problem of multiple goals, having large numbers of stakeholders means that every option involves a series of trade-offs. And it greatly adds to complexity.

So what? Why does complexity matter? It matters because of this:

> The most important expectations citizens have of public and nonprofit agencies are to solve complex, cross-cutting issues, but such issues can only be dealt with through collaboration across agency boundaries.

Our most pressing problems, like crime and pollution, don't honor organizational or geographic boundaries. The pressure to solve complex problems is forcing us to seek collaborative solutions.

### The Blurring of Boundaries

"Wherever we look the walls are coming down. The old barriers are fading." So writes Frances Hesselbein of the Drucker Foundation (Hesselbein, Goldsmith, and Somerville, 1999, p. 6). The walls and lines separating organizations from one another, separating public from private sector, separating agencies from their customers and clients, are certainly blurring—if not coming down altogether. This is one of the most powerful and fascinating stories of our new organizational society. It's happening in a wide variety of settings. And when such blurring occurs, it creates a need for collaboration. A few examples of blurred boundaries and collapsing walls:

*Blurring of Boundaries Separating Organizations and Their Competitors*

When Wally Stettinius, former CEO of Byrd Press in Richmond, Virginia, was conducting workshops in the 1980s on innovations in printing *and invited his competitors to attend,* he seemed to be breaking the rules. But the rules have changed; we're now in a world of *co-opetition*, in which competitors sometimes cooperate with each other. Stettinius argued that his real competition didn't come from other printers; no, it came from other types of media (network TV, cable, and now the Internet) that competed for the attention of potential magazine readers.

### Blurring of Boundaries Separating the Public, Corporate, and Nonprofit Sectors

In this age of contracting out, privatizing, and devolution of services from federal to state, local, and nonprofit agencies, it's often not clear where the public sector ends and the private one begins. In Maine, the Occupational Safety and Health Administration (OSHA) has transformed itself. Selected Maine employers are given the option of doing self-inspections on their own premises, using their own employees to prevent, find, and remove health and safety hazards. And the OSHA office's inspectors act more like coaches and advisers to the private firms, helping them understand OSHA's standards and providing them with information on best practices. The firms are responsible for cleaning up their work sites.

The results have been impressive. In two years these firms found five times the number of hazards on their premises that OSHA inspectors had found in thousands of workplaces around the state during the preceding eight years. Moreover, the participating firms corrected 70 percent of those hazards quickly, and 65 percent of them had significant reductions in work-related illnesses and injuries. In relationships like this, where does "public" end and "private" begin?

### The Move from Mechanistic to Horizontal and Networked Structures

The Orpheus Chamber Orchestra is the only orchestra in the world that plays without a conductor. Founded in 1972, it has twenty-six musicians who are passionate about practicing and playing beautiful music in a democratic fashion, and its many international awards attest to its success. A core group of musicians is nominated to plan a given concert, and that leadership rotates among several musicians. One of the Orpheus violinists notes that when she played in an orchestra with a conductor, she had to cut her bangs so that she could look up. She doesn't do that now; with Orpheus, it's all about peripheral vision.

Orpheus is a good metaphor for the emerging organizational world. No, organizations aren't all going to become democracies by any means, but many are moving toward a more horizontal style of management in which leadership is shared and decisions are often made on the basis of expertise rather than position.

Public administration giant Harlan Cleveland predicted this transformation in 1972: "The organizations that get things done will no longer be hierarchical pyramids. . . . They will be systems—interlaced webs of tension in which control is loose, power diffused" (Cleveland, 1972, p. 13). It's taken four decades for most of us to understand and start acting on Cleveland's prediction. We have little choice today; the new economy is forcing us to change.

The new economy places a premium on speed, agility, responsiveness. Customers today demand what I call the 3 C's—they want *control* over the product or service (that's one reason why e-commerce is so popular), they want multiple *choices*, and they want those choices *customized* to their own preferences. Old-line hierarchies can't satisfy these demands.

A symbol for organizations today needs to include customers and other stakeholders, suppliers and vendors, formal and informal partners. The traditional pyramid that usually portrays organizations is internally oriented; customers, partners, and other stakeholders are rarely depicted. But few important things get done wholly by one agency anymore. A rendering of today's interconnected organization might resemble a cell swimming in its environment, as shown in Figure 1.1.

**Figure 1.1. Organizing for a Networked Age.**

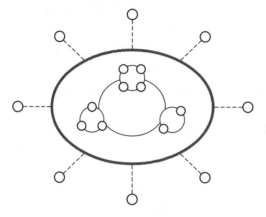

Notes:

1. Outer circles represent customers, special interest groups, unions, media, citizens, vendors, and other agencies and stakeholders.

2. Inside circles are organizational units (divisions, departments, and so on); those with related missions are shown as connected.

The figure is meant to show permeable boundaries and multiple connections. The internal and external units are connected by a web of collaborative relationships and by the information that flows between them. The boundaries are permeable to allow a free flow of information while maintaining the organization's identity.

## A "Nobody in Charge" World

As Don Kettl writes, "From Medicare to Medicaid, environmental planning to transportation policy, the federal government shares responsibility with state and local governments and with for-profit and nonprofit organizations. . . . The result is an extended chain of implementation in which no one is fully in charge of everything" (2001, p. 25).

Most managers can relate to Kettl's statement. The networked structures described here often emerge because no one person or entity can deal effectively with important societal issues. But this "nobody in charge" world is hardly new: "I do not rule Russia," Czar Nicholas once said in a moment of great frustration. "Ten thousand clerks do!" (quoted in Cleveland, 1972, p. 33). Czar Nicholas faced the same reality, so what's new? What's new, or different, is that the world is much more interconnected now than in the past. Technological advancements, improvements in transportation, the rise of an information age, the lowering of trade barriers—these and other factors create a world in which we all feel the consequences of actions that occur elsewhere very quickly and strongly. Fareed Zakaria, editor of *Newsweek International,* calls this the "CNN effect"; events in one place are immediately known and felt worldwide (Zakaria, 2001a).

The implications of this "nobody in charge" environment are clear. To deal with the critical issues of urban sprawl, to work with multiple constituencies who care passionately about our public schools, or, since September 11, 2001, to get our law enforcement and intelligence agencies to work together and share information, leaders need to enhance their skills at collaboration.

**Technological Advances**

Another factor driving collaboration today is the revolution in information technology. If you have children you understand this well. My kids Becca and Josh don't need a sermon from their dad about the benefits of sharing, at least not when one of them is on the computer. The generation now coming of age, sometimes dubbed Generation D (for *digital*), collaborates and shares information as a matter of course. Whether it's sharing music files through Napster or its successors, sharing ideas for a group project, or gossiping via instant messaging, collaborating for many of these kids is a no-brainer.

Author Tom McGehee puts it well: "People will soon be expected to work in more collaborative ways because collaborative behavior is the only way to maximize the value of these sophisticated enterprise-wide information systems. . . . We are moving from a work culture in which hoarding information is a source of power to a work culture in which hoarding information is impossible (and useless)" (2001, pp. 48–49).

## A Public Unwilling to Accept and Fund Poor Performance

When Congress passed the Government Performance and Results Act (GPRA) in 1993, it was responding to a public that is demanding more from its government. It's no longer enough for public agencies or nonprofits to publish data concerning inputs and outputs—number of police department arrests, number of kids enrolled in school. Today the public demands to know whether the streets are safer, whether those kids are reading at age-appropriate levels. GPRA reflected a revolution in societal expectations of organizations that focus on public concerns. We expect these agencies to be accountable for *outcomes*—results.

And that's a recent phenomenon. When I directed a nonprofit organization that served handicapped people and their families back in the 1970s, I simply had to show an increasing demand for my nonprofit's programs in order to justify a budget increase from its funding agencies. If ten more adults wanted to live in its group homes, if fifteen more families with delayed infants needed its infant stimulation service, my staff and I were confident that more money would flow in (and it usually did). But what about results? Were the adults becoming more self-sufficient? Were the infants developing faster once the nonprofit's teachers started to work with their parents? I used to wonder why nobody asked those questions.

Today that's changing. Human services leaders, as well as university presidents, medical providers, environmental protection administrators, and most other professionals, are being pressed to document results—not just numbers in and out. When you're accountable for real results, and the issue is complex, the best way to achieve them is often through collaboration with other professionals.

Some United Way boards now encourage or require active collaboration among the recipients of the funds. At the federal government level, several laws covering mental health, early intervention, workforce development, and rehabilitation services require collaboration by grant recipients. Minnesota is a leader in pushing for collaboration at the state and local level; it has encouraged collaboration in the human services field since the late 1980s. In 1989 the Minnesota legislature passed the Comprehensive Children's Mental Health Act, which asked communities to establish local coordinating councils to coordinate services from child-serving agencies. Then in the 1990s, two laws were passed that went further than coordination, encouraging system integration through intensive collaboration. Many human services professionals are behaving in more collaborative ways because of these laws, and children and families are benefiting.

## Some Personal Assumptions

Finally, a statement about my own beliefs concerning collaboration. I began this research with no preconceived notions of what I'd find, except the sense that collaboration is both difficult and of increasing importance in the public and nonprofit worlds. Through dozens of interviews and observations, however, I began to form some assumptions about this topic. I make them explicit here so that you can examine them as you read the book and determine for yourself if they appear valid.

- Collaboration can provide impressive, even extraordinary results. It's often the best way to deal with complex challenges. But it isn't the only way, and it isn't for everyone.

- Effective collaboration requires careful attention to the process being used. However, an obsession with process can sap the parties' energies and reduce chances for concrete results. My bias is for action.

- "You know more than you think you know" (Spock, 1945, p. 3). That is the opening line in Dr. Benjamin Spock's most famous book. Spock was urging new

parents to trust their own common sense, and empowered millions of them to do so. I encourage you
to do the same concerning your instincts about collaboration. Reflect on your experience, consider the
key factors cited in this book, and use your own best
judgment.

- The organizational barriers and hurdles to collaboration are large. Larger still are the barriers *in our
  minds*—fear of loss, the need for autonomy and control,
  hierarchical thinking, and the like. Learning to think
  in more collaborative ways can provide some of the
  biggest benefits of all.

---

Collaboration is a riddle. It's as old as our species, yet remains a mys-
tery to many. But as we enter a networked age that requires and
rewards collaboration, leaders and managers no longer have a real
choice. When they learn the lessons from those who are succeeding at collaboration (as well as those who are struggling), they and
their organizations benefit greatly. If they don't develop the ability
to collaborate, they risk becoming irrelevant or worse.

Learning to collaborate is an exciting, challenging, difficult,
sometimes scary yet extraordinarily rewarding journey. As with most
journeys, it's easiest to learn from concrete examples. The next
chapter offers one, an alliance involving social workers and police
officers who are collaborating around the issue of child sexual abuse.

**2**

# One Example of Collaboration
# That Makes a Difference

*Police are paramilitary, social services is looser, and
these two types of organizations collide.*
> Police sergeant in the Baltimore County
> Child Advocacy Center

*It helps when one of our supervisors reminds us that
we're here for the kids.*
> Social worker in the Baltimore County
> Child Advocacy Center

Take the discussion out of the abstract and put it in concrete
terms: What difference does collaboration make for those who
receive certain services? For the recipients' families? For those providing the services? For others in the community who would like to
help? This chapter presents one successful example of collaboration
across two very different settings.

## Dealing with Sexual Abuse of Children

The crime is the lowest of the low—sexual abuse of a child. In
prison, such perpetrators are at the bottom of the hierarchy; other
prisoners view them with disgust. The victims' experiences are horrific enough, and the last thing such children need is to be put
through a cold, bureaucratic process by the investigating authorities.

Many communities are taking steps to make the investigation process easier on the child, and to improve the chances of successful treatment for the victims and the perpetrators. One of the most promising approaches is called the Child Advocacy Center (CAC) model, which brings social workers, police detectives, and health department staff together in one location, providing an integrated approach to children who are victims of sexual abuse.

In the CAC model, there's no need for repeated interviews covering the same information, no parade of strangers asking children the most intimate questions about their abusive experiences. The police and social work professionals do joint interviews with the kids in a child-friendly atmosphere; they work together to identify the suspected perpetrators, they share information and engage in joint training. It's an excellent model that is spreading around the country. And it requires a high degree of collaboration among professionals from extraordinarily different cultures and backgrounds, as the Baltimore CAC example demonstrates.

## The Baltimore CAC

"People drive things, not ideas," states Mark Vidor, assistant director of the Baltimore County Department of Social Services. "In 1983 we hired Kris Debye, a very talented social worker who was extremely interested in the child advocacy center model. She spearheaded the effort to start our CAC. The model is simple to understand—you co-locate police, social workers, and health professionals, provide space for the state attorney's office, and they work together to identify child sexual abuse (and sometimes physical abuse) problems."

A Maryland law passed in 1985 mandated written agreements among police, social services, state attorney's office, and health department officials for the coordination and joint investigations of child sexual abuse cases. "Before that law, relations were strained between our two departments," Debye recalls. "We signed an agreement with the police in 1985 to improve communications on child sexual abuse cases, and we started working together better.

"Then in 1988 we learned of a federal grant to establish child advocacy centers. The grant required co-location of services. I can tell you, we wouldn't have been able to try co-location if we hadn't already been meeting with the police and talking together. The police captain running the family crimes unit liked the idea of co-locating our services and he sold the chief on the idea. That was critical. But relationships between the two departments still had a long way to go. We approached the state attorney's office (which is involved with child sexual abuse cases) about the co-location idea, and they were very supportive. That support proved important, because the state attorney had solid relationships with the police department.

"We talked with the health department leaders, told them we might apply for a grant to pay for a doctor's salary, and asked if they would hire the doctor as part of their staff (if we got the grant). They agreed, and also contributed a health department nurse to the team. In this way, the health department would cover the medical liability insurance as well. We had the support of each agency's director, and that was a key." The agencies received the grant, social services offered space in one of its buildings, and after several months of planning, clarifying roles, establishing shared goals, deciding funding issues, and working out the procedures, the new center opened its doors in June 1989.

### How the Child Advocacy Center Model Works

The Child Advocacy Center Model (see Exhibit 2.1) allows different professionals to share their insights, information, and hunches in a way that helps everyone involved. "The social worker and police do joint interviews when they get a report of sexual child abuse," Vidor explains. "The social worker usually takes the lead when interviewing the kid, and the police generally lead when they

**Exhibit 2.1. The Child Advocacy Center Model.**

- Co-location of services
- Child-friendly place (police not in uniforms, interviewing and waiting rooms designed for kids)
- Joint interviews, so victims don't have to keep repeating their horrific stories

meet the suspected offender. Our social workers can provide preventive services and treatment to both victims and offenders, and they place abused kids in foster care if need be. The police determine if there is enough concrete evidence on the alleged perpetrator to recommend that the state attorney try him for child abuse and determine the punishment if he's guilty. It's a very good model, but it's filled with tensions."

### Working Across Very Different Organizational Cultures

Kathy Miller is a police sergeant in charge of the sexual abuse unit. She says collaborating with social workers is a mutual challenge because of the differences between the two organizational cultures, summarized in Exhibit 2.2.

"Police are paramilitary, social services is looser, and these two different types of organizations collide sometimes," Miller says. "Our cops call the social workers 'tofu eaters'! They see them as overly focused on the victim's feelings. See, our cops are trained to do law enforcement. They don't get trained in dealing with relationships— they don't think they have *time* for that. They're moving fast out there, they have to track down the suspect, get the facts on him, and to our cops it's a black-and-white world. Either he did it, or he didn't.

"Social workers are from a different world. They're trained to connect with people, to form relationships, to identify with feelings, and to see the world from the client's point of view. So the social

**Exhibit 2.2. Two Different Cultures.**

| Police | Social Workers |
|---|---|
| **View of Other** | |
| Social workers are too focused on victim's feelings; they're soft-hearted liberals | Police are in a black-and-white world; they just want the facts |
| **Training** | |
| Law enforcement; separate self from others' feelings | Interpersonal skills; tune into their feelings |
| **Method** | |
| Don't trust, be wary, stay factual, get evidence, don't get taken in | Form relationships, understand client's point of view, connect |
| **Pecking Order** | |
| See themselves as higher up the food chain | Feel they must prove themselves (even though they tend to have more formal education) |
| **Joining the CAC** | |
| Most are assigned; it's not seen as career enhancing | They choose it |
| **Attitude Toward Perpetrators** | |
| They should be locked up | They can be rehabilitated |

workers come across to the cops as soft liberals who just want to talk about feelings, and the social workers see the cops as people who have no heart, who can only see things in cold factual terms. . . . The social workers want to give treatment to the proven offenders; our cops just want to push those guys off a roof! We don't think they can be rehabilitated. But we can't focus on that, because we have to work together. And we do.

"These cultural differences are reinforced by the system we're in. See, the police are governed by certain laws. There must be 'probable cause' to make a criminal charge against the suspect. Social workers aren't required to provide concrete evidence. They can go with their gut, and sometimes they do. They'll say, 'This guy did it! Go after him!!' But if the cop doesn't have any hard evidence, he can't go with it."

Somehow, Miller says, it works. "We share information this way, we have two sets of eyes and ears working together. And being together and working cases together, you develop relationships, you get a comfort level with the social workers and learn from them, and that wouldn't happen if we weren't co-located in this space. And despite the tensions and teasing, both groups are trying to make a difference."

## It's Mainly About Relationships

And what is it that keeps these two very different groups working together? Miller says it's many things—being co-located, agreeing to disagree on cases, learning how to keep an open mind about each other. But mostly, she says, it comes down to relationships. "If the supervisors on both sides work well together and have a positive attitude about the other group, it works fine."

The center's social workers agree about this clash of cultures, but they say that they are usually the ones trying to bridge the divide. One says, "We make it work, frankly. We put a tremendous amount of effort into these relationships. . . . They see us as soft-hearted liberals trying to save the world, and they don't respect that. In fact, some cops say, 'I only respect you if you have more stripes on your sleeve than I do.' So we work at building friendships with them, sometimes doing 'informal social work' with them (listening to their complaints), making time to eat lunch with them, humoring and kidding them. We stroke their egos a lot.

"It helped when we started getting the same investigative training that they get, although even that can lead to problems. If these investigative techniques help us gain a confession from a suspect, it can threaten the cops. These are mostly guys, and they don't like it if 'one of those social workers' gets a confession before they do. That leaves them feeling one down." What's the bottom line for the social workers? "It helps when one of our supervisors reminds us that we're here for the kids."

Debye, who has been the coordinator for sexual abuse services since the CAC opened, reinforces that point. "Relationships are a key, no question about it. And building relationships involves seeing what we have *in common*. We both want successful prosecution of sexual abuse offenders, we both want to protect kids. It helps to acknowledge our differences, to joke about them and be able to vent together as well. But through co-location we bridge many differences because we've become like family. In the early phases, we used to have end-of-the-day sessions where we'd vent and talk about what happened that day. It got us closer. . . . I think over time we've learned to look beyond the near term, we take a longer view, and we're aware of our commonalities. That really helps."

## Other Issues and Hurdles

The police and social workers' radically different cultures presents a major hurdle to the CAC staff, but they must deal with other issues as well.

### State and Local Funding Streams and Mandates

The Social Services Department is 80 percent state funded and state supervised; the Police Department is a local agency. The difference can create problems. One Social Services manager notes that there is far more flexibility in the county budget than in the state's; "that's why we usually try to get the county to pay for certain costs like our office lease. It's just much easier to get that through the county." It's a complicated arrangement; many social workers use state-funded computers that sit on furniture funded by the county! There's no simple solution to this challenge. CAC leaders negotiate with each funding entity annually and try to keep them informed of the overall CAC needs. "And when there's a need that neither agency can fund, like for some equipment," says Debye, "I'll sometimes write a grant. There's no set formula stating who pays for some items. We work it out."

### Different Incentives and Levels of Choice

The social workers in the CAC usually choose that role; the police are assigned to the CAC. Further, a tour in the CAC may not be career enhancing for cops. As one social worker notes, "It's not considered 'real police work'; some call it a 'kiddie cop' job." The police have no lack of motivation to do their job well; they are just as committed to helping the victims and catching the perpetrators as the social workers are. But they may not feel as committed to collaborating initially; that's a major change for them, and it requires constant work and attention. "And some people don't have the stomach for this, frankly," says Miller. "Most of our officers stay here for several years, but dealing with these kinds of problems can be a shock at first."

"It helps when our social workers have joint training sessions with the police," notes Vidor. "That, plus the shared experiences of investigating the cases together, help the police see the value in collaboration here. But it takes constant attention and work . . . and accommodation." A colleague of mine likes to say that there are two types of problems. Some problems get solved, other problems have to be managed. Vidor's response: "If you think you've solved this problem, then you *really* have a problem! We have to manage it over and over."

*Who's in Charge?*

There is no one position designated as the CAC director or coordinator. Debye and her police counterpart oversee the operations of the CAC on a daily basis. A committee has responsibility for longer-term planning and policy matters. It is made up of a police commander, Debye, representatives from the health department and state attorney's office, Mark Vidor, and a senior police department official. The absence of a CAC director doesn't seem to be a problem, according to some middle and senior managers of the key departments. (One called it a "perceived problem.") There are frontline staff people who do worry about this, however, especially the social workers. With two different cultures and different levels of motivation, it seems that some of them would appreciate having one senior CAC manager to resolve conflicts and emphasize the importance of collaboration. Lacking that, they are frequently negotiating issues and relationships at their own level. "I just wish we had more involvement from our senior leaders," is how one frontline worker put it.

"I don't think it [a single CAC director] would ever work," is Debye's response. "Each department wants to maintain its own leader and its own accountability here. I don't think either department would want to give that up." She notes that a CAC administrator who manages facility and other administrative items might be helpful, but not a true center leader. The two cultures need their own designated leaders, it seems.

**Results**

It's clear that the CAC model offers many potential benefits to the staff and the people they serve. What are the results? There's been a large increase in confession rates and in arrest rates, and these are occurring without the victims testifying in court. "That's very important because the perpetrator is usually the father or another family member, and having to testify against a family member would only add to their trauma," Debye explains. The CAC opened in 1989. Table 2.1 presents the numbers for "indicated cases" (those in which the staff believe that sexual abuse did occur).

Debye cites three ways that the CAC model helps produce such positive results:

- Co-location and integrated teams increase the timeliness of response.

- The model also increases the percentage of coordinated responses. Coordination prevents one person (police officer or social worker) from preceding the other and tipping off the offender prematurely.

- The model increases the emphasis on training and professionalism by improving the staff members' skills at forensic interviewing and interrogations.

Debye also notes that the joint interview approach has radically reduced the number of victims who must tell their stories repeated times. And, interestingly, fewer victims are being placed in foster care. "Because of this model, the mom now *sees* that the dad did it. Without the confession (and subsequent successful prosecution), and without being able to incarcerate the perpetrator, we sometimes had to put the child in foster care."

Human services professionals are learning that child sexual abuse is a complex challenge, and like other complex issues, it is best han-

Table 2.1. Concrete Results for the CAC Model (percentages).

|  | Baseline | 1992 | 1999 |
| --- | --- | --- | --- |
| Arrest rate | 27 (1988) | 73 | 95+ |
| Confession rate | 20 (1990) | 40 | 50 |

dled through a multidisciplinary approach. It can be tough to get people from very different disciplines to collaborate. The CAC model fosters collaboration when the professionals have the support of their leaders, when they have a common project, and when they use co-location to support their working relationships.

---

This case, like the others in this book, demonstrates the power as well as the challenges of collaboration. The leaders and staff members who created the CAC worked at it for years; their passion, political smarts, and people skills were demonstrated over and over. And their collaboration is working. The huge increase in arrest and confession rates is impressive. Harder to quantify but equally important is the fact that the victims of sexual abuse now experience a far more humane process. The children only tell their story once, in a supportive setting that includes a trained social worker. Fewer of them are being sent to foster care. The family is more likely to acknowledge what happened, get needed treatment, and begin a healing process.

Some of the key elements in this success include the presence of a champion (Kris Debye), open relationships among the frontline staff, the high stakes involved in this work, and collaborative leaders who support the approach. These and other key elements and skills involved in collaboration will get a careful review in Chapters Four through Nine. Before going there, however, it's necessary to take a clear-eyed look at the world of collaboration. For, as in this case, true collaboration across agencies is very hard work. The differences in organizational cultures, values, training, background, reward systems, and professional approaches are continual challenges to the CAC staff. And these are only a few of the collaboration challenges. Many other hurdles confront people working across boundaries, and they're detailed in the next chapter.

# 3

# The Challenges of
# Successful Collaboration

*The streets department does not talk to the planning
department. The planning department does not talk
to the housing department. Nobody talks to police.
Nobody talks to fire. Nobody talks to social service
agencies. Everything is done in isolation and often at
cross-purposes.*

A municipal leader

Sure it's hard, but look at the results we're getting!" That is how
one staff member at the Baltimore County Child Advocacy
Center summed up her experience with collaboration. When the
effort pays off, it makes all the hard work worthwhile. But some
alliances struggle for months and years without achieving significant successes. To fully appreciate the potential challenges involved
in collaborating, it's useful to look at a more complex situation, one
involving many parties who hold different values, disagree about
data, and have a history of failed efforts and distrust. I know of no
better example than the ongoing efforts to protect the wild salmon
in the Columbia River Basin of the Pacific Northwest.

Consider: The wild salmon have been experiencing problems
here for over 125 years, and twelve salmon populations are now
listed as threatened or endangered under the Endangered Species
Act. These populations could become extinct unless concerted

actions are taken by all elements of the region—local communities, five state and ten federal government agencies, thirteen Indian tribes, thousands of large and small landowners. The issues are extraordinarily complex. Four interrelated factors determine the salmon's fate: hydropower, habitat, hatchery, and harvest. (This story focuses only on hydropower.) The key parties have a long and painful history of distrust and poor communications. And there is no one "salmon czar" to call the shots; each agency has responsibility for only part of the problem. Other than that, things are going beautifully!

### Saving the Wild Salmon

The Columbia River Basin extends from Montana and Idaho west through Oregon and Washington, and includes the Columbia and Snake Rivers. Efforts to rebuild the salmon populations here were initiated as early as 1877, when the first fish hatchery was created. During the next century many dams were built on the Columbia and Snake Rivers, each posing threats to the salmon and their ability to safely migrate. Young salmon swim out to sea where they mature for two to four years, then return to fresh water where they spawn and die. If they can't return, they won't reproduce. A variety of methods have been used to help the salmon bypass the dams, but those efforts haven't done enough.

In 1985 the United States and Canada signed the Pacific Salmon Treaty, which tried to deal with the overfishing of salmon. But by 1992 four Snake River salmon species were on the endangered species list. In 1992, 1993, and 1994 the National Marine Fisheries Service (NMFS) required changes in hydropower operations to protect certain salmon species. It called for changes in the river flow volume and the amount of water spilled over dams, and for alterations to the dams.

The agency's 1994 action was challenged in court and found inadequate. It issued new requirements in 1995 (called a Biological Opinion) that required stronger protections; this time the courts upheld it. One element of the 1995 requirements called for inclusion of a larger number of stakeholders to negotiate the ongoing protection efforts.

## Many Stakeholders, None of Them in Charge

By the mid-1990s, two things were becoming evident. First, the steps being taken to save the salmon weren't working; more salmon populations were listed as threatened or endangered. And second, no one agency could take action that would deal effectively with the entire problem. The Army Corps of Engineers and the Bureau of Reclamation manage dams and deal with flood control, as do the public utility districts that manage five non-federal dams on the Columbia. NMFS is charged with enforcing the Endangered Species Act. Bonneville Power provides electricity generated by the Corps and Bureau dams. The states are responsible for fisheries management. But nobody goes to work each morning in the "Office of Salmon Protection." There is no such entity. The salmon problem is complex but is managed in a fragmented way. It's the classic case of multiple stakeholders with nobody fully in charge.

And the stakes in this effort are huge. Over nine million people live in the region. They're all stakeholders, whether they care about salmon or not. Most get electricity generated by the dams, and when dam operations are altered to protect the salmon it can affect the residents. Many use the river basins for recreation; some are employed by the barges that carry food and natural resources on the rivers, and others work for companies that use the materials those barges carry. The economic, cultural, and recreational implications of protecting the salmon are enormous.

## The Columbia River Regional Forum

In 1996 the NMFS convened a meeting of twenty-three key parties and formed the Columbia River Regional Forum. The group represented six federal agencies: EPA, NMFS, Bonneville Power Administration (a government agency, similar to the Tennessee Valley Authority), the U.S. Fish and Wildlife Service, the Army Corps of Engineers, and the Bureau of Reclamation. It also included five states (Washington, Montana, Oregon, Idaho, and Alaska) and thirteen Indian tribes.

The Forum's purpose is to implement the terms of a Biological Opinion on protecting the salmon. (The 1995 version has been replaced by a 2000 Opinion that's even broader in scope.) It quickly became apparent that the Forum members were having problems working together. In 1998 the Forum retained a professional consultant to guide its efforts—a smart move given the difficulties it was experiencing:

- Each agency or group has its own statutory responsibilities, its own processes and culture. Communication among members has been difficult and time consuming.

- The parties don't agree on the causes or remedies of the salmon problem; they all believe in using scientific data, but the science isn't clear yet.

- Trust is a long-standing problem among many of the parties. Even when independent scientists agree on certain issues, some Forum members dispute the findings, questioning whether the scientists are simply reflecting the interests of the agencies paying them.

- The scientists and other technical people in the Forum have difficulty communicating with government and tribal policymakers, who aren't scientists but must make sense of the data and their implications in order to take constructive action.

- The parties have strongly held and very different values. Some would save the fish at any cost, whereas others put a higher priority on economics.

- Because of the trust problem, small things get magnified and misinterpreted. One person's absence from a meeting, for example, is taken by some as a statement that the person's agency is no longer committed to the Forum.

- Some individuals in the Forum see themselves as advocates for specific remedies and courses of action; others believe they are there to pursue a larger good. There was no initial agreement on their roles and goals, or on their mutual expectations of each other.

- The historical relationships among the groups pose another never-ending challenge. The tribes' experience with government officials has been difficult, to put it mildly. They don't see much reason to trust the government agencies in this endeavor.

- Most of the professionals in the Forum are scientists and engineers. They have deep knowledge of the technical issues, but few have a background in the interpersonal aspects of working collaboratively. One observer notes that "when the agenda has technical items on it, the members really want to meet; that seems like 'real work.' But the biggest problems and challenges are the process issues, and many of them have a difficult time discussing process."

And there's more. The engineers and scientists use different problem-solving approaches. Once, several engineers in the Forum come up with what they considered to be a creative engineering solution to an apparently intractable problem. They were ready to give it a try in the absence of any other option. But the scientists objected, insisting that several biological tests be done to provide the scientific evidence that it could work. And the tribes said that the fix would disrupt natural environmental processes. All had valid points, and none of them wanted to give up anything.

## Hurdles and Why They're So Important

The effort to protect the salmon demonstrates many of the key hurdles to collaboration: communications problems and value differences at the interpersonal level, distrust at the organizational level, and systemic problems such as the fragmentation of responsibility. Although the salmon case is an especially difficult one, it reflects an important reality that collaborators must understand: *the forces that pull people apart are very strong, some of them are wired into the very DNA of organizations, and it takes far more than good intentions and kind-hearted people to make collaboration work.* As professor Eugene Bardach puts it, "Almost nothing about the bureaucratic ethos makes it hospitable to interagency collaboration" (1998, p. 232).

Unfortunately, it's easy to put together a long list of collaboration hurdles. If you ask several veterans of collaborative efforts what makes the work so difficult, they won't have to pause to gather their thoughts. For example, when I posed this question to Kerwyn Keith, associate deputy state director for the U.S. Bureau of Land Management (and collaboration veteran), he immediately launched into an impressive catalogue of reasons to avoid collaboration:

> *People worry that this means more work and more time.*
>
> *They think this will get them in trouble.*
>
> *They wonder, "How would I explain this (time invested in it) to others?"*
>
> *They worry they'll have to give up something in the process.*
>
> *They focus on their turf.*
>
> *They think, "Now that I've worked so hard to get to this position, why start collaborating and sharing what I've got with others?"*
>
> *People worry they might give up possibilities for promotion.*
>
> *Collaboration isn't as clear a way to work as the old bureaucratic ways.*
>
> *Some people aren't comfortable with uncertainty and ambiguity.*

He pointed out that many people simply fear the unknown, and continued, "Bottom line: collaboration is a change that doesn't seem (to some people) to have anything in it for them." And he was just getting started!

Keith identified a number of the biggest collaboration hurdles. He focused primarily on the individual (and interpersonal) challenges to collaboration, and those are considerable—but only the beginning of the wide range of hurdles that await the effort. My point isn't to take the wind out of your sails. Quite the opposite; all these hurdles can be overcome. Indeed, this book is filled with inspiring examples of people doing just that (and they're even starting to make some progress in the battle to save the salmon).

## Individual Hurdles to Collaboration

Success is more likely when you can anticipate the "speed bumps" coming your way and have a plan for addressing them. I've divided the hurdles into four broad types: individual, organizational, societal, and systemic.

### *The Need for Power*

Author Michael Shrage tells a story about a man being interviewed for a senior executive position in a large firm. The interviewers told him that their company used the team concept, and that it was important to hire people who valued working on teams. One of them asked the man if he was a team player. "You bet," he replied, "team captain!"

We've all worked with people like him. They're strong and capable, usually have solid accomplishments to their credit, but are only comfortable being numero uno. They can give enormous amounts of energy, focus, and drive to an organization, but you don't want them involved in a project that relies on good peer interaction.

One way to understand such people is to use a framework developed by psychologist David McClelland of Harvard. McClelland spent years developing and testing a "theory of social motives," a way to understand people's behavior, especially at work (McClelland, 1975). He came up with three primary motivations: achievement, affiliation, and power, as summarized in Table 3.1.

**Table 3.1. McClelland's Primary Motivations.**

| Achievement | Affiliation | Power |
|---|---|---|
| Concern with standards of excellence | Concern for inter-personal relations, well-being of others | Concern with influence over others for benefit of self and own organization |
| Takes intrinsic satis-faction in doing things well; likes to work alone and be accountable for challenging tasks | Contact with others is intrinsically satis-fying; likes to work in groups; likes tasks that serve others | Gains satisfaction by increasing span of control and having position of authority and leadership |
| Focuses on the tech-nical aspects of the job; likes to get it right | Focuses on the inter-personal climate of the office | Focuses on patterns of influence, making an impact, status and recognition |
| Likes to be seen as doing things in unique, innovative ways | Likes to be seen as a helpful, supportive, cooperative team player | Likes to be seen as important |

McClelland's three words—*achievement, affiliation, power*—sum-marize these three motivational states very nicely. And which of them would you want in your alliance? Well, there may be roles for all three. But if you consider a different question—Which one poses the greatest challenge to a collaborative group?—the answer is clear. Power-oriented individuals can be very difficult in collaborative set-tings. Jacki Bryant, a human services professional with extensive experience at facilitating collaboration among nonprofit and pub-lic agencies, makes the point well:

> People with big needs for power are likely to feel threat-ened by collaboration. They'll worry about losing power

because of the partnership. When that's the case, they aren't likely to join. Or, they might join, but do so *to undermine and slow down the effort*. This need for power is hard to address directly; most people with high power needs don't say so explicitly and it's hard for others to tell the person that his need for power is getting in the way of the group. So power-oriented people do things indirectly to keep the collaborative from reducing their individual power.

Some power-oriented people have a difficult time seeing an answer to the WIIFM (What's in it for me?) question in collaboration. And that difficulty can be a big loss for the parties, Bryant says. "Collaborative groups don't usually have one central authority, one person in a decision-making role to make the decisions for the group. Sometimes it's hard for the collaborative group to come to agreement on important issues." It's at these very times, of course, that power-oriented people often shine, because they step up and take control and help people come to closure. And that brings up one last, ironic fact: McClelland's research on more than five hundred managers from twenty-five different companies revealed that the most effective managers have high needs for power. They don't tend to have high needs for achievement or affiliation (see McClelland and Burnham, 1976). So the very people who can be most effective at moving people to action (in a hierarchical setting) may also be the ones most likely to turn others off in a collaborative context. The key is whether the power needs are primarily for personal gain or are focused on organizational improvement. McClelland points out that the need for power can work for the good of the whole, if that need is conditioned by maturity and self-control.

### Self-Serving Bias

The term *self-serving bias* refers to our tendency to value our own contribution more than that of others. It's related to our exposure to people outside our immediate space. When we don't work next to another group and therefore can't see its actual performance, we tend to place a lower value on what it produces than on what we do ourselves.

"That's why people working on one shift often badmouth those on another shift," notes Steve Schwartz, former director of a state-funded addiction treatment center in Buffalo. "I saw it in my own clinic. The people working there are very talented, very committed, and they do great work. But those working during the day don't actually see what their colleagues are doing in the evening shift (and vice versa), and they assume that their own work with the clients is greater."

The implications of the self-serving bias in collaborative projects are obvious and must be anticipated. One of the most effective ways to do so is to use short-term rotations in one of the other participating agencies or units. When staff spend time working in another office, they typically gain a much broader awareness of the people in that unit and of their challenges.

*Fear of Losing Control, Autonomy, Quality, Identity, Resources*

When considering a collaboration, people ask themselves several questions. One of the most important questions is, What might I lose?

Don't despair. That's not as negative as it may seem. Management sage Peter Drucker notes that entrepreneurs also ask this question up front when confronted with an economic opportunity. Now entrepreneurs are optimistic by nature, but they're hard-headed optimists and they need to assess the benefit/risk ratio before investing energy in a project. Drucker writes, "The innovators I know are successful to the extent to which they define risks and confine them" (Drucker, 1985, p. 139). It's the same with collaboration. Unless you have a history of working with someone, collaboration is a risk to be managed.

Some of the biggest questions have to do with the fear of loss: of control, autonomy, quality, and resources. As noted earlier, many effective managers have relatively high needs for control. So are you ready to let go of control and put some of your fate in another's hands? Autonomy can be another concern. Professionals tend to have high needs for autonomy. Think about the nature of most professionals—attorneys, physicians, accountants, teachers—they do most of their work alone. Some people worry that a partnership will greatly reduce their ability to control their own work and style.

Quality presents another concern. This is related to the self-serving bias discussed earlier. When it comes to quality, I'm OK, but I'm not so sure about you. Entering into an alliance with others means being judged, in part, by the quality of the others' work. Are they up to our standards? Identity also presents concerns. When the Forest Service and Bureau of Land Management began active collaboration in Oregon and Colorado in the early 1990s, many BLM staff worried about losing their identity. The Forest Service is about three times as large as BLM, there's a history of efforts to merge the two, and BLMers naturally wondered if this was going to end their independent identity.

Finally, people worry about losing resources in a collaborative effort. What do you do if the other party is half your size? You'll probably invest more money and time than the other. Which means you'll be wondering if you're getting your money's worth out of the effort. Or what happens if the collaborative is successful and results in certain efficiencies. Are you "rewarded" in the next budget by receiving a reduced appropriation? These concerns need to be addressed. One very effective method is a Partnering Workshop, discussed at the end of Chapter Five.

### Lack of Trust and Confidence Among the Principals

My daughter Becca had a great school project in the eighth grade. She was going to write about an innovative transportation strategy that some cities are using to reduce the numbers of cars clogging the roads. She was excited but frustrated. I asked what was going on.

"It's supposed to be a group project, but one member of our group isn't doing her part."

"How do you know?" I asked. As soon as the words were out of my mouth and she started rolling her eyes, I figured it wasn't one of my more inspired questions. "Because when we get together, Amy's not prepared, *that's* how! Besides, ask anyone in class and they'll tell you that she's not reliable. She just tries to slide through on others' efforts . . . and when she finally does contribute something, it's lousy work, and that reflects on the rest of our group. I wish she'd 'honor' someone else with her presence."

Trust and confidence form the soil from which collaboration grows. The essence of collaboration is joint effort toward a common goal, which means we're reliant on each other. If we don't trust the other to follow through, if we don't have confidence in the other's abilities, it won't work. It's as simple, and important, as that. Detailed memos of understanding won't replace mutual trust and confidence. I'll describe several ways to foster trust in Chapter Six, on relationships.

### Turf Concerns

This is sometimes related to issues of trust and confidence. The human need to define and protect one's space, or turf, is as old as the species. In organizations, of course, turf also refers to your functional or technical area, your work unit, your own job. Turf can also refer to a narrow mind-set. Author and human relations guru Stephen Covey has an interesting name for this: he calls it a "scarcity mentality" (Covey, 1989, p. 219), and others use the term *zero-sum*—your gain is my loss. Whatever the label, a major focus on personal turf is surely a critical hurdle to collaboration. When discussing efforts to share information in the war against terrorism, Ann Arbor Police Chief Daniel Oates describes the FBI as "obsessed with turf" (Novak, 2001). Whether that's a fair description or not, it's a widely held perception and it limits many agencies' willingness to cooperate with the FBI. Why should we work with you to meet some important societal need, if we're looking to the higher good while your main interest is to protect your power and reputation? Why indeed?

## Organizational Hurdles to Collaboration

A variety of organizational dynamics create challenges to collaboration. Here are some of the most powerful ones.

### Immediate Costs, Remote Benefits

The costs of collaboration are clear and are borne up front; the benefits appear fuzzy and come later. We seem to live in an increasingly impatient society, one driven by expectations for real-time communications, instant solutions. But collaboration doesn't meet the need for instant gratification, as the following example illustrates.

### The EARN Partnership

In southern Maryland, an alliance of state and local government human service agencies called EARN began in 1997 to create customer-focused, one-stop service for those needing workforce development assistance. Many of the six agencies involved serve common customers and there's no question that their customers are starting to get better services as the partnership grows.

But the leaders of the agencies often feel frustrated by the process. The leaders meet monthly for a half day, as they've done since 1997, and work on follow-up tasks between meetings. And then there's what economists call the opportunity costs. Every hour devoted to EARN is an hour not devoted to something else these busy leaders could be working on. It can be difficult to justify the ongoing investment of time when concrete results come very slowly.

In the business world, partnerships are far easier to justify. As Bill Gray, a former legal counsel for General Electric, puts it, "Collaboration in the private sector is based primarily on economics: Can I make more money by working together with a third party or parties? Is this a win-win, in financial terms? Either the joint venture makes money for us or we don't continue." In the public and nonprofit sectors the payoffs are usually much less precise. And they often come later, sometimes much later. This is the reason that collaboration, like other change efforts, benefits when the parties create early and visible wins.

### Differing Goals and Measures

It was the middle of a workshop on collaboration, and the police lieutenant was starting to look agitated. I asked him what was on his mind. He was frank: "Look, Russ, collaboration is great, I'm all for it. But how do you collaborate with people who have different goals? Right now I'm running the traffic division. When a new subdivision is being planned for our community, we work with the traffic engineering folks, but it's always a struggle. See, they're measured on designing new roads and intersections that provide for the *maximum traffic flow*—they want to move as many vehicles per hour as possible. But that's not our priority. Our first job is to ensure *traffic safety*. And sometimes the safest design means you get fewer vehicles per hour through the intersection, not more. How do you collaborate when you have different goals?"

It was a reasonable question. The fact remains that some units are rewarded for pursuing diverging or even opposing goals. When trust is low, people are inclined to see each other as having different goals (and turf to protect), whether such differences exist or not. That's one of the issues involved with the effort to protect the salmon. Some members of the Forum are perceived to be participating in an effort to protect their organizational interests, not the larger interest of saving the wild salmon. I'll return to this in Chapter Five, taking up the basics that are needed for collaboration to begin. One of those basics is the presence of common interests.

## Low Credit or Reward

In the late 1990s, a team from the U.S. Forest Service redesigned the process of communicating with external customers in the field. After several months, the team started to realize that an important cause of the external customer communications problem was internal. One veteran customer service staffer laid out the problem frankly:

> It goes like this: You're a front-line employee working directly with customers. You spend most of your time answering customers' questions and providing them with guidance and information. Sometimes you get questions you can't answer. If your supervisor doesn't know the answer, you might call someone in one of the operating divisions. How quickly does that person return your phone call? Maybe right away, maybe later . . . maybe never. If the answer is "later" or "never," it's probably because your need isn't his priority. There's nothing in it for him to respond. He's a scientist, an analyst, a planner, and there's lots of people waiting for his work who are higher on the food chain than the lowly customer service worker out at the front desk!

This isn't an isolated instance. The customer service worker needs information from someone higher up. But that higher-up has bigger fish to fry; there's no credit or reward for taking the time to provide the information so the request simply slips out of memory. I usually find more collaboration among the frontline staff in most agencies than at middle and senior management levels. Using the traditional organizational model, it appears as shown in Figure 3.1.

**Figure 3.1. Usage of Collaboration.**

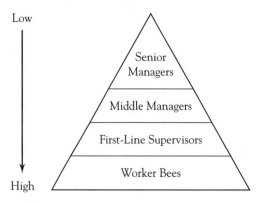

Why? One reason is the lack of rewards. Most frontline staff get promoted for technical skills and demonstrated competence at getting things done, which often involves short-circuiting the organization chart and working directly with others who can influence the situation regardless of where they work. What gets them from first-level supervisor to middle manager? Running their assigned unit, not necessarily sharing time and resources with others. And the same criterion applies in the move to top management. The worker bees collaborate because it's the only way they can get some of their work done. As people move up, there are fewer (perceived) benefits to collaborating in most agencies. Jay Coles, a manager working on a virtual team in one of the U.S. government's intelligence agencies, describes collaboration on the virtual team this way: "This is always a collateral duty. It would really help some of these guys if they just got a letter from a senior leader acknowledging their work and their contribution. We need to do more of that."

*Individually Oriented Appraisal Systems*

This hurdle is related to the preceding one. Many leaders and managers today preach the value of team play and collaboration. New employees find these listed in the organizational values statement.

And then comes the performance appraisal, and the major focus is on your *individual* accomplishments. One of the more humorous examples I've seen is in a conference center where I teach. In the lobby is a large plaque listing the names of exemplary employees. There's a big, beautiful graphic dominating the middle of the plaque with the word "Teamwork!" displayed proudly. And how are the honored employees listed? They're listed as the *individual* "employee of the month."

If it's true that "what gets measured gets done," and I believe it usually is, our appraisal, measurement, and reward systems need to change in major ways to support a collaborative ethic.

*Line-Item Budget Systems*

Another internal administrative system that inhibits collaborative behavior is the classic line-item budget. When your program's funding is noted as a line item on a budget, it gives you two things: the amount of money you can expect to receive—and an identity. What happens if several line items are lumped into a large block grant? The purpose could be laudable: greater flexibility, possible collaboration across program boundaries. But many program managers will feel threatened. With no line-item figure, they worry they'll lose funding. And their constituents may raise hell because there's no written guarantee that the program will be maintained. So we continue with line-item budgets and make it harder to share resources between programs. One example: the Service First initiative between the BLM and the Forest Service in the western United States involves the sharing of staff. In some cases a BLM manager supervises Forest Service staff, and vice versa. It literally took an act of Congress to make such sharing legitimate.

*What's in It for My Organization?*

The lack of rewards for collaboration applies at the organizational as well as individual level. Lane Hurley, a colleague of mine, likes to say that WIIFM is the most popular radio station in the country.

WIIFM? is a very appropriate question when it comes to collaboration. Collaboration only makes sense when it helps the participating organizations do something they couldn't do individually, or couldn't do as well, or as quickly, or as cheaply. *Collaboration is a means, not an end.* It must pass the WIIFM? test from an organizational standpoint: Does a given alliance help the organization perform better? Does it improve service to customers, lower costs, achieve better overall outcomes, attract more talented staff? When I'm inviting someone to collaborate on a project and the other person hesitates, it's usually because they don't see an obvious answer to the WIIFM? question (that, or the perceived costs of collaboration are too high). It's in your interest to learn whether others see collaboration in their interest.

*Different Rules, Different Cultures, Different Values*

Collaborating across organizations with different cultures and rules always places a huge emphasis on personal relationships, as it did in the Baltimore County Child Advocacy Center. The CAC helps bridge the gap in the police and social work cultures through its colocation of staff, as well as the conscious attention to relationships. But most organizations don't find it realistic to merge their staff members when they work collaboratively. The committees working to save the salmon meet monthly or quarterly. They work on the issues in between, but their face-to-face contact is occasional—which doesn't make it easy to deal with their agencies' very different cultures and with the values differences among many of the parties.

Even when relationships are very positive and people meet frequently, it's difficult to work together when there are different cultures with different rules, values, and pressures. In the salmon case, values differences are tough to resolve. Such differences must be understood and respected if the parties are to make progress.

### Societal Hurdles to Collaboration

Some of the organizational hurdles to collaboration reflect broader dynamics in American society.

*The American Ethos of Individualism*

Consider this comment from the provost of a large research university: "All by yourself you write a masters thesis. All by yourself your write your dissertation. All by yourself you spend about six years doing research, writing, and teaching. All by yourself you build a case for tenure. All by yourself you're evaluated for tenure. And, if you're successful and get tenure, suddenly we expect you to be a part of a collegial community!"

Most modern organizations place a tremendous emphasis on teams and teamwork. When that team focus is difficult to achieve, it's often because the organization's systems, rewards, and culture are built on an ethic of individualism. That shouldn't surprise anyone; our organizations reflect the larger society in many ways. And American society has long been characterized by a strong individualistic spirit. Jefferson spoke eloquently about his vision of a nation of sturdy yeoman farmers. The French nobleman and political scientist Alexis de Tocqueville, who visited America in 1831–32, helped popularize the term "individualism" when he described the new American in his classic, *Democracy in America*. He wrote, "As social conditions become more equal, the number of persons increases who . . . acquire the habit of always considering themselves as standing alone, and they are apt to imagine that their whole destiny is in their own hands" ([1835] 1956, p. 194).

Tocqueville also observed a very different tendency in the society, which was our habit of forming voluntary associations. These two forces, individualism and collectivism, have formed a duality in America since the dawn of the republic. The problem, from a collaboration standpoint, is that individualism often trumps our collectivist instincts. Sociologist Robert Bellah and his colleagues documented this tension in their wonderful commentary on American society, *Habits of the Heart* (1985). We cherish our individual rights, and we like to join with others. But, they wrote, "we are hesitant to articulate our sense that we need one another as much as we need to stand alone" (p. 151).

This individualistic tendency has a very real and practical influence on our behavior. Until the 1990s, few elementary and secondary schools placed an emphasis on group learning activities. We learned, or failed, by ourselves. (Happily, this is changing in some school systems.) Our greatest corporations reflect in word and action their commitment to the individual. In *Built to Last* (Collins and Porras, 1994), a widely acclaimed book about eighteen extraordinarily successful companies, the authors list the "core ideologies" (key values) of each company. Among the seventeen American firms on the list (the other is Japanese), one value shows up more often than any other: respect for the individual employee. It is cited by nine companies. Integrity/honesty comes in second (listed by seven). Our movies and literature tend to venerate the ideal that one person can make a difference. *The Lone Ranger* is a classic American story; it wouldn't be popular in Japan and other countries that emphasize group norms.

Perhaps the most eye-catching title to come out of academia in many moons was written by Robert Putnam. The two-word title said it all: *Bowling Alone*. Putnam documents in extraordinary detail the drop in the number of voluntary associations, in church attendance, in fraternal organizations like Elks and Jaycees, in PTOs and PTAs, and in mainstream volunteer organizations like the Boy Scouts and Red Cross (Putnam, 2000). But beyond all of the numbers lies that stark image conveyed by the title, the solitary bowler standing there alone in what we think of as an eminently social activity.

Individualism continues to be a dominant element in American society. It contributes to many of our greatest strengths. It doesn't make collaboration impossible at all, but it does make such behavior more difficult.

*The American Bias for Competition*

Consider these two stories:

1. When I was growing up, my family was often invited to spend a vacation week with close friends who had rustic cottages in the

quiet hamlet of Northport in northern Michigan. In the early mornings I'd go out on the beach when the water was quiet to skip stones. As I got better, I started counting the number of "skips" the stones made. And that led to a classic young boy's fantasy: I imagined being in a "National Stone Skipping Contest" and going for the gold! Now this was the mid-1950s, a "simpler time," as we often say; this contest only existed in a child's mind, or so I thought. Imagine my surprise when I read the results of the *real* National Stone Skipping Contest held two years later!

2. An American was visiting London for the first time in the 1960s. He went to Hyde Park and saw the famous Speakers Corner, the children playing, the lovers walking hand in hand, families picnicking. Then he noticed something he hadn't seen before: two young men gently tossing a Frisbee back and forth. He watched, fascinated, for several minutes (he'd never seen a Frisbee before). Finally, unable to restrain himself any longer, he approached one of the men and asked, "Excuse me, who's winning?"

We Americans can find a way to make most any endeavor into a competition, and that competitive spirit has served us well in numerous ways. But it poses a challenge to collaboration. As Alfie Kohn writes in his analysis of competitive behavior, "Life for us has become an endless succession of contests" (1986, p. 1). Collaboration—literally to labor together—is based on a win-win assumption. Most competitive endeavors are win-lose, zero-sum activities. That's not always true; high-performing athletes sometimes collaborate even as they compete. Author Tim Gallwey makes this point nicely in *The Inner Game of Tennis* (1974). High-performing athletes are actually working together (through competition) to bring out the best in each other. But when the participants in a competitive activity believe that it's in their interest for the other person or group to do poorly, then the chances of collaboration are nil. And that's how the majority of competitive activities are structured.

To say America is an extraordinarily competitive society isn't a value judgment, it's a comparative assessment. As Kohn puts it, "We are systematically socialized to compete" (1986, p. 25). And for some, that socialization begins at very early ages. Case in point: preschools that market themselves for "college-bound" children. How did we come to this?

It's not only higher education that has become so competitive. Win-lose competition characterizes most other aspects of our society: economics, politics, the adversarial assumptions of our legal system, agency procedures, the list goes on. Competition is usually embedded in organizations' "employee of the month" awards. Like the hotel I described earlier, only one person (or, on some occasions, one team) can excel each month; everyone else loses by comparison. I once asked a manager at the local phone company why nobody parked in the space reserved for its employee of the month. She paused, smiled, leaned forward and said softly, "The winners of that award got tired of coming out at lunch and finding a big dent in their door from someone parked next to them who thought the wrong person got the award!"

Our competitive bent is so ingrained that most of us can scarcely imagine another way to function. But some people are operating under different assumptions. Professor Jerry Harvey is one of them. Well known in management circles for his article and video "The Abilene Paradox," Harvey teaches a most unusual graduate management class at George Washington University. His definition of cheating goes like this: you are cheating when another student asks you for assistance on a paper or exam, and you refuse to provide it! Harvey understands something that many of his colleagues still don't get: most students leaving an MBA or MPA program will enter a world in which they have to collaborate in order to succeed. Harvey's helping them get started on this path.

### Systemic Hurdles to Collaboration

Finally, certain collaboration barriers are structured into the very nature of government and of the funding systems that support public and nonprofit agencies.

*Constitutional Separation of Powers and Fragmentation*

Public administration and political science has taught us very well about the core genius of American governance—our separation of powers, checks and balances, and division of authority between the federal and state levels. The framers of the Constitution were primarily worried about tyranny—of another King George, of the majority over the minority, or of one part of government over the others. Their main strategy was *separation;* they separated powers so that no one person or unit could do very much harm. James Madison's comment after the Constitutional Convention in 1787 was telling: *"We have consciously designed an inefficient government to keep men free."* Given the framers' goal, it's clear that the model has been a brilliant success. Fragmentation and separation meant freedom to the founders of this nation.

Unfortunately, our fragmented government also puts serious obstacles in the way of public servants who want to get things done. When power and authority become diffused, the task of managing complex problems gets tougher. This problem is a major factor in the effort to protect the wild salmon, where formal responsibility for salmon protection is thoroughly fragmented.

It's the same at the state and local level. Power is dispersed and fragmented among oversight agencies, review boards and commissions (often with their own independent authority), inspectors general, civil service commissions, not to mention all of the other constituencies that can exert pressure and veto initiatives they don't like—unions, special interest groups, business associations, and so on. Separation and fragmentation make collaboration more important—no one agency can handle the problem alone—but they also pose some of the biggest hurdles to collaboration. When "a hundred people can veto a project but no one person or office can move it forward" (to paraphrase the late Cabinet secretary and founder of Common Cause, John Gardner), getting agreement can be an enormous challenge.

*Narrow Categorical Funding Programs*

Nonprofit agencies aren't a part of government entities in the tech-nical sense, but they are surely affected by it. They frequently must go to multiple governmental bodies, each with its own application process and funding categories, its own priorities, and its own requirements for measuring results.

The field of human services is a huge example of fragmentation. All levels of government are spending upwards of $600 billion annually on programs for children and families; this is a big busi-ness. The hallmark of this (non) system is the wide use of categor-ical programs. These are typically narrowly defined initiatives that focus on a single problem (say, dealing with the large number of teenage pregnancies). Agencies that want to grab some of the fund-ing must demonstrate what they will do to address the problem. All too often, the categorical program is written in such a way that it virtually guarantees that grant recipients will take a very narrow approach to the problem.

Social scientist Lisbeth Schorr has researched the problem of categorical programs in human services. She writes: "Workers con-centrating on specialized functions often lose sight of the family as a whole" (1997, p. 82). She cites an example of a meeting with three professionals who were working with the same family. The social services worker was concerned about the teenager's involve-ment in gangs; the school nurse noted that the kids came to school wearing dirty clothes; the school social worker worried about the seven-year-old's frequent absences from school. And the mother? Her major concern was the fact that the home had been without electricity for six weeks! Turns out that each of the professionals knew of that problem, but they noted that "it wasn't in their job description" to call the power company and get the electricity flow-ing again.

Are these simply narrow-minded bureaucrats? Probably not. A more likely analysis is that *they are doing precisely what they're hired to do, trained to do, and measured on,* which has to do with one specific aspect of a family's life. Schorr got it right when she said categorical programs mean that "we often lose sight of the family as a whole."

Just how pervasive is the problem of categorical programs? Professor Sid Gardner, an expert on the subject, decided to document it for himself. He found 238 separate programs for students defined as being "at risk"—*in the city of Los Angeles alone.* Former Secretary of Health, Education and Welfare Joe Califano recalls his federal experience: "When we discovered that poor students needed a good lunch, we devised legislation for a school lunch program. When we later found out that breakfast helped them learn better, we whipped up a law for school breakfasts. . . . When my son, Joe, swallowed a bottle of aspirin, President Johnson sent Congress a Child Safety Act" (Schorr, 1997, p. 75).

---

The list of collaboration hurdles, from individual and organizational to societal and systemic, is long. But, as noted earlier, there are many people who overcome these hurdles and succeed at collaboration. In the next section I'll start presenting lessons from their experiences. I've organized their similarities into a collaboration framework. The next six chapters describe the framework's elements.

# Part II

# A Framework for Collaboration in the Real World

# 4

# A Framework for Collaboration

*Behind all the current buzz about collaboration is a*
*discipline. . . . If it contained a silicon chip, we'd all*
*be excited.*

*John Gardner*

The promise of collaboration is great. The hurdles are significant. And successful efforts can provide key lessons to those
who are trying to make collaboration work for themselves and their
own organizations. No, there's no quantitative formula for success
here; as Buz Cox, director of a city social services department points
out, "this is an art, not a science." But art forms are based on certain principles, and accomplished artists use those principles flaw-
lessly. There is, as John Gardner said, a discipline to this work.
Exhibit 4.1 presents the essential elements of that discipline.

---

**Exhibit 4.1. Framework for Collaboration.**

- The basics are in place.
- The principals have open, trusting relationships with one another.
- The stakes are high.
- The participants include a constituency for collaboration.
- The leadership follows collaborative principles.

---

The *basics* include the following elements:

- The parties have a shared purpose or goal that they care about but cannot achieve on their own.

- The parties want to pursue a collaborative solution now and are willing to contribute something to achieve it.

- The right people are at the table.

- The parties have an open, credible process.

- The initiative has a champion, someone with credibility and clout who makes this a high priority.

A word about the other elements. *Open, trusting relationships* form the glue for most collaborative ventures. Since we're talking about co-labor, people naturally wonder if they can trust the other parties to share information, to follow up on their tasks, to equitably share the credit for success and stand together when things get tough. The need for *high stakes* refers to the factor that, perhaps more than any other, pulls individuals together when it seems easier to work separately. High stakes occur when the task at hand is very important to employees and outside stakeholders, the results are visible to others, and the consequences of getting it right (or wrong) are large and will be felt directly by those doing the work in the near term.

High stakes are a powerful force to bring people to the table. But collaboration also needs *a constituency*—a group (or several groups) who strongly believe that a collaborative effort is in their interest, who want to support it, and who have influence over the parties involved—to keep people at the table over the long haul. Effective collaborative leaders find ways to help stakeholders see it in their interest for the collaborative effort to succeed. And that leads to the final element, *collaborative leadership*. This is the way you need to work when you want to provide leadership and have no formal authority over your peers. Collaborative leadership is required when people from different agencies or agency units work on a common project. And it's different in fundamental ways from hierarchical leadership styles.

Each of these collaboration elements is present in the following case. See which ones you notice as you read through; I'll discuss them at the end of the chapter.

### JNET: Information Sharing in a Low-Trust Environment

On August 19, 1994, patrolman Willis John Cole was murdered in New Cumberland, Pennsylvania, while responding to a robbery in progress. The killer had many arrests, under at least six different names. Five days before the shooting he had been picked up on a parole violation, but then let out on bail. If law enforcement and court personnel had known of his complete history, he would have been behind bars on August 19. The tragedy of Cole's death led to several changes in Pennsylvania. One, called JNET, involves unprecedented information sharing.

Pennsylvania's JNET (for "Justice Network") was launched in 1996. It's an impressive example of information sharing among sixteen state agencies, some federal agencies, and over twelve hundred local police departments spread around Pennsylvania's sixty-seven counties. JNET's goal is to enhance public safety by providing a common online environment that helps authorized federal, state, and local officials access each other's offender records and other criminal justice information. Through JNET, agencies can better track potentially dangerous individuals (like the man who killed officer Cole) by exchanging information. This is critical in the criminal justice area, but turf protection and lack of trust among these agencies have historically limited their willingness to share information.

Before JNET, state agencies couldn't share data electronically. It took several days to obtain hard copies of photos, suspects' addresses and criminal histories, outstanding warrants, and the like. That's why nobody caught officer Cole's killer in time. Through JNET, this information is now available in real time to those JNET members who need it. Exhibit 4.2 summarizes the functionalities JNET provides for its member agencies.

JNET uses open Internet and Web technologies and standards to link information from each agency using common Web browser and messaging interfaces. *Each participating agency controls what information it chooses to share and also who is authorized to see it.* That has been essential to getting agency support. Network firewalls, secure communication protocols, data encryption, and digital signatures protect information on JNET from unauthorized use. Agencies can share extremely sensitive information by using encrypted authenticated e-mail over JNET.

"That's one of the real keys to JNET's success," says Martin Horn, who was secretary of administration in former governor Tom Ridge's second administration and a key JNET leader. "Each agency maintains its own autonomy, its own legacy systems. Our Web-based solution allows agencies to convert their data to an XML format—that really helped gain buy-in." You don't have to know anything about technology to understand Horn's point. He's talking about Control (with

**Exhibit 4.2.  What JNET Helps Its Users Do.**

- Share offender information.
- Access driver license information.
- Access digital mug shots.
- Exchange photo images.
- Use secure e-mail.
- Use various criminal justice Web sites not available to the public.
- Access searchable online reference libraries.

a capital C). That's a biggie when you're dealing with criminal justice agencies that often have trust issues with one another and haven't shared information openly in the past. JNET assures agencies that they can maintain their own autonomy, control the information shared, and maintain their own computer systems.

Horn emphasizes that no single authority can force people in the criminal justice system to share information. They had to develop a strategy that allowed trust to build slowly. "And that's exactly what we did with this program. We took a gradualist approach, and it's working."

## A Little History

State officials had been looking for an integrated system in criminal justice since at least 1988, but earlier efforts failed due to lack of funding or inadequate telecommunications capacity. Other false starts occurred when a vendor or state agency tried to impose a standardized, one-size-fits-all solution on others. Tom Ridge made crime reduction a priority in his 1994 campaign, and stressed that to his cabinet. The actual work on the JNET system itself began in 1997 when the state Office of Administration designated $11 million to begin designing and building a justice network. A contractor worked with officials from participating agencies to develop a high-level architecture for the proposed system, which was in place by November 1997. One participant noted that the funding was an important factor for the agencies early on: "They didn't need to ask their own organizations for money—they could rely on the central fund. The participants could then worry about creating a safer community instead of who would have to pay for it." The governor's strong support also made a big difference.

A steering committee started meeting in 1997, to oversee design and operations of the system. A "JNET lab" was in place by May 1998, providing an environment to deploy and test a proof-of-concept system. That system was released to a pilot user group in

October 1998. By May 1999, the first phase of JNET was completed. "The contractor really played a key role in the development of JNET," remarks Terri Savidge, JNET's first executive director. "Those early, tangible successes were an absolute requirement for the continued support and growth of JNET."

### Another Key Element: The Governance Structure

In June 1999, Tom Ridge issued an executive order establishing the JNET governance structure shown in Figure 4.1, which created a JNET executive director position and a high-level Executive Council (made up

**Figure 4.1. JNET Governance Structure.**

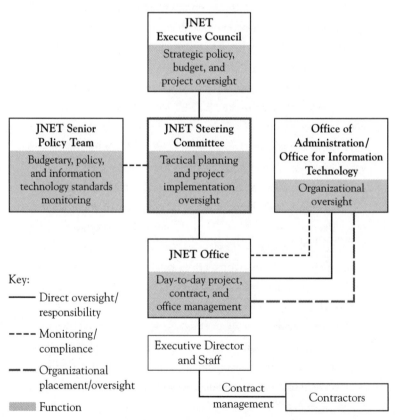

of the chief executives from participating JNET state agencies). The Executive Council establishes policy and strategic direction. A Steering Committee was also authorized; it handles the more tactical, day-to-day decisions and operational matters. It turns out that the Steering Committee has been a key to JNET's success.

All but one of JNET's sixteen agencies are represented on both the Executive Council and the Steering Committee (the Commission on Sentencing has a seat only on the latter). The Executive Council meets about twice a year to deal with high-level policy matters. Its members are elected officials or gubernatorial appointments. The Steering Committee, however, is made up of career civil servants. It meets every other week to deal with the ongoing operational issues that make or break the system. It's been meeting this frequently since 1997 (its members were working together before being given official status through Ridge's executive order).

"The beauty of JNET is that it has 'joint ownership.' All sixteen agencies own it; no one single agency controls it. The JNET Steering Committee manages JNET on an ongoing basis, and it represents all of the players," Horn explains. "You see, *there is no one authority that can force JNET on everyone.* The Steering Committee is the way it works . . . it provided a formal venue in which the informal relationships could take root and blossom. You could say we kind of force people to get to know each other." Table 4.1 outlines the differing composition of the Executive Council and the Steering Committee.

### Developing Trust on the Steering Committee

A key to the Steering Committee's success is its composition; it includes only people with managerial (as opposed to political) concerns. Horn says, "We took the 'big guns' out of the room. The elected and appointed officials who run some of the JNET agencies aren't on the Steering Committee. We got the big egos out, and that allowed trust to grow slowly, over time and out of shared successes."

Another key to trust was the decision to build JNET slowly, one phase at a time. Terri Savidge emphasizes that "functionality got

**Table 4.1. The JNET Governance Structure's Two Key Groups.**

| JNET Executive Council (policy, strategic direction) | Steering Committee (implementation, operations) | |
|---|---|---|
| | Core Member | Ex Officio |
| Department of Corrections | X | |
| State Police | X | |
| Board of Probation and Parole | X | |
| Board of Pardons | X | |
| Office of Attorney General | X | |
| Governor's Office of General Counsel | | X |
| Administrative Office of Pennsylvania Courts | X | |
| Office of Administration | | X |
| Juvenile Court Judge's Commission | X | |
| Department of Public Welfare | X | |
| Department of Transportation | X | |
| Office of Inspector General | | X |
| Commission on Crime and Delinquency | X | |
| Office of the Budget | | X |
| Governor's Policy Office | | X |
| Commission on Sentencing (not on Executive Council) | X | |

delivered. Otherwise, people would have given up." JNET was built in chunks, and every time a new function was added to the system, it built confidence among the users. The pace did one other thing. It allowed relationships among those on the Steering Committee to grow and strengthen. Linda Rosenberg, executive director after Savidge left, stresses that "relationships are the key here. Relationships have been so important in building JNET, especially given that this is a criminal justice system, where trust is a huge factor."

## How JNET Makes a Difference: Some Examples

It's not collaboration for collaboration's sake. The question is, Does JNET make a difference in terms of public safety? Thus far, the indicators are impressive:

- *Screening prison visitors.* JNET has helped prison officials catch people with false IDs trying to access the prison illegally.

- *Apprehending dangerous criminals.* Using JNET, state troopers have pulled down a suspect's photo from the state's driver license photo database. That allows them to immediately identify suspects and arrest them on the spot.

- *Identifying suspects, locating offenders.* Several state agencies and the FBI use the JNET photos to identify parolees, suspects, prison visitors, and others. Some counties use JNET to find current addresses of absconders.

- *Protecting the innocent.* When an Alabama state trooper pulled a driver over at a stop light, he suspected the man was wanted by Pennsylvania authorities for violating parole there. Using JNET, the picture of the actual parolee was quickly faxed to Alabama, showing clearly that the driver wasn't the suspect. JNET's speed and accuracy prevent innocent people from being falsely detained and charged.

- *Pardons decisions.* When someone with a criminal record asks for a pardon, JNET's notification system lets the Board of Pardons know if the person has been arrested on other charges. This helps the board make smarter decisions.

JNET was selected as one of the top fifty government technology projects in the country in 2000 by the *Civic.com Magazine* National, State and Local 50 Awards program.

## Speed Bumps

So far, the development of JNET seems to be problem free. Brilliant strategy, flawless execution, happy customers. Well, not exactly. There have been many speed bumps and issues along the way, and some continue still:

- *Who's in, who's out?* Many agencies outside of criminal justice and law enforcement have an interest in JNET information. The Public Welfare Department is one; it has a "need to know" when it comes to child-care providers. What if providers get arrested after the state has licensed them? Welfare officials must learn about that. But bringing in "outsiders" isn't easy in the criminal justice arena. In the Public Welfare case, the JNET agencies came up with a compromise. Public Welfare is included for current information about people's criminal records.

- *Preserving agency autonomy, and the risk of losing important information.* Giving participating agencies control over the data they share was critical to JNET's success. Nobody lost control. But the wide autonomy also limits the breadth of the information available; some agencies want and need information that others won't provide. JNET leaders use informal peer pressure to deal with this one.

- *Differences in member agency automation and agency resources and capacity.* Some of the smaller JNET agencies have little automated data, so they have little to contribute to the system. (Of the twelve hundred local police departments in the state, many are townships and boroughs with only one or two officers and little or no computerized record keeping.) Among those fully automated, some are more willing to share information than others. JNET reaches out by paying the costs for certain counties to connect to the JNET system. That county then is expected to pay for connecting its smaller jurisdictions to the county. Once they're connected, JNET requires these localities to start contributing data within two years. As a former JNET director puts it, "Dollars do wonders!"

- *Executive Council involvement and activity level.* "Until recently, the Executive Council wasn't as active as it might have been," Martin Horn noted in 2001. JNET needs the political people's involvement, which is why the Council was created. But its members are incredibly busy people who often face complex external pressures. Some have plans to run for higher office (and may be rivals). The politics of their lives has slowed down the pace of their involvement and decision making.

There seems to be no obvious solution for that last point. Executive Council inactivity is trade-off that JNET leaders have accepted. It's also resulted in the Steering Committee's becoming more active, which is critical because that is the group that will continue on with JNET when a new administration takes over.

It's reasonable to ask, if JNET is so wonderful, why isn't it the national model? And the answer is, states love their autonomy as much as individual agencies do. Many other states are developing their own integrated justice information systems, with goals similar to JNET's (check them out at http://www.search.org/integration/default.asp). What's clear in Pennsylvania is that local and state agency leaders are finally able to get real-time information on the critical aspects of their work, which means greater safety for their citizens. For the first time, the walls separating agencies are being replaced by networks. For more on JNET, try http://www.pajnet.state.pa.us/.

## Analysis

I like the JNET example for many reasons. It reflects the complex realities of collaboration across multiple agencies (and across all three levels of government); strong leadership is needed, the politics

must be managed, compromise is often required with so many players and interests involved. The case illustrates a truism about change
in social systems: *most change is pain driven*. That doesn't mean
change must be painful, it means that we are far more likely to
change our organizations (and ourselves) when we get very uncomfortable with the status quo. The pain involved in sharing information across criminal justice agencies was evident here, especially
after a tragic death. And this case demonstrates that collaboration
can produce significant change that affects everyday people.

I also like the case because it highlights well the key elements in
my collaboration framework. Each of the basics was in place in the
JNET example. First, the criminal justice agencies had *a shared interest* in obtaining real-time information on suspects and criminals.
Prior to JNET they were operating with partial information, which
reduced their efficiency and effectiveness. Second, *they wanted to find
a solution* to the information problem, soon. After patrolman Cole's
death and Tom Ridge's campaign emphasis on battling crime, there
was greater awareness of the problem, greater commitment to work
on it. The third basic—*the right people are at the table*—is one of the
most important factors in JNET's success. The governance structure
was cited over and over as the glue for JNET's many constituents.
It kept the key players involved, communicating, and in control of
the network. Previous attempts to share information among these
agencies were perceived as top-down control moves by one agency
or individual. JNET is just what the name suggests, a network of
agencies, and the governance structure provides a seat at the table
for their leaders.

Fourth, JNET's development was a model in using *an open and
credible process*. A steering team was formed in 1997 at the incep-
tion of the project, and that team managed the process throughout.
Consultants were used, but they didn't control the process. The
state's information technology office was involved, but it didn't call
the shots. Nor did the governor, even though his help was indis-
pensable. The parties at the table crafted their plan and imple-

mented it, and that ownership was critical. They sold it to their colleagues in other state and local agencies, and they provide subtle peer pressure on each other to share more and more information through the network.

The final basic has to do with the *champions* who are typically present in successful collaborations, people who have clout and credibility, who care passionately about the initiative and will make it a high priority. That was Tom Ridge in this instance. His priority on public safety was well known. He spent time with his cabinet on the issue, found the funds to support JNET's development, and frequently reminded senior officials and the public why this network was so important. Some of the JNET members don't report to the governor, but they were influenced by his public and sincere commitment.

JNET also reflects the other key elements in this framework. *Open, trusting relationships* are important in collaboration because the parties depend on one another for their mutual success. The Steering Committee members developed that trust over the course of their work on JNET's design and implementation. Another key element was the presence of *high stakes*. The governor's active involvement and clear expectations raised the stakes for his direct reports while creating a public expectation that affected others. Moreover, the tragic murder of a cop, which could have been prevented through effective information sharing, raised the stakes for everyone.

Further, JNET's leaders did a superb job of creating a *constituency for collaboration*. Recall Martin Horn's words: "there is no one authority that can force JNET on everyone." JNET's leaders needed to sell their colleagues in other agencies on its value. In the criminal justice world, peer pressure and interpersonal relationships are among the few means for breaking down the walls of turf and mistrust. JNET's Steering Committee members became strong advocates for the system as they saw it develop, chunk by chunk, and experienced the benefits it brought to their agencies. They created a larger JNET constituency when they talked it up in their agencies and with their colleagues in local and federal agencies.

Finally, JNET was led by people with *collaborative leadership* skills. As I'll discuss in Chapter Nine, this isn't the dynamic, charismatic, crisp leadership style you get in John Wayne movies or in some business books on the topic. Collaborative leaders are able to pull others in because they can keep their own egos in check. They're not primarily motivated by personal power needs—instead, they see possibilities through collaboration that excite others, and they are passionately driven to see the project succeed *through others*.

———

Each of these framework elements will take center stage in the next five chapters. As you read, I invite you to do two things. First, use the framework as a diagnostic tool. Assess your own organization's collaborative initiatives, or potential, with this framework. What's in place? What's missing? What needs to be done better, or differently? You can use the assessment checklist in Resource C, which includes each element of the framework, as well as the hurdles identified in Chapter Three. Second, use this framework as a starting point, not a rigid formula. Customize it to your own experience and agency culture. Become a "co-creator" with me and determine which of these lessons are more or less relevant to you. And if you're involved in collaborative efforts now, discuss the framework with your colleagues and test it against your own shared experience. What you come up with may be somewhat different, but it will be yours, and you'll be committed to it.

# 5

# Getting the Basics Right

*The* main thing *is to keep the main thing the* main thing!

*Jim Barksdale, Former Netscape CEO*

S ome leaders use a football term to refer to it. They call it "block-ing and tackling." They're talking about the basics of their busi-ness, whatever those basics are. As legendary football coach Vince Lombardi taught his players (and opponents), it doesn't matter how fancy, fast, or creative you are on the football field. If you don't do the basics well on every play, the other team will usually prevail.

I draw the same lesson from studying collaborative efforts. They tend to be founded on certain fundamentals, or basics. Knowing what constitutes those basics is an important start. Knowing how to create the basics (if any are missing) is even more important. This chapter will address both needs. Exhibit 5.1 outlines the basic elements required for collaboration.

## Shared Purpose

The first basic is a shared purpose or specific goal that the parties care about but can't achieve on their own.

If there is no shared purpose or goal, why collaborate in the first place? Good question—and one not always asked. The corporate world is littered with failed examples of companies that merged or took each other over, only to realize that they had little or nothing in common. Many in the public and nonprofit sectors can recall sitting through nonproductive meetings among would-be partners who thought they saw potential for win-win initiatives but couldn't pull them off. Frequently, the reason is that they had no shared purpose or goal to coalesce around.

---

**Exhibit 5.1. The Basics.**

- The parties have a shared purpose or specific goal that they care about but cannot achieve on their own.
- The parties want to pursue a collaborative solution, now, and are willing to contribute something to achieve it.
- The right people are at the table.
- The parties have an open, credible process.
- There is a champion for the initiative, someone with credibility and clout who makes this a high priority.

---

Sometimes the common ground is obvious. That was the case with the Child Advocacy Center case discussed in Chapter Two, where the shared interests were very specific. The county police and social services department don't have the same overall mission (except in the most global sense, to serve the county's citizens), but they do have one specific goal in common: to prevent child sexual abuse and deal with the perpetrators and victims effectively when it occurs. Recall the statement from one of the social workers: "It helps when one of our supervisors reminds us that we're here for the kids." Each can accomplish part of their shared goal, but neither can be fully successful on its own.

Many collaboration veterans believe that this common interest is most powerful if it's narrowed down to something concrete, even measurable. Con Hogan, who helped lead an impressive statewide collaborative effort to improve the health and education of Vermont's children in the 1990s, puts it this way: "What's often missing, and what's most important, is for the collaboration partners to agree on a short, declarative sentence stating the purpose of the collaboration. If the group can say that we all want babies to be born healthy, then that's very clear, and it also sets up expectations among community members, expectations that help hold the partner group accountable and responsible for their work. And it's important for this discussion of common purpose to occur before any discussion of organization, structure, bureaucracy, etc."

And how do you identify common interests? Sometimes the shared interest isn't obvious. The parties may not know what they want to achieve at the outset. In other instances the parties' goals for the effort will be in conflict. Jacki Bryant, a professional with experience at coordinating several human service collaboratives, sometimes has to deal with this problem. Her solution: confront the issue directly. She meets with each party individually, asks what they think the effort is supposed to accomplish, then gets the full group together to discuss their responses. This helps the group learn if they're together on goals, which leads to more open and direct communications.

Another method is to ask the parties this question: What will it take for you to consider this effort worth your while? That's not a question about measures of success (though success is also important to determine), it's a question about bottom-line interests. I once saw a group that was muddling along but not getting very far. At one meeting, the members were asked to identify something concrete that, if it occurred, would justify the time and energy they were investing in the effort. They went around the table, responding one at a time. One said, "I need to see some action; I'm tired of all the meetings." Another replied that after a half year, she still wasn't clear on the initiative's goals. After the last person spoke, they started to understand, for the first time, the underlying needs of each member. Happily, several of those were shared needs. In the language of negotiation, they were moving from *positions* to *interests,* and the group started to gain momentum. Whether through such direct discussion or more formal written statements, the parties need to put on the table what they hope to gain from the effort and the respective interests of their organizations and key stakeholders.

A third approach is to allow the parties a certain amount of time to determine their shared interest or goal. The purpose may not emerge for several meetings, as the members learn about each other's operations and explore their possibilities for joint action. Also, some of them may keep their interests to themselves because they're not sure of the trust level. I've seen cases in which a group agreed to meet for a specific period of time, or until a certain piece of work got done (say, a review of each entity's programs, customers, internal culture, and values), before trying to articulate mutual interests and purpose. It pays to be patient and not force this. It's also very helpful if a strong, committed champion for the initiative exists at the start. Such champions can play a central role in helping define shared purpose. Champions are one of the five basics, and are discussed later in the chapter.

# Desire for Action—Now!

The second basic is that the parties want to pursue a collaborative solution, now, and are willing to contribute something to that effort.

The key words here are *want*, *now*, and *contribute*. The fact that common interests or goals may exist doesn't guarantee that the principals will collaborate. There must be a desire, a sense of importance, and a willingness to invest in the effort. Without these, the group is only mouthing generalities.

When I ask if the parties want to pursue a collaborative solution now, it doesn't mean that every one of them must be ready to sign on the dotted line. Most groups include some individuals who have mixed feelings about the effort, especially at the start. Some parties attend knowing only that their past efforts going it alone didn't work. They may come in a defensive posture, interested primarily in protecting their interests from the collaborative, not in contributing to it. The real question is, Does a core of principals exist who want to pursue a collaborative solution? If there is, then the others can test the waters while the core moves forward.

And does the core group want to work on a collaborative solution right now? Timing is critical in collaboration. If the proposed collaboration doesn't address a real and compelling need for a given agency in the near future, its leader may relegate the effort to a priority B or C. Words are far less useful than actions when discerning a task's importance to someone. It's helpful to end a meeting with a list of specific follow-up tasks. Those who place a high priority on the initiative are most likely to sign up for the tasks. Often, one or two people who feel real passion for the effort will step up and demonstrate commitment and leadership.

Finally, a core group of the parties needs to be willing to contribute something to the effort. The contribution might be staff time, money, or other resources. In the Baltimore case, the social services and police departments provided staff to the joint center. And sometimes the contribution is less tangible. One of the keys to JNET's success with the criminal justice agencies in Pennsylvania has been the members' willingness to share information in the JNET system. Those who did this at the outset sent a strong signal, and created subtle but real peer pressure on others to do the same.

## Proper Representatives

The third basic is getting the right people to the table.

By *right people* I mean the people who can represent the key stakeholder organizations and interest groups involved in the issue or project, who can make agreements and influence others in their group to come along. Jim Pipkin, a veteran negotiator for the U.S. State Department, remarks, "You must get all of the right people to the table, which requires getting all who need to be there to believe that they can't get what they need to by going it alone."

Sometimes, the "right people" are brought together through a governance structure. This is especially important when several agencies are involved and an element of formality is required to ensure everyone's voice is heard, as is the case with JNET. By contrast, the Child Advocacy Center involves only two major entities; a formal governance structure there would probably be overkill.

Sometimes different people need to be at the table for different activities and functions. Once the superintendent of a national park held meetings with the park's key partners, six nonprofit organizations that provide a variety of services for the park (volunteer services, funding, sales of items related to the park, and so on). The goal was to clarify roles and responsibilities among the partners. Before the sessions began, the park's superintendent and staff realized that the major sticking points involved just two of the partner organizations. They decided to hold two separate meetings. The first included the executives and board presidents of those two parties and the senior staff of the park. Once their issues and conflicts were dealt with, the larger meeting was held for all the nonprofit partners. The "right people" were at the table, but in this case there needed to be two tables at two different times. It worked well.

And there are times when the "right people" should not be limited to the obvious people, as this example illustrates.

### Joint Venture: Silicon Valley

Home to more than seven thousand technology-based companies (Cisco Systems, Hewlett-Packard, and Intel, among others) that employ 1.2 million people, this region has become a symbol of the new economy. Over 2.5 million people live in the Silicon Valley area of California. Its residents enjoy a wonderful quality of life. But the 1991–92 recession hit Silicon Valley hard. It lost forty thousand jobs. The real estate market slumped. Job growth was flat after growing 7 percent annually through most of the 1970s and 1980s (Joint Venture, 1995). Moreover, the region started to suffer a lack of self-confidence. It lost competitions to house three major federally funded centers; one of those failed because the region couldn't even put together a credible proposal.

In January 1992, the San Jose Metropolitan Chamber of Commerce created a "coalition of partners" called Joint Venture: Silicon Valley (JVSV). It was made up of the region's major business organizations. "The initial purpose was to bring the business community together," according to Doug Henton, who has been a key player in JVSV from the start. "We had no common vision back then, no real identity. We had lost our ability to solve our own problems." The board chose to start by commissioning a $75,000 study of the region's economy. The resulting report, "An Economy at Risk," identified the region's warning signs and documented immediate and long-term problems. It got people's attention, as did a JVSV conference held in June 1992. Over a thousand regional leaders came to discuss the report and find solutions. It seemed to be an impressive start.

But the JVSV board faced serious criticism. The board and its initial working groups included only business leaders; none of the
region's twenty-seven cities was represented, nor were any of its educational institutions, nonprofits, or community groups. "Some in the
region started asking, 'where are the rest of the players?'" Henton
notes. The *San Jose Mercury News* (largest daily in the region) edi-
torialized on July 12, 1992, "[But] some skeptics fear it is an attempt
by business and industry to gang up on local government, trampling
environmental regulations and restrictions on growth."

The JVSV leaders quickly got the message and expanded the
board and working group membership. Soon, a new board was
formed, one fourth each from business, education, government, and
the community. And it greatly expanded its purpose. The vision was
broad and intriguing: "to build a community collaborating to compete globally." The new board incorporated as a 501(c)(3) nonprofit
in 1993.

The Joint Venture leaders learned that it was both right and
smart to take a very inclusive approach to its work. Their initial
motives were benign and sincere, but others wondered if the organization's business-only membership meant that it was primarily in
business to *protect* business. The lesson for would-be collaborators:
when there's low trust (and even when there isn't), consider broad-
ening the core group of members to include a broad range of perspectives and voices. JVSV experienced extraordinary successes
after it broadened the core group membership.

### Getting Appropriate People to the Table

And how do you get the right people to the table? This can be very
difficult. It's always important to clarify the type of people you want
other parties to send (that is, those able to speak for their agency)
but you may not get people at the level you need. Sometimes other
parties place a relatively low priority on the proposed effort; they
may send people who aren't high enough in the agency to represent

it; they may feel threatened and send people to observe and slow the process down if necessary. One solution is to meet with the other parties, one at a time, and listen carefully to their needs and reservations. See if they believe that, as Jim Pipkin put it, "they can't get what they need to by going it alone." And explain why it's so important to send someone high enough to represent the organization's needs and interests accurately.

In some instances it helps to get the most prestigious potential party to commit first; that can put pressure on others to join. Another strategy is to seek some new funding for the proposed initiative, as Kris Debye did when starting the Baltimore Child Advocacy Center. Getting a grant signals one partner's seriousness and capabilities, and others may follow the money and join. This step requires care. Take time to learn why some potential partners may be reluctant; gaining that knowledge will provide very useful intelligence down the road.

## An Open Process

The fourth basic is that the parties have an open, credible process. In their study of effective community-based collaborations, David Chrislip and Carl Larson include the "credibility and openness of the process" in their list of ten keys to success (Chrislip and Larson, 1994). I found this true of interagency collaboration as well. Now, it's true that the "P word"—*process*—turns many people off, often for good reasons. Process too often becomes an excuse for a lack of action and results. Robert Schaffer and Harvey Thomson call this the "activity-centered fallacy" (Schaffer and Thomson, 1992). They're referring to organizational change efforts in which the change leaders confuse activities (number of people trained, number of quality teams in place, and the like) for real change. An obsession with process for its own sake has doomed many potentially effective change initiatives. Remember: *the process is the means to the end;* it most certainly is not the goal.

But the process used to engage the principals is an important basic, because nobody knows whether a new collaborative will work. When starting out you only can assess its prospects by the nature of the process being used, the quality and reputation of the people in the room (which is another reason why it's so important to have the right people at the table), and the history of past efforts on the same issue. Here are some of the elements that help create an open and credible process for a collaborative group:

- Joint ownership

- Agreed-upon norms or ground rules

- Knowledge of each other

- Transparency

- Skillful convening

**Joint Ownership**

City officials will tell you that homeowners take better care of their properties than renters do. This is true in collaboratives as well. If the entire approach has been determined by one or a few people, the rest of the parties may assume that the whole thing is *wired*— that is, the results are predetermined, and their participation is unnecessary, or, worse, it's for show only.

When the parties have a sense of joint ownership they tend to see the process as open and credible. Joint ownership can be achieved in many ways—by seeking group consensus on the goals and outcomes of the effort, jointly deciding who should be at the table, getting everyone's input on the agenda for each meeting, or jointly determining measures of success. Joint ownership can also be achieved through a governance structure. Joint Venture's early struggles reflected the need for broader inclusion to achieve joint ownership from all segments of the community. It revamped its board and created that sense of ownership, which gave its process far more credibility and openness.

### Agreed Norms or Ground Rules

Norms and ground rules can be specific (for example, don't send a substitute if you can't make a meeting), or more general (treat each other with respect). The point is to invite the parties to articulate the standards of behavior they want to maintain. Doing so helps create an open and credible process. One way is to ask participants to reflect on previous group experiences they've had. What made the positive ones work well? What made the others less successful? Their responses will provide some of the behaviors and attitudes that can become group norms. The one norm I insist on when I'm convening such groups is candor. And I'm often struck by how powerful this (obvious) ground rule is. Inevitably, someone will say, "Well, since we're being candid, I want to point out that—" This person probably would have been quiet had we not agreed on a norm of candor.

For an excellent discussion of collaboration ground rules and how to develop them, see Appendix H in *Collaboration: A Guide for Environmental Advocates* (Dukes, Firehock, Leahy, and Anderson, 2001; call 434-924-1970 for a copy).

### Knowledge of Each Other

This is a main topic of the next chapter, on relationships. For now, suffice to say that group members are usually much more effective— and feel that the process being used is more open—when they exchange some information about each other. This was the case in the national park partnership mentioned earlier. Just as the first meeting was starting, in which the two principal nonprofit parties were present, one member suggested going around the table to learn about the participants. Nobody objected. Several of the participants took three or four minutes to talk about their work lives, college attended, non-work activities, family, and the like. The group "lost" about twenty-five minutes doing this exercise, but the members frequently referred to something they knew about each other in their later discussions, and after the session ended they stated that the initial exercise set an excellent tone that opened them up for in-depth discussions. A little patience and openness at the beginning creates credibility later.

## Transparency

This may seem like a trendy term, but I like it very much. It perfectly reflects the kind of process that fosters collaboration. In a transparent process, what you see is what you get. There are no surprises, at least no deliberate ones. Statements, commitments, disagreements are out in the open. Changes in course are discussed at the table, not in sidebar negotiations. When the process is transparent, it builds trust and confidence, the ingredients from which successful collaboratives grow. There is a very useful ground rule to adopt to ensure transparency: make all decisions and changes at the table.

## Skillful Convening

One of the best ways to ensure the existence of the first four items in this list is by using an experienced, skillful convener. This function can be performed by one of the parties, it can be rotated among many or all of them, or it can be performed by an outside consultant. If a consultant is hired and is paid by one of the parties, it's critical that the person be seen as working for all parties, not just the one footing the bills. As collaboration veteran Steve Schwartz suggests, the convener must be perceived as fair and effective, having the interests of the whole group at heart, not just the sponsoring agency's interests.

This isn't the place to detail the many tasks, behaviors, and functions that fall to a convener. That's been done ably by others (see, for instance, Schwarz, 1994—*The Skilled Facilitator*). Suffice to say that the convener's work sends an early and important message to the parties. That message will build credibility and confidence if people see the convener engaging the whole group in its work, helping them make the ground rules real, keeping the agenda open for all to influence, and above all moving the group continually forward without overly controlling it.

One effective method for developing an open and credible process is called a Partnering Workshop. It's described at the end of this chapter.

## A Strong, Committed Champion

The fifth basic is a champion for the initiative, someone with credibility and clout who makes this a high priority.

The overwhelming majority of successful collaborative efforts I've studied were marked by one or more strong, energetic champions. Someone with real passion for the issue must articulate the goal and demonstrate its importance. And, if that person has credibility and clout, and shows that this is the highest priority, you can start without several other basics and still have success.

Champions are usually peers, members of the core group that's doing the collaborative work. For instance, Kris Debye was an excellent champion for the Baltimore CAC initiative. More than a decade after she led the drive to create the center, people still point to her early efforts as the key ingredient to their success. One observer of the efforts to save the salmon in the Pacific Northwest notes that the parties have made reasonable progress when they had an internal champion. Unfortunately, it's been difficult to keep a champion over any extended period of time, which has slowed their progress somewhat.

Sometimes the champion is a senior leader who is in a position to foster collaboration without forcing it on people. That's the role former governor Tom Ridge played with the JNET information-sharing program in Pennsylvania. Governor Jim Hunt was the same kind of champion for Smart Start, a program serving kids up to age five in North Carolina. Hunt emphasized the need to do more for young children during his campaign in 1992, and after he won he convinced the legislature to fund it and helped rally the business community to support it. Smart Start operates through state-local-private sector partnerships in every North Carolina community.

## What Champions Do

The champion's job has no detailed position description; the role will vary with each effort. Certain tasks and roles seem to be common, though. These include the ones listed in Exhibit 5.2.

A colleague of mine says that the most important thing he's learned since joining a venture capital group is that venture capitalists "bet on the rider, not the horse." The point is that even the savviest businesspeople can't determine with confidence whether a

---

**Exhibit 5.2. The Roles and Tasks of Champions.**

- Articulating the project's purpose and importance, the benefits of succeeding and the costs and risks of failing.

- Helping the parties see that they can only meet the identified need through joint action.

- Seeing that someone attends to the rest of the basics.

- Being a downfield blocker. The champion anticipates hurdles, gets support for removing (or leaping over) those hurdles, and deals with people who are standing on turf and ego.

- Keeping senior leaders informed and involved, asking for their help selectively.

- Reminding the parties what they have in common, especially when conflicts and differences threaten their progress.

- Helping the parties engage in joint problem solving and visioning tasks.

- Taking a risk when moments of truth arrive.

- Providing confidence, hope, and resilience (perhaps the most important characteristic).

business plan is likely to succeed. So venture capitalists decide how to invest money by focusing on the person presenting that plan. If that person has a good track record (pardon the pun), a passion for the project, and the energy and connections to bring in very talented people to run the new venture, the investors are more likely to invest in the person (and thus the project). Members of a collaborative, especially in the early phases of the effort, are likely to "bet on the rider" if they believe they're looking at a committed, focused champion. Such champions give others hope and confidence.

### Finding a Champion

How do you find a champion for an initiative? You don't. Champions aren't found. They usually emerge in one of two ways: they nominate themselves, or they're already at the table and are invited to play a key role in the initiative. The Joint Venture: Silicon Valley initiative had both kinds.

> The initial idea for JVSV actually began in the spring of 1992 when John Kennett, the chairman-elect of the Chamber of Commerce, provided real leadership to the business community when it needed a lift. He invited representatives of twenty-six different business associations to the planning conference. Their input convinced the Chamber of Commerce board that "coalition building" should be a top priority. Several meetings later, Joint Venture was created. Kennett exemplifies the self-nominated champion.
>
> He then decided the group needed its own leader, and asked Tom Hayes, corporate affairs manager at a large semiconductor firm, to head up the coalition. Hayes (an invited champion) was an excellent choice. He served on the Chamber of Commerce board and knew many of the business leaders in the region. He worked for a leading firm in a key industry. And in an earlier life he'd been active in politics, working for a U.S. senator. His community organizing skills, knowledge of technology, and relationships with business leaders gave him excellent tools and background to be the next champion.

Hayes was the person who proposed commissioning a study of the region's economy, to document the problems and spell out the needs. But the board balked at the $75,000 price tag. Hayes, knowing his boss would support him, committed $25,000 of that amount *on the spot.* That changed the tone of the debate and created momentum. The board ultimately approved the expenditure, and the "Economy at Risk" report was produced. Hayes later noted that committing the $25,000 was the first "moment of truth" for JVSV. "We could have lost it right there, but someone had to step forward and make a dramatic statement that this effort was going to be real and world class" (Joint Venture, 1995, p. ii/7).

Sometimes, nobody steps forward to champion the effort, and nobody is recruited. At such times I've found it's often better to move forward in small steps and wait for a champion to emerge, rather than force the action with no willing leader. And if no champion emerges after many months, it's reasonable to consider waiting until the timing improves. It's also reasonable to ask the group members if collaboration is a high enough priority to continue meeting.

## Partnering Workshops

Partnering workshops, a structured method for helping several agencies work together, have been used successfully by dozens of private and public organizations since the 1980s. The goal of a partnering workshop is to establish a long-term relationship between the parties based on trust and a win-win mentality, in order to achieve their common objectives. It helps them master the basics of collaboration. For example, say an agency needs a new building. Once the contract is signed, but before the work begins, it holds a partnering workshop. Participants are the leaders from each organization, in this case they come from the agency requesting the work, the general contractor, the architect's firm, the engineering firm, and possibly some subcontractors. The deliverable is a partnering contract or charter, detailing the goals of the project, time line, work processes to be used, methods for dealing with change orders and conflicts, the key roles in the project, how communications will be managed, how an ongoing evaluation process will be managed, and the like.

But the session isn't all focused on the work project. It's largely about building trust and relationships. Thus, activities include the following:

- Trust-building tasks

- Discussions of personal and leadership styles

- Conflict management exercises and instruction on interest-based negotiations

- Discussions of organizational and personal values

- Discussions of communications styles and methods

The session lasts one to three days, usually in a setting away from the organizations. It's best to use a neutral facilitator.

The Army Corps of Engineers is given credit for the evolution of the partnering approach, and it swears by the process. Navy facilities regularly use partnering workshops on construction and long-term services contracts. The Associated General Contractors of America strongly endorses partnering, as does the Arizona Department of Transportation. ADOT has used partnering sessions since 1992 with excellent results. The number of claims on its projects has been radically reduced; the number of projects finished on time has increased (there is far less time spent in disputes and in court); and ADOT is saving hundreds of thousands of dollars through ideas generated at partnering sessions—money that it splits with its contractors (Cole, 1993).

Another agency with considerable experience in the partnering process is the U.S. Army Materiel Command. You can learn about its partnering methods and lessons learned at http://www.osc.army.mil/others/gca/partnering/index.htm. A detailed partnering workshop agenda is given in Resource A.

## Assessment: Are the Basics in Place?

It's useful to pause early on in a project and ask some questions to determine if you have the basics in place. Exhibit 5.3 provides a checklist for this effort.

———

The basics provide an excellent foundation for collaborative work. These factors don't ensure success, however. They simply provide the setting in which interested parties are most likely to achieve their goals through joint effort. The collaboration framework has four other key elements, and they're described in the following chapters, starting with the ingredient that gives partnerships their glue—open, trusting relationships.

---

**Exhibit 5.3. Checking for the Basics.**

Have you

- Discussed the parties' interests and goals regarding the collaborative?
- Agreed that there is a compelling, shared interest that the parties want to pursue, now?
- Felt comfortable asking questions and discussing doubts and concerns?
- Got people at the table who can speak for all of the stakeholder organizations?
- Considered forming a smaller core group to take on certain leadership and management tasks (if the number of people involved has grown into the double digits)?
- Spent time in the early phases getting to know one another?
- Periodically asked if the process is clear, and if the parties are comfortable with it?
- Established a few simple ground rules?
- Identified and supported those who will function as champions for the effort?

# 6

# Forming Open, Trusting Relationships Among the Principals

*The longer I work in this business, the more I'm
convinced that it's fundamentally about managing
relationships.*
      Bob Stripling, City Manager, Staunton, Virginia

*There is no magical leadership structure—just people
and relationships.*
      Neal Peirce and Curtis Johnson

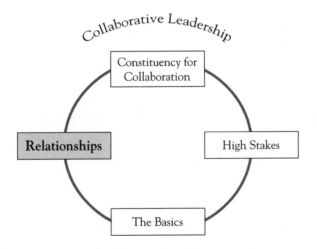

H ere's a pop quiz. What do the following have in common?

- Diplomats

- Some insurance companies

- University development officers

If you said, "They're all in the relationship business," you passed with flying colors. That word *relationship* may not appear on any of their job descriptions, but it's fundamental to what most of these people do (if they're good at their jobs). They each offer different products and services, but they achieve their goals largely by form-ing and sustaining positive relationships. Development officers, for instance, are measured on the amount of money they raise for their institution; it's a quantifiable, bottom-line job. But they don't usu-ally start talking about money when they visit a prospect. No, the good ones cultivate prospects by building relationships. They spend time learning about their prospects, about their experience at their alma mater, about their values and aspirations. Later, once the rela-tionship is established, they start discussing the university and what it's doing (or could do) that furthers the prospect's values (say, inter-national affairs), touches one of their concerns (cure for cancer), or demonstrates their appreciation for their school.

## Relationships: The Glue to Most Collaborative Efforts

Consider the following:

> Joe Wienand is the director of the Western Management Develop-ment Center, which serves senior federal managers. Earlier in his career, when Joe managed projects as a civilian in an army R&D lab, he frequently received requirements from military officers to design a piece of equipment for troops to use in combat. For instance, a gen-

eral might order lightweight chemical decontamination equipment that soldiers would use to clean toxic agents (like deadly nerve gas) from themselves and their equipment after an attack. A team of technical specialists from different disciplines would be assigned, and together they designed, tested, and evaluated the prototype equipment.

It was high-pressure work: the equipment often was urgently needed to protect troops deployed in action, and it had to be completed on a strict time frame. To keep funding available, the project had to hit specific milestones on schedule; failure to do so could delay the project five years. Moreover, the project team had to defend its status routinely at military "murder boards," where the customer and other senior officials would ask tough questions about the project. These inquisitions determined whether projects continued to be funded or not.

Sounds challenging, and it was. But to hear Wienand tell it, the technical work and time pressures and budget uncertainties were the easy part:

My main job was managing relationships among the project team members. It was usually a team of people who hadn't worked together before. They came from different units and technical specialties. I had people from testing, quality assurance, production engineering, drafting, computer and engineering specialties, numerous contractors . . . and they all reported to other managers, not to me. So it was the classic matrix approach. But we somehow had to work together very well if we were going to stay on schedule, keep our funding, and design the equipment to the needs of the ultimate customer—the soldier in the field.

And I'll tell you, keeping the technical people on the team happy and working together wasn't easy. In fact, it was by far my toughest job, dealing with those relationships. Project managers who don't have real good people skills don't succeed.

Wienand learned the same lesson that people in a variety of businesses are discovering: when you're trying to get individuals from different technical areas, professions, or organizations to work together, you need to develop and support the interpersonal relationships involved. Harvard Business School professor Rosabeth Moss Kanter (1994) learned a similar lesson from her research on alliances among thirty-seven companies in eleven countries. After conducting over five hundred interviews, she found three major themes. One of them: alliances can't be controlled by formal systems. Rather, they require a "dense web of interpersonal connections" (p. 97). Her key point: "Successful partnerships manage the relationship, not just the deal" (p. 96).

## Why Are Relationships So Critical to Partnerships?

Vantage Partners conducted a study of 130 companies to determine the major causes of failures in collaboration. Sixty-four percent of the respondents cited poor working relationships among the parties (Tischler, 2001). Poor relationships will kill almost any alliance; without strong relationships there's no trust, and without trust there will be no collaboration. When trust has been built, people are usually willing to give one another the benefit of the doubt and take small risks with each other. As one veteran collaborator puts it, "Collaboration involves giving up some control. You won't give up control if you're worried the other guy will rip you off."

Another reason that relationships are critical to collaboration: collaborative efforts aren't a straight line to success. There are many meetings and periods when little seems to happen, there are surprises that don't always delight. Relationships can carry the partners through difficult and unpredictable times. Nancy Carstedt, executive director of the Chicago Children's Choir, notes, "As we venture into unknown territory, it's critical to have that support [of a good relationship]" (Austin, 2000a, p. 48).

A third reason: collaboration requires considerable give and take, and that's more likely when good relationships exist. Some of the best—and worst—examples of give and take occur in legislative bodies. When Representative Mike Simpson was elected to the U.S. House of Representatives from Idaho in 1998, he was struck by the level of acrimony in Congress. One of Simpson's Idaho colleagues told him that, in the 1970s, congressional members went home to their districts only two or three times a year. Their families lived with them in Washington. Members spent time with each other on weekends; they got to know one another.

Today, most members of Congress leave their families at home. Members return to their district virtually every weekend. And while that keeps them in touch with their constituents, it means they have little time to develop the bonds that are required for compromise and effectiveness in Congress. Simpson saw a far more effective legislative process during his fourteen years in the Idaho state legislature, where members got to know each other. He sums up his two different experiences this way: "If I've learned anything, it's that a legislative body is built on relationships" (Simpson, 2000).

## Forming and Sustaining Relationships

"The touchstone of partnership is an understanding of the business needs and the self-interest of your potential partner," writes Bill Shore, an expert on the growing trend toward entrepreneurship in the nonprofit world (1999, p. 216). And how do you learn about another's needs without having formed a relationship with that person? You don't. Exhibit 6.1 lists some of the ways people develop relationships in their collaborative efforts. This is, of course, only a starter list. Please customize it to fit your needs.

### Begin Meetings with a Simple Check-In

Starting meetings by getting reacquainted came up in the last chapter, but it bears repeating here. I learned the wisdom of giving people an easy way to check in during a series of team meetings at the

**Exhibit 6.1. Building Strong Relationships.**

- Begin meetings with a simple way to check in and get people reconnected.

- Model open, candid communications; use self-disclosure.

- Build trust by giving the parties a chance to be accountable.

- Do some informal exploring and careful listening.

- Share accurate information, both requested and unrequested.

- Make conscious use of stories.

- Set aside time to work explicitly on relationships and trust.

- Find ways to create a sense of an "entity."

Federal Executive Institute. We were working on the design for a new program. Terry Newell, the FEI faculty coordinator, began each session with a question attributed to poet Ralph Waldo Emerson: "What has become clear to you since we last met?" People responded at different levels; some talked about business insights they'd had, others discussed something personal (such as the folly of making suggestions to an adolescent son), and some kept their remarks on the surface. It didn't matter what level people addressed: what mattered was that we had a consistent way to check in. Terry's question was a great one, and helped connect a group that only met every month or two.

There are other ways to check in when a group begins a meeting. The convener may ask members to say a few words about something going on in their nonwork life. Some conveners start by telling a story about themselves that others can relate to, like an instance of terrible customer service they received. There's no magic to this. All that's required is a simple question or comment that relates to where people have been since the last meeting, or where their minds are right now.

## Model Candid Communications

Anyone can provide a model of open communications; it needn't be done by the person theoretically in charge (and in collaboratives, everyone is "in charge" in various ways). Self-disclosure is almost always disarming; it puts people on a common human level and implicitly gives others permission to be open themselves.

Self-disclosure can be as simple as saying, "I'm confused about where we are right now; can someone help me?" It can quickly unearth issues that are easy for groups to avoid. For instance, someone says, "I want to be positive about the idea we're discussing, but I'm worried that maybe in the interest of consensus we're all being a bit too polite. Frankly, I don't think that this idea is going to fly! Am I the only one who feels this way?" Chances are, that person isn't alone at all, and the confession helps everyone else avoid the pitfalls of *groupthink* (agreeing because it looks as though the whole group wants something).

Another way to model open and candid communications is to acknowledge another's point of view, even though you disagree with it. Tim Reeves, president of Neiman Communications, says he learned that lesson well when he served as press secretary to former governor Tom Ridge of Pennsylvania. "You can't be an advocate for only one position. In a large public enterprise, no one point of view is determinative. You have to show respect for different perspectives—legal, legislative, policy, media. You serve your boss best when you remind him or her that there are other important perspectives. And your colleagues will love you for it. This kind of candor builds relationships."

## Give the Parties a Chance to Be Accountable

Collaboration inevitably involves giving up something—some control, autonomy, flexibility—in exchange for an outcome we can't produce alone. It's the giving up part that worries us. "All change involves loss," teaches Alec Horniman, a professor of business administration at the University of Virginia's Darden School, "and collaboration is a major change in most organizations." Horniman is right on the mark. But our fear of loss decreases when we're with people who demonstrate accountability through their actions.

That may sound obvious. How to put this insight into action? One way is to identify specific, short-term tasks that need to be done, invite the core members to volunteer for certain activities, and then discuss the results at the following meeting. It works even better if the members divide into small groups to do the work, because that gives them a chance to do real work together. *Few things cement relationships as well as working on a common task that the people care about.* Following through on tasks gives people an opportunity to demonstrate accountability. And when the core group works on a task like a common assessment form for shared clients or a joint training session for staff from each agency, it builds a sense of identity. People start talking more about "us" and "we," less about "you" and "me." As collaboration veteran Steve Schwartz says, "Never underestimate the power of a product." Creating one together generates confidence in the accountability and credibility of the members.

### Listen Carefully

Ron Redmon, a leadership coach and former government executive, tells a story about management guru Peter Drucker. Drucker visited a client organization and observed its top leadership team. When the CEO asked him for an assessment of the team, Drucker said, "Your people don't communicate well with each other. They don't listen to one another."

"And what do you suggest we do about that?" asked the CEO.

Drucker's reply: "Stop talking."

There probably aren't many senior managers who believe they got to the top by talking less. But that's an important part of collaborating, *if* it's accompanied by careful listening. When a group meets and discusses goals and strategies, when it looks for win-win opportunities, when it discusses what each party hopes to achieve and worries about losing, it's time to do some very careful listening. That's not about being nice, it's about being smart. "Collaboration is more likely when one party understands the other's needs, and wants to do what's possible to help the other meet those needs," says Bob O'Neill, who was a city and county manager before becoming executive director of the International City/County Management Association. Careful listening will help you determine the agencies' comparative strengths and shortcomings. And it will give the group a sense of whether it is ready to move forward.

### Share Requested and Unrequested Information

People in many regulatory and oversight agencies often say, "You just can't win." Whatever you decide, someone will be upset. If a local government planning commission gives approval to a "big box" department store, some people are delighted at the new offerings they can buy while others may be angry because of increased traffic near their homes. One of the most important things such agencies can do to maintain their credibility in the face of constantly angry constituents is to ensure that the information they give out is absolutely reliable. What you want is for people to say, "I don't always agree with them, but at least I know they're honest with me."

Providing credible information when it's requested is important; providing it *before* it's requested is even more so. As Richard Axelrod says, "Holding information creates dependency, while sharing information creates initiative" (Axelrod, 2000, p. 150). When the Bureau of Land Management and Forest Service offices in Missoula, Montana, decided to integrate their two weed management programs into one, they did a number of things to build relationships among the people involved. One of the most powerful steps they took was to watch out for each other. Once, a Forest Service supervisor learned that the local BLM office was going to be publicly (and wrongly) criticized. He got on the phone immediately and gave his BLM counterpart a heads-up. The BLM staffer was better able to handle the problem when it surfaced, and a relationship was cemented.

## Use Stories

Rick Stone is a consultant who teaches managers and others how to use stories to communicate their important messages. He calls stories "the core tool to relationship building." Rick says that when people tell a story, those listening often try to find something in common with the story or storyteller. And that builds common ground. Exhibit 6.2 summarizes the functions storytelling can serve in a business relationship.

The head of one Department of Veterans Affairs Benefits office used a powerful story to reinforce the office's purpose and importance. The movie *Saving Private Ryan* portrayed the attempt to retrieve a soldier whose brothers had been killed during the D-Day assault on Normandy. The office manager was moved by the movie, and he paid to have all two hundred of his staff see the film and discuss it afterward. His reasoning? "They [the soldiers] are who we're working for, they are the reason we do our jobs here each day." The movie's story gave staff a common experience, a way to connect their daily work to their ultimate purpose.

---

**Exhibit 6.2. Uses of Stories.**

Stories do many things:

- Signal to people your priorities and values.
- Make the organization's or partnership's mission clearer and more compelling.
- Help people be more open to change.
- Give others information about who you are, what you value, and why you're there.
- Help people find common ground.

---

## Make Time for Relationships and Trust

In the southern Maryland workforce development partnership called EARN, the key players have made much progress but occasionally feel frustrated that things haven't moved faster. At one monthly meeting, a core group member suggested taking a boat trip together! It wasn't quite as strange as it sounds. The group's leaders hadn't gotten to know one another outside their business meetings, and this individual emphasized that only through stronger personal relationships would they develop the trust and confidence to succeed. The group didn't quite find a boat, but they did devote a full day to a retreat at one of their homes, where a consultant helped them lower their guard and form stronger connections.

Sadly, collaboratives that set aside time to work on relationships and trust are the exception. This task is too important to be left to chance. Taking the time to build relationships doesn't have to involve a full-day retreat (although that certainly can help). It can happen at meetings that include a meal. There's something about breaking bread with others that allows people to lower their guard and find common interests. That's what Rod Collins, retired Forest Service administrative officer (and former member of Vice President Gore's National Performance Review team), concluded from one of his collaborative experiences in Oregon:

### Friday Chowders

"In the early 1990s, our local Forest Service leadership team and the leaders of the local Bureau of Land Management used to hold a formal meeting once a year to discuss common interests and concerns (and our offices were only about two hundred feet apart!). But we weren't making progress in these meetings; they were too formal, and not frequent enough to get into the real issues." One day Rod made a proposal to his colleagues in the BLM office: "We all eat lunch every day. A restaurant here serves a nice chowder on Fridays, our leadership team is going to eat there this coming Friday. Want to join us?"

The two teams met, had a good talk, and soon the "Friday chowders" became a regular on everyone's calendars. For over four years, in fact, the leaders of the offices met monthly at a restaurant.

These lunch chats produced many results. At one they decided to stop using three different permits for citizens who wanted to cut firewood on national forests, and agreed on a single permit form and uniform cost. That one item had been batted around for years; it was dealt with in ten minutes during a lunch. On other occasions frontline employees came and proposed certain changes, sometimes getting approval on the spot.

Collins believes the chowder lunches worked well for several reasons:

- They offered an informal setting to discuss important issues and make decisions.

- They provided the social lubrication to form relationships.

- They helped the leaders think in broader terms— which can be difficult sitting at your desk, trying to deal with ongoing and sometimes urgent operational issues.

- They were based on an age-old principle of building friendships and alliances that is common across cultures: breaking bread together.

Whether it's at a retreat, a series of informal lunch meetings, or an occasional team-building session, partnership groups gain strength when they take time to work explicitly on relationships.

### Create a Sense of an "Entity"

Just before I joined the faculty of an executive development institute some years ago, I learned that someone on the faculty was spreading an untrue (and not terribly flattering) story about me. Lane, one of the other faculty members, heard the story and immediately told the deputy director that they had to stop the rumor quickly. Now, Lane barely knew me; we'd met only once. Why was he so concerned? He said he was acting "because this kind of thing will hurt the *system* if we don't catch it right away." His commitment wasn't to me, it was to the institute, to the "entity" that he cared about.

The notion of relationships as an entity is a powerful one. Steve Nock is a sociologist who has researched relationships for years. After doing countless interviews and surveys of over fifteen thousand couples, he concludes that "the most successful marital relationships involve three elements; there's me, you, and the 'entity' which is our relationship. And in positive relationships, people are more willing to compromise and go with the other person's preference, in the interest of preserving the entity" (personal communication).

Nock's research led to an intriguing finding. Couples who are cohabiting but not married tend to focus on the present. They report how things are going today, they talk about how much equality there is in their everyday actions and decisions, right now. Happily married couples don't think and talk as much about the present. Rather, "marriages—happy ones, at least—do not exist in the present so much as in a more expansive time frame that incorporates past and future. Obligations, the threads from which intimacy is woven, are both debt and promise. Obligations exist only in the past and future, not in the present. I feel obligated to perform some duty in my marriage today because I was the beneficiary in the past or believe that failure to perform my obligations may jeopardize our common future" (Nock, 1998, p. 240).

People in good relationships seem to organize their lives around a "shared past and imagined future," Nock writes. They've created something together (experiences, a home, perhaps children) that they value, and they envision events they hope to experience together. Couples in good relationships don't pull up the flower each day to see how it's growing. They've created an entity that they're committed to; it reflects their past and foreshadows their future.

Here are some approaches for making a collaborative initiative into an entity:

### Create a Brand

The concept of *branding* may not be well received in some government and nonprofit agencies; it may seem too corporate, too commercial. But even if the word bothers you, its meaning should excite you. After all, a brand is a symbol and reminder of the defining elements, the essence of an organization or its products. The brand represents the agency's distinctive core; it's an important and powerful notion. Collaborators can nurture relationships and strengthen their commitment to their common purpose as they build a brand, an identity, around their initiative.

One way to create a brand has to do with the conscious use of language. The research on fourteen communities engaged in collaborative civic change supported by the Pew Partnership showed that people in these communities developed certain "watchwords" to describe their mission accomplishments. "In Western North Carolina, people talked about 'revaluing the crafts worker.' In Charleston, South Carolina, people wove the phrase 'youth as assets' into conversations" (Dewar, Dodson, Paget, and Roberts, 1998, p. 39). A memorable catchphrase helps to promote a sense of identity.

So do logos and themes. When NASA initiates a space project, the crew assigned to it creates a logo that goes on the patch on their sleeves and becomes an informal trademark for the venture. It may be round, octagonal, or some unconventional design. The point is, it's *their* design, their brand, and they take it whenever they meet with employees around the country who are working on some aspect of the mission. In the southern Maryland EARN collaborative, erasers were given out at early meetings with the words "Erasing the Lines" on them (see Figure 6.1). As the erasers found their way back to staff members' desks, they served as useful reminders of one of the initiative's goals: to eliminate the lines between agencies serving the same clients.

**Figure 6.1. The EARN Eraser.**

*Generate Opportunities for Success*

Finally, the simple fact of succeeding at a common effort helps create a commitment to an entity and to a shared purpose. Many research studies demonstrate people's desire to identify with a winner. One of the most creative involved university students and their football team. One fall, psychology professor Robert Cialdini interviewed students at Arizona State University and asked about the outcome of their school's football games. In the great majority of cases, students used the pronoun "we" after a win: "We beat Houston" or "We won." After a loss, students used a different pronoun: "*They* lost to Missouri, 30–20." Cialdini's conclusion: There's a strong human desire to "connect ourselves to winners and distance ourselves from losers." One student summarized both needs nicely—after noting the score of a home team defeat, he said "*They* threw away *our* chance for a national championship!" (Cialdini, 1984, p. 196).

Smart collaborative leaders find relatively simple ways to help the parties experience successes. When the initiative produces positive results, it helps create a sense of an entity and moves people from "me" and "them" to "us."

---

If you're trying to collaborate with people who worry about what they or their agency might lose, it may help to use the metaphor of personal relationships. Relationships, or at least good relationships, don't take away from our individual identities. They *add* a new element, an entity, that we grow to value. There's still me, and you, but now there's also us. That's how collaboration works when done well. It gives far more than it takes.

# 7

# Developing High Stakes

*The only thing more challenging than a crisis may be its absence.*

> *Neal Peirce and Curtis Johnson*

M ost adult Americans recall the horrors of April 20, 1999, when two sick boys opened fire at students and teachers inside Columbine High School. We know all too well the statistics, and we know the faces of many victims. What most of us don't know is a very different story that unfolded over and over during those hours of terror. Nancy Gibbs, senior editor of *Time,*

has described it eloquently in print and also in this speech at the Chautauqua Institution:

> We would be missing an opportunity if we didn't realize that this generation of teenagers right now, is a generation that has gotten a very bad rap of being spoiled, and untested, and their brains sodden by popular culture, and they've never faced anything like the trials of the "greatest generation" who have been so at the forefront of our imagination. . . . And yet on that day in April, a bunch of privileged, suburban high school kids who by any measure of any past generation had never had anything asked of them, were put to a test that none of them could have anticipated . . . and look at what they did:
>
> You had bigger kids lying on top of little kids, to protect them from being shot. You had kids holding doors open and ushering other kids out and showing them a safe way to get out of school. You had children barricaded in the choir room, who were lifting their asthmatic classmates up over their heads, where the air was clearer up closer to the ceiling.
>
> You had a bunch of students up in a classroom where their teacher was bleeding to death, on the phone with the 911 operators trying to guide the SWAT teams to where they were, so that they could rescue Dave Sanders, and *refusing* to leave him until someone had come to help him.
>
> Everywhere, all through that day, there were stories of heroism like, thank God, we haven't had occasion to see in this country. But we saw them. And to only focus on what two sad, monstrous young men did, and not on what *hundreds* of young men and women did that day, is to miss one of the great lessons of Columbine, and the one I take the most heart from [Gibbs, 2000].

There seems to be something in the way we human beings are wired that pulls us together when we're faced with an emergency or crisis. Think about this question: When does your organization perform at its best? When I ask the managers who take my classes, over 90 percent of them reply with statements like the ones in Exhibit 7.1. And when I ask my students to explain why people pull together in such situations, they say the following:

"Everyone pulled together; for once there was no problem of 'my unit versus yours.'"

"We knew what the priorities were, so everyone was on the same page."

"The consequences of getting it wrong were very big."

"The challenge was so enormous that the usual egos and turf didn't get in the way; all we knew was that we had to solve the problem."

"People who didn't respect each other were thrown together and amazingly they found strengths and positives that they'd never seen in each other."

"It was 'us against the problem'; we had a common enemy."

A pessimist could look at these quotes and (being a pessimist) conclude that only in crises are people willing to collaborate. It may

---

**Exhibit 7.1. When Is Your Organization at Its Best?**

Most common responses:

- In a crisis or emergency (the most frequent answer).
- When there's a complex task that has a sense of urgency to it and nobody can do it alone.
- When we feel threatened by the loss of funding, customers, important projects.

be true, as the old joke goes, that many pessimists got that way by betting on too many optimists! But I'm a hard-headed optimist, and I find a different message here. My experience tells me that these quotes reveal some very powerful insights about crises, insights that can help us collaborate when there is no crisis. Think about the words—people "pulled together"; people were on the "same page"; they were "thrown together" and found strengths in each other. There's a common thread here: something about high-stakes situations reveals our common humanity and overcomes the forces that pull us away from one another.

## What I Mean by "High Stakes"

People experience high stakes in the types of situations outlined in Exhibit 7.2. When we look around, we see high stakes in a variety of human situations that elicit collaborative behavior: a colleague suffers a heart attack in the office and people drop what they're doing to help out; a child is missing and hundreds of strangers volunteer to join the search effort; a city applies to host the Olympic Games and can barely handle the hordes of volunteers who offer their time and talents to the cause.

Most of the collaborative efforts I've studied were initiated because the stakes were too high to allow current problems to con-

---

**Exhibit 7.2. What Creates High Stakes.**

- People are working on an activity that is very important to them, their leaders, their customers, or other key stakeholders (such as funders).

- The activity is visible to others.

- The consequences of doing the activity well or poorly are very large.

- Those doing the activity will feel the consequences directly, in the near term.

---

tinue. The intelligence community's virtual teams developed after Congress made it very clear that it was upset with some costly and highly publicized intelligence mistakes that might have been avoided had the agencies collaborated. Joint Venture: Silicon Valley began during a deep recession when local business leaders became convinced that they had to do something to deal with it. It's a common story: when faced with a shared crisis or challenge, people often pull together in extraordinary ways.

But you can't rely on crises (or create them) to stimulate collaboration; doing so would burn out your staff and lead to cynicism. On the other hand, it is possible to learn important lessons from urgent situations and crises, and to find ways to apply such lessons when there is no emergency. I find four insights from crises that relate directly to collaboration during more normal times:

CRISIS INSIGHT No. 1: *People usually work best together when they have a common project, product, or program to work on that involves high stakes.*

Recall Steve Schwartz's comment: "Never underestimate the power of a product." From the playground to the boardroom to the battlefield, people with a concrete goal—a game to win, product to get out, an enemy to defeat—find that they can get the job done even if they can't stand each other personally. Consider this story told by a twenty-eight-year-old female manager in a large bank:

> There was something that used to bother me. I can remember when I was about ten, my brother . . . used to play on Saturdays with a gang of boys down the street. He'd come in for lunch and we would hear every single Saturday about two of these boys. They were just terrible. He couldn't stand them. But he'd be back out playing

> with them after lunch. . . . One day I said, "If you don't
> like them, why do you play with them?" He just stared
> at me and said, "You've got to be crazy! We need eleven
> for the team!" [Hennig and Jardim, 1976, pp. 51–52].

In a way, this story seems to contradict the importance of interpersonal relationships I've been emphasizing. This woman's brother
had a terrible relationship with two members of his football team.
He couldn't stand them. Yet they had a common project that the
boys considered important: winning on the field. It's not that relationships didn't matter; rather, the stakes were high enough to offset their mutual dislike.

CRISIS INSIGHT NO. 2: *Crises tend to clarify the goal, the objectives, and
the priorities.*

The beauty of a crisis is that it usually simplifies things—at least if
the group is somewhat prepared. People may have different agendas and conflicting egos; they may differ over the agency's priorities,
but crises cut through that. If a high-priority report must be produced by close of business tomorrow for a nonprofit's board of directors and the agency will be judged by it, people usually put aside
their differences and get the job done well. Other tasks become
lower priority.

One exception to this insight is the extreme situation that catches
people totally by surprise. Tragically, many emergency personnel per-
ished on September 11, 2001, for this reason (Dwyer, 2002).

CRISIS INSIGHT NO. 3: *People's capabilities often count far more than
rank during a crisis.*

Think about your own organization. If the computer system is down
and a high-priority report must be produced quickly, do you look
around for the most senior manager to solve the problem? Chances

are, you grab the person who's got the skills and experience to get the system going, even if you have to phone someone who's called in sick that day.

CRISIS INSIGHT No. 4: *Many crises create incredibly close bonds because there's a common challenge or enemy.*

That's why so much military training simulates combat; it helps the troops bond in powerful ways. They establish relationships that enable them to do literally anything for each other. As one retired general observed, in the foxhole your real loyalty isn't so much to flag and country, it's to the guy next to you. The person who used to seem so different has demonstrated talents and guts and helped you survive.

Well-coached sports teams experience the same phenomenon, as do political campaign teams. After a successful season or campaign, the members of the team talk about "all we've been through," about being "family" and the closeness they feel for each other. By the way, this is also why winning politicians often feel closer to and more trusting of those who served with them on their campaign than those who didn't. They've been through a war together.

## Raising the Stakes Without Burning People Out

How do we create a sense of high stakes without burning people out? That's the big question. Most people cannot live in a state of perpetual crisis. Some do thrive on the rush of constant challenge, but the majority get overwhelmed or exhausted if they work in perpetual crisis. How to apply the insights from crises on an ongoing basis—how to create the feeling of high stakes—without burning out your staff and yourself? Exhibit 7.3 outlines some approaches that often do the job.

---

**Exhibit 7.3.  Creating High Stakes.**

- Help others develop a line of sight.

- Develop a sense of urgency.

- Make current performance visible and accountability real.

- Identify a higher purpose.

---

## Help Others Develop a Line of Sight

*Line of sight* is a term used most often in the private sector. People with a line of sight see the connection between their work and some larger purpose or impact on others. For a variety of reasons many employees lack a line of sight, which makes it difficult for them to understand how their efforts connect to real people.

Bill Leighty, former director of the Virginia Retirement System, tells this true story about helping employees in one office to develop a line of sight and see their impact on others.

### Form 47

When Leighty became deputy commissioner of the Virginia Department of Motor Vehicles in 1990, he did what many new leaders do, he went around the building and visited different units to find out about their missions and people. Every visit proved extremely helpful, all but one. That office was depressing. Two supervisors' desks faced a sea of workers sitting in neat rows. Bill introduced himself, explained why he was there, and asked what this unit did. The reply: "We process Form 47." (The Habitual Offender Status Form.) As he asked more questions about their work and about their customers, he got increasingly frustrated. The staff had no sense of goals or priorities. These poor souls knew little about their role or mission at the DMV.

Leighty asked one more question: "How do you know when you're successful?" That they could answer. They told him that if they kept the backlog of forms under six weeks, "nobody bothers us." That was all they knew. Leighty left, depressed.

Some time later Leighty was talking with a member of the state police. He told the man about his experience with this work group. The trooper got excited: "They don't know what this is all about? They don't realize how important this is?? This form gets filled out when a driver is caught driving under the influence for the third time. Three DUIs and that allows us to take his license away; it lets us get dangerous people off the road! We can't do our work without that form, it's critical to us in law enforcement!!!" Leighty asked the trooper if he would be willing to meet with the unit and explain the impact of the group's work on the police and on road safety. He quickly said yes, and soon met the staff.

Several weeks passed and Leighty met a woman who headed up the Virginia chapter of MADD—Mothers Against Drunk Driving. He told her the story about this unit and what it did. Her eyes got teary. She described numerous examples of habitual offenders who'd had more than three DUIs but were still on the road, and of the people she knew personally who'd been killed by them. She was astonished that the staff didn't know the importance of their work. When she regained her composure, Leighty asked her if she would meet with the unit. She agreed, and soon was talking with them about her own personal story.

A few months later Leighty came back to visit with the unit. He asked them how they viewed their job. The staff no longer said, "We process Form 47." No, they looked Leighty right in the eye and said, "We save people's lives." And that's not all. They had taken it upon themselves to do more than asked. They developed charts and graphs on productivity; they created a "Ten Worst Offenders" list for each state jurisdiction and gave them to the police there. They automated their processes, dramatically reducing the time to process information even though that was a threat to the job security of some in the office. They had been transformed from mindlessly filling out forms to passionately pursuing a noble mission.

Bill Leighty is a delightful, creative, and high-energy public executive (in December 2001 he was appointed chief of staff by

Virginia's new governor, Mark Warner, an unusual promotion for a career civil servant). But all of us can do what he did if we think about it. He helped create a line of sight, a connection between what people do every day and their impact on real human beings. He did it by taking two steps. First, he showed his own interest by personally visiting with the staff, in their office. That gets most people's attention, especially if it hasn't been done in years. Second, he brought in key customers to tell the staff how that unit's work touched them and others. It was that direct, and that powerful.

When people have a line of sight, when they see the connection between what they do and an important outcome, it often creates high stakes that pulls them together. Here are some of the many ways to create a line of sight:

- *Offering voluntary, short-term rotations.* Staff can experience what others do and how the pieces fit into the whole.

- *Experiencing the organization as a customer.* When you get outside the system you see it more clearly. That's why airline execs fly unannounced on their planes.

- *Flow charting important work processes.* Meeting with people from different units and mapping out a business process exposes numerous delays, redundancies, opportunities for improvement. It helps staff see their connection to the larger whole.

- *Meeting with customers to learn how they experience the work.* When this isn't possible, some organizations develop alternatives to capture the voice of the customer. A student loan office in the U.S. Department of Education has large pictures of some students who received the office's assistance, sometimes accompanied by letters explaining the difference that a college education is making for them.

- *Seeing the ultimate outcome of the organization's work.*
  Staff can gain a line of sight by experiencing an activity that represents part of the agency's mission. That's why NASA routinely brings a cross-section of employees (from support staff up) and their families to Cape Canaveral to observe its big launches.

There are other ways to help people see their connection to something larger. The point is, *most people need that connection*. They need to feel and touch and see it. Mission statements don't do it. Experiences do it.

### Develop a Sense of Urgency

Many people use the word *urgency* when describing the conditions that led to an organizational change. But how do you create that sense of urgency? It usually develops when one or more of these conditions exist:

- Employees come to believe that the way they're doing business is hurting themselves or their customers (in terms of quality, financial condition, timeliness, interpersonal relationships, or efficiency).

- Employees face a deadline that they believe is real, and a significant amount of work must be done by that time.

- Powerful external stakeholders demand that the organization make an important change.

- There is competition to determine who will get the contract and funding to perform a service.

Joint Venture: Silicon Valley is a prime example of the first cause. Business leaders in the region were convinced by 1991 that they had to change. The region is filled with high-tech entrepreneurs who excel at start-ups but don't always work well across boundaries.

When the region's economy went south, when it lost bids for large federal installations, the leaders knew they had to change. Their report, "An Economy at Risk," helped to convince thousands of others that they all had to make some changes. It identified a major problem in the region, a "culture of blame," and helped people realize they weren't taking responsibility for solving their own problems.

Deadlines help create a sense of urgency. When the champion of the Baltimore County Child Advocacy Center was trying to put it together, she learned of a grant available to agencies willing to co-locate and provide services to victims of child sexual abuse. Having to meet a deadline for the grant proposal helped spur four parties to come together. Powerful external stakeholders also can create pressures that lead to a sense of urgency. In the late 1990s, congressional hearings into alleged abuses by the Internal Revenue Service led to changes in the IRS that have amazed many. After a series of taxpayers told horrific stories of IRS mistreatment, the agency began placing much more emphasis on customer service and less on collections.

Finally, competition can provide a powerful sense of urgency, even in the nonprofit and public worlds. David Osborne, coauthor of *Reinventing Government* (1992) and *Banishing Bureaucracy* (1997) among other well-regarded books, describes the use of competition to improve service delivery in one-stop career development centers in Massachusetts. The centers were designed to help people find jobs and the education or training they needed. Providers were invited to compete for the opportunity to run the centers. The winners received funding and three-year charters, but would have to compete to keep the charter after the third year. Most of the winners were collaboratives, and, as Osborne noted, "the competition really worked. It created very good business plans, and then it kept the pressure on because every center staff knew that the other center operators might compete to run their center when their charter expired in three years" (personal communication).

Competition isn't a new concept to public and nonprofit agencies. They are used to competing informally for resources, talent, and attractive programs. But few are used to formal competitions for the right to run core services, or even to stay in business. It's a coming trend, and it helps create the urgency that can lead to collaboration and results. (See Chapter Five of *The Reinventor's Fieldbook* by Osborne and Plastrik, 2000, for more on competition in government.)

## Make Current Performance Visible, and Make Accountability Real

When my corporate colleagues complain about government waste and inefficiencies and conclude that "government should be run just like a business," I tell them to review their Civics 101. American government was never intended to run like a business. On the contrary, the framers wanted to make it relatively slow. Recall Madison's comment after the Constitutional Convention: "We have consciously designed an inefficient government, to keep man free." The cost of preventing tyranny was a fragmented, separated government system in which everyone seems to check everyone else.

But, when it comes to making government and nonprofits more *businesslike*, I'm all for it. The fact that we separate powers of government is no excuse for shoddy quality or inattention to results. The fact that nonprofits have important social missions is no reason to overspend a budget. And the most powerful method I know to ensure a more businesslike agency is to measure performance, make the results visible, and hold employees accountable for results, regularly. The city of Baltimore is demonstrating this very well. Its sixteen-thousand-employee workforce used to be considered one of the least responsive and least productive in the country. That's changing, primarily because of a new mayor and a system called CitiStat that requires accountability for results.

## CitiStat

CitiStat is a citywide application of the heralded Comstat system pioneered by the New York Police Department in the mid-1990s. Every other week in Baltimore the first deputy mayor, city department heads, and most of the mayor's cabinet meet for an hour and a half in a room filled with graphic presentations that depict how each city department is functioning. Mayor Martin O'Malley, who created CitiStat after taking office in January 2000, attends as many sessions as he can.

The CitiStat room has two computers projecting interactive graphic information. On a large wall behind the podium are two six-foot by ten-foot projection screens, each filled with spreadsheets, maps, graphs, and other visuals that capture key data on the agencies: number of complaints about missed trash pickup in a given neighborhood, crime trends, amount of overtime for a particular unit, and the like. The CitiStat leaders ask questions about these trends, and demand answers.

For instance, Figure 7.1 presents a CitiStat graphic from Public Works, showing amount of overtime, lost workdays (employees couldn't work for reasons beyond their control), and number of complaints in the refuse collection unit over a four-month period.

CitiStat uses numbers, lots of them, to identify the performance level of each unit. Managers are put on the spot by cabinet members who pepper them with questions. You don't want to come to these sessions unprepared, and you don't want to see your numbers revealing constant trouble. "Having everybody in the room, looking at the same data, with the built-in follow-up component [of meetings every two weeks] really contributes to a sense of urgency," says Matt Gallagher, CitiStat's director of operations. "The system really compresses decision making" (personal communication). It also allows effective managers to shine. O'Malley sends personal notes or even Orioles baseball tickets to employees who do exceptional work (Clines, 2001).

**Figure 7.1. Extended Mixed Refuse Collection Overtime, Lost Workdays, and Complaint Trends.**

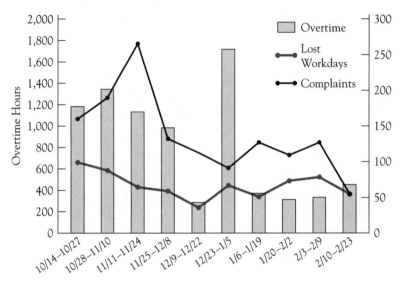

Baltimore is the first city to use CitiStat for all city operations, and it seems to be helping. In its first two years the system saved the city over $13 million, mostly in overtime costs. The city now collects 65 percent more garbage than it did before CitiStat. And the number of murders went down 14 percent during the first year of CitiStat operations. In 2001 Baltimore experienced a 30 percent reduction in overall crime. Further, home sales were up in 2001, after years of decline.

Equally important, CitiStat has department and agency heads talking and working together. They no longer circulate endless series of e-mail messages among various departments when an issue is a hot one and nobody wants to take control. "There is a great creative dynamic because all of the principals are in the room," says Baltimore's first deputy mayor, Michael Enright. "We don't need twenty-two memos to get an issue resolved." CitiStat creates an environment fostering direct, nondefensive *conversations* among the principals of each important city operation. There's enormous value in that.

> Lead paint poisoning is a good example of collaboration through CitiStat. Not a single case of lead poisoning had been abated in ten years prior to CitiStat. Worse, the city hadn't even gone after any landlords who owned buildings where children were being poisoned with lead paint in the whole decade; not a single one. A "LeadStat" team was pulled together with officials from eleven agencies (housing, health and environmental, and justice) and from some community organizations. Six of the agencies are state and federal, but they all started attending LeadStat meetings in city hall. The team identified cases of child lead poisoning and posted them on the map with red dots. They also started meeting regularly to find solutions and turn the red dots to green ones. They identified many of the barriers that had prevented them from working together in the past. Health and housing inspectors were cross-trained, ending the overlap in their enforcement duties.
>
> In LeadStat's first year (2000), the team filed 121 cases against landlords of buildings where lead poisoning was occurring. They also prevented 482 properties from being rented to new tenants until the landlords eliminated the lead paint. And the City Council passed legislation requiring universal lead testing for one- and two-year-olds. Results: In the first year, the number of children tested for lead poisoning went up by 51 percent. By December 2000, 124 red dots (contaminated properties) turned green. The statistics for 2001 were even more impressive, as Figure 7.2 illustrates.
>
> It's clear that CitiStat has city officials' attention, largely because it makes performance visible in a quantifiable way. A few agency heads left once the system was introduced; most are stepping up and learning to respond. And several have instituted their own versions of CitiStat within their agencies. For more on CitiStat, see Resource A, and check its Web site at http://www.baltimorecity.gov/news/citistat.

**Figure 7.2. Cumulative Abatements.**

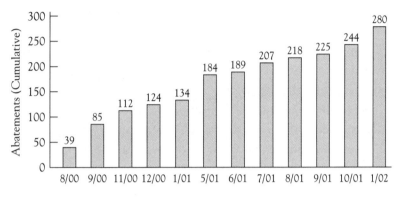

*Note: Abatements* are contaminated properties made lead-safe.

## Identify a Higher Purpose

"Great Groups think they are on a mission from God." That's one of the defining elements of high-performing teams, according to Warren Bennis (1997, p. 204). He studied several great teams, including the group that worked on the Manhattan Project (which built the atom bomb) and the team that came up with the first personal computer. Bennis continues, "People in Great Groups often have the zeal of converts. . . . Great Groups are engaged in holy wars. . . . People know going in that they will be expected to make sacrifices, but they also know they are doing something monumental, something worthy of their best selves. . . . Their clear, collective purpose makes everything they do seem meaningful and valuable."

People working on collaborative ventures usually experience high stakes when they believe that their effort serves a higher purpose. Sometimes that higher purpose is obvious, and the partners need no reminders of its critical nature. Medical researchers seeking a cure for a disease don't need a reminder about the urgency of their task; nor do NASA engineers and scientists working on a space shuttle launch. There's an old joke: Why are the passions of academic politics so high? Because the stakes are so low! But the stakes (and ultimate purpose) are not at all low in the physical sciences, and that's the place you're most likely to find true collaboration in many universities.

Sometimes, the higher purpose isn't so obvious to the staff involved. When state law enforcement officials meet to discuss their information-sharing needs, they understand its critical importance to public safety. But does the frontline clerk who does the data entry understand how that repetitive chore connects to a larger purpose? That's a classic management issue, one touched on earlier in the discussion about creating a line of sight.

Some leaders make conscious use of language to emphasize the higher purpose of their work. Those involved with the war against terrorism frequently talk about a struggle to preserve our freedoms, about a fight between good and evil. Bill Leighty's DMV staff decided that they weren't there to process Form 47, they were really in the business of saving lives.

Speaking from the heart can demonstrate your belief in the higher purpose of a collaborative effort. The question isn't so much what technique you use; the question is, do you *see* a higher purpose in the work? And if you do, are you willing to talk, with passion, about that higher purpose? When partners believe that their work aims to change the world (even in some small way), and when they communicate that belief to others, their words and actions often instill the high stakes that help people cross boundaries and find common ground. When people on a team are challenged to produce something that leaves a legacy, something that will touch others' lives for years, it raises the stakes and creates a higher purpose.

This kind of communication requires collaborative leaders to show their emotions, to talk personally and from the heart about their commitments and beliefs. And that's unusual for most of us. Indeed, in many organizations such talk is frowned upon. Or so it seems. What's intriguing, however, is the number of people who have a real yearning to hear such talk in their agencies. When collaborative leaders shed their impersonal, professional role and articulate the values and principles that move them, it usually strikes a responsive chord. Speaking from the heart about a higher purpose in work raises the stakes and helps people work across boundaries.

---

President Kennedy once told a story about a French general who asked his gardener to plant a tree. The gardener told the general, "This tree grows very slowly. It won't mature for a hundred years." "Then there's no time to lose," the general responded. "Plant it this afternoon."

Like that tree, collaborative work often takes many years before it matures. That awareness could lower people's sense of urgency. But most organizational members work with heightened energy when the stakes are high and the consequences are visible and attach personally to those staff members. If you're convinced that your collaborative project aims to make a difference in the world, the stakes are too high to wait. The leadership challenge is to help others feel those same high stakes.

Another important leadership challenge is to create expectations among key stakeholders that the collaborative effort is in their interest. Developing such a constituency is the topic of the next chapter.

# 8

# Creating a Constituency for Collaboration

*There is no "constituency for the whole."*
*David Chrislip and Carl Larson*

*There's very little constituency out there for collaboration.*
*Bob O'Neill*

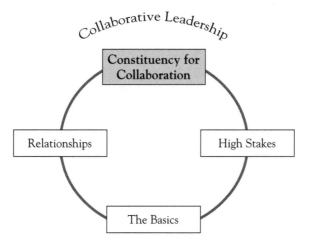

You don't need to convince *me!* It's those guys who don't want to play. How do I get them to see the mutual advantages of working together, and how do I do that when I have no authority over them?"

That's a classic question many would-be collaborators ask. The hurdles to collaboration are ever present. High stakes often help overcome these forces, as discussed in the last chapter. But although high stakes can bring the parties to the table, they don't necessarily keep them there. To *sustain* collaboration, when no one party has authority to lead, you need to create a constituency for it, a strong base of support among many stakeholders. That requires the use of influence and political smarts, as the following story demonstrates.

### Cleaning Up the Lower Charles River

On October 22, 1995, John DeVillars, the EPA regional administrator for New England, made a surprising and bold announcement to the press and public: the Lower Charles River would be clean enough for swimming by 2005. Many people were skeptical, or just didn't believe it. After all, the Lower Charles had been too dirty to swim in for almost fifty years. Most of its pollution came from unknown sources. Yet on Earth Day in April 2000, less than five years after DeVillars's announcement, the Lower Charles River was already clean enough for swimming 65 percent of the time, up from 19 percent in 1995.

### A History of Fragmented Responsibility

Prior to 1995, many environmental offices and groups had been concerned about the river's quality, but nobody felt the full responsibility for taking care of it. Five federal and state agencies had some responsibility and ability to help, but none had ownership for the whole problem. Over a dozen local governments, educational institutions and corporations owned land along the Lower Charles and were contributing to the problem, but nobody had stepped up to offer leadership.

The EPA had spent over a decade trying to force the Massachusetts Water Resource Authority to invest in controls of sewer overflow problems, but MWRA had resisted, claiming that such actions wouldn't improve water quality significantly. Members of the nonprofit Charles

River Watershed Association had often tried to offer their services cleaning up the river, but could never seem to find the unit within the EPA with which to collaborate. The situation had many of the classic collaboration hurdles: turf, fragmented responsibility, no obvious incentive to collaborate (Metzenbaum, 2001).

## Creating a Coalition Effort

But today the Lower Charles is getting cleaner, for several reasons. One is the creative use of a clear goal that resonated with the public: *a swimmable Lower Charles River by 2005.* Everyone could understand and relate to it, and there was a potential constituency to achieve it. But the EPA lacked full regulatory authority to require the landowners on the Charles to take corrective steps. Collaboration was required.

The EPA office used a mix of enforcement, education, and incentives to gain cooperation from landowners along the river. It educated and instructed communities on the Lower Charles to inspect their storm water pipes for illegal sewer connections—and levied no penalties when communities took such action. It notified two hundred probable polluters in the area that they were likely sources of water pollution, and gave them two months to clean up their act, again without penalizing them for past sins. It sent inspectors and lawyers to the sites of those that didn't take action, and the press gave that big coverage.

The EPA also went after Boston University for two major spills in the river in the past four years. BU ended up paying a $2 million fine, the largest ever levied by a federal agency against an educational institution. Perhaps influenced by that fine (and its negative media coverage), Harvard helped to organize sixteen landowners on the river into the Clean Charles Coalition, which provided assistance to help smaller polluters reduce their emissions into the river.

The EPA enlisted many environmental organizations to help in the effort. One nonprofit monitored water quality on a monthly basis, a second built political support in local communities, which put pressure on local political leaders to take aggressive action on storm water problems. DeVillars's office invited the state's environmental agencies to join the effort. Convinced that the EPA was serious, they did join—including the MWRA, despite its long-running dispute with the EPA. One state official said that the act of publicly stating an important goal and measuring progress toward it "made people more aware of the efforts to clean the Charles. . . . Gathering stakeholders helped bring more money" to the cleanup effort (Metzenbaum, 2001, p. 36). To coordinate efforts, the EPA named two seasoned and respected staffers to be "goal managers." They convened the agencies quarterly to review results, learn together, and plan next actions.

To build a scientific database, make better decisions, and increase public support, the EPA started monitoring Lower Charles water quality regularly at thirty-seven different points. This helped staff spot locations and timing of problems. It also allowed them to track cause-effect relationships when pollution abatement equipment was put into place. The U.S. Geological Survey started to monitor water quality, as did one of the nonprofits. They each posted their ratings of the river's quality on their Web sites. They came up with the same data that the EPA was obtaining, which improved the EPA's credibility with the public and media.

### One of the Keys: Pulling the Media In

The EPA made creative use of a clear, simple goal, and its clever invitation to the press and others to help monitor progress was critical. The 1995 announcement of the goal was made at an annual regatta that attracts 300,000 spectators and all Boston media. They played it up big. On Earth Day, 1996, six months after the "swimmable by 2005" goal was stated, EPA gave the Lower Charles a D in water quality.

The press was intrigued with the candor and simplicity of the measure, and the Earth Day timing of the water quality grade again got the media's attention. The EPA office became very astute at working with the media. Office staff would brief media personnel the day before they gave out new announcements on river water quality. That resulted in more accurate stories and also enhanced relationships with the media. Because the information was credible, and because the "swimmable by 2005" goal was so simple and important, the media became an ally in creating a constituency for this collaboration. The papers and TV cited organizations that were reducing their emissions as well as those that weren't, and kept the report card grades in the public's eye. The *Boston Globe* ran a major Sunday magazine story on the cleanup, "Renaissance on the Charles" (Howe, 1997).

And on Earth Day in 2000, the EPA delighted many when it announced the water quality in the Lower Charles had gone from a D to a B.

For an excellent account of this story, see "Measurement That Matters: Cleaning Up the Charles River" (Metzenbaum, 2001).

## Creating a Constituency for Collaboration

The regional EPA leaders took a number of smart and creative steps that led to the improvements in the Lower Charles River. Their overall strategy, however, was clear: they needed to create and tap a broad constituency of players to clean up the river. No one agency or group could do it alone. How do you get others to collaborate when they show little interest, and you have no formal authority over them? One of the most powerful answers to that question is to create a constituency for collaboration among the stakeholders.

A *constituency for collaboration* is a group (or several groups) of people who strongly believe that a collaborative effort is in their interest, who want to support it, and who have influence over the parties involved. Just as constituencies form around particular interests and specific programs—women's health needs, the environment, a weapons system for the military, international trade, and so on—collaboration needs strong constituencies to overcome the individual self-interests that can prevent it. There are many ways to create and sustain constituencies for this work; this chapter will look at the six outlined in Exhibit 8.1.

### Create Signs of Success and Share the Credit

What's your reaction to the common assertion, "Good work speaks for itself"? In a perfect world there might be no need to publicize the quality work that goes on every day in countless organizations. I've worked with some agencies where marketing was a task that the highly skilled professionals who toiled there thought was beneath them. They truly believed that others would quickly see the obvious superiority of their products. Alas, would that it were so. In our world of information overload, even the best initiatives require skillful marketing to get attention and develop a loyal constituency.

In the Charles River example, the EPA staff kept the public focused on the results they were getting by using ongoing measures and periodic grades to let people know if they could swim in the river. And the media helped publicize those who contributed to improvements. Another good example of creating visible successes and sharing credit comes from the leaders of the Comprehensive Performance Partnership (CPP) in Chautauqua County, New York.

---

**Exhibit 8.1. Strategies to Create a Constituency for Collaboration.**

- Create visible signs of success and share credit widely.
- Set clear, simple goals that resonate with the public; invite outside groups to help and monitor progress.
- Use symbols to reinforce the partnership's power.
- Involve stakeholders at every step.
- Educate stakeholders to see the connection between collaboration and their self-interest.
- Think politically, without becoming political.

---

## Developing "Broad Shoulders"

Chautauqua County (population 139,000) is a rural county in the southwest corner of New York State. In 1998 its residents approved a new county charter, which requires a performance-based government that uses partnerships to achieve measurable results and accountability. This led to the creation of the Comprehensive Performance Partnership (CPP), a commitment by the county executive, elected officials, and five public and nonprofit organizations to deliver services with the highest quality. The parties' main role was to help the county develop its workforce's ability to focus on results and performance (rather than internal bureaucratic rules) in order to better serve customers. To accomplish their goal the parties adopted certain principles, began intensive staff training, and focused pilot efforts on two departments, hoping to demonstrate some quick and measurable results.

After the first two years the CPP produced some visible successes in the Public Facilities Department. When it did, County Executive Mark Thomas wasted no time sending out a press release to inform his constituents of the good news. Here's an excerpt from one:

August 13, 2001

GERRY—Chautauqua County Executive Mark W. Thomas today officially re-opened a section of Route 380, which has been closed for over four weeks due to a bridge reconstruction project. Thomas was joined by county public facilities director Ken Brentley to recognize the county bridge crew who completed the scheduled eight-week reconstruction project in nearly half the expected time.

Thomas praised the work crew assigned to the project from the Sheridan DPF facility, including foreman, Rusty Gross; carpenter, Marty Miller; skilled road maintainer, Vince Bomasuto; road maintainer, Jake Porpiglia; motor equipment operator, Bob Gunnell; and seasonal employee, Dustin Arnold.

The county executive said allowing Gross and his team to utilize their judgment and expertise to complete the project in the most efficient manner was key to the early re-opening.

The construction crew originally slated to construct the Route 380 project was not going to be able to start until late August. This delay would have meant the road would still be closed when area schools re-opened in September. . . . That was determined to be unacceptable to Gross and his crew.

Brentley said successes like the . . . Route 380 projects are examples that the department's move to performance-based government through the Comprehensive Performance Partnership (CPP) is working. "In the past . . . if the project was scheduled to take eight weeks, that's how long it took. Clearly, this is another example that our CPP training is beginning to pay dividends . . . for the residents of our county."

Who is the audience for this press release? Obviously the public is one, but notice the amount of space given to the names of the work crew and the support for the crew's use of its own judgment to expedite the project. This release is also targeted to the workforce and to the Department of Public Facilities. The county is building an *internal* constituency for its performance partnership.

But that's not all. Mark Thomas also needs the support of his elected officials and their constituents. Whenever a project is completed or a goal achieved, Thomas finds ways to share the credit with them. As Len Faulk, one of the early champions of the CPP notes, "Mark is relentless in involving legislators whenever there's a success. He continually involves them in the projects that are completed, he brings them in when the media are informed about our progress."

Thomas won reelection in November 2001 with 53 percent of the vote, despite the fact that his opponent claimed the CPP was a failure. Thomas seemed to relish the fact that his opponent picked on the CPP:

When you're creating this kind of effort, you have to develop what I like to call "broad shoulders." That is, you need strong, wide support from the community. And that's how the CPP started. We had the Chamber, State University of New York (SUNY), our community college, the Chautauqua Institution, and a local foundation [the five CPP partners] all working together to help us. So when my opponent criticized the CPP leaders as "rookies," I just countered by saying, "I don't think you ought to brand the president of Chautauqua Institution, the President of SUNY, and the Chamber of Commerce as 'rookies.'" It didn't get him very far!

For more on this story, check out http://www.nlma.org/cpp.htm.

### Set Clear Goals and Monitor Progress with Outside Help

Most agencies set goals, but the public often has trouble relating to such goals because they're usually written in bureaucratese. The EPA's annual performance report for fiscal year 1999, for instance, notes that it met this goal: "11 states submitted upgraded non-point source programs for a cumulative total of 13" (reported in Metzenbaum, 2001, p. 19). Now, does that make you want to get out of bed early and charge up the hill? Compare that to the regional EPA administrator's goal for the Charles River: "The Lower Charles River will be clean enough for swimming by 2005." People living in the area connect with that. It's clear, and they care about it. It's written in terms that mean something to them—they'll be able to swim in the river. It's about outcomes, not bureaucratic inputs and activities. It's specific in time and place; everyone knows when it's supposed to happen, and where.

Most managers would be delighted to find simple, clear ways to state goals that capture the public's attention. But inviting outsiders to monitor progress? That strikes many as risky. And it is, if done poorly. If you identify people you trust, people who will call the shots fairly, however, it can be a powerful strategy for building a constituency. Public and nonprofit leaders know that they aren't the most effective or believable people to proclaim their agencies' successes; those with no vested interest have more credibility. So consider bringing in a special interest watchdog group, some academics, an oversight body, or the media and inviting them to monitor an important goal. It can create a broader constituency to support the initiative and its purpose.

## Use Symbols

We all know the old saying, "A picture is worth a thousand words." Some elected officials build on that, saying that a symbol is worth a thousand pictures. Symbols play very powerful roles in our culture, and they resonate in our politics. For instance, on October 8, 2001, former Pennsylvania governor Tom Ridge was named the nation's first director of homeland security. Many wondered if he'd have the power to coordinate all forty-eight federal agencies involved in counterterrorism. Paul C. Light, director of governmental studies at the Brookings Institution, noted that the symbols of Ridge's office would tell others whether he was a heavy player or not: "This is a town that reads the tea leaves. . . . Does he have one bodyguard or two bodyguards? Does he sit down the hall from the president or is he condemned to the Old Executive Office Building? . . . The FBI . . . Customs Service, the CIA, these are agencies that have been in business a long time, and they pay attention to symbols. If he doesn't have the right symbols, he's getting nowhere" (Light, 2001b).

One way to create a constituency for collaboration, and to manage the political pressures that can undermine it, is to make skillful use of certain symbols.

### Service First (continued)

The Service First alliance between the BLM and the Forest Service (introduced in Chapter One) sometimes involved the bold step of allowing a supervisor from one agency to oversee staff from both agencies (to get the combined staff working more closely and to save money). They called it "dual hatting." This kind of innovation required special approvals from several offices. Many employees felt threatened; they doubted that headquarters would support such major changes.

In the fall of 1995, Bill Delaney (Forest Service) and Kerwyn Keith (BLM) went to their agency leaders and urged them to sign a letter announcing a new initiative that would formally recognize the collaboration in the field. Delaney and Keith wanted the senior leaders' support to provide the cover needed to cut through the bureaucracy and support the changes in the field. The leaders agreed, and two months later sent the letter out to all employees in both agencies.

The letter came out on joint letterhead, and that symbolism was deliberate and powerful. In it the two leaders announced a national initiative to encourage collaboration, improved customer service, and cost savings. They called it the Trading Post, named after the one-stop centers of the nineteenth century where settlers in the West purchased products and got commonsense service. The headquarters invited local BLM and Forest Service offices around the country to nominate themselves for Trading Post designation. On March 5, 1996, Forest Service Chief Jack Ward Thomas and BLM Director Mike Dombeck announced the first sites designated as Trading Posts: central Oregon and southern Colorado. (Exhibit 8.2 shows the opening of that letter, printed on a letterhead combining the logos of the two agencies.) "The 'Trading Post' designation was an opportunity to legitimize what we were already doing," says former Forest Service supervisor Jim Webb. "It didn't necessarily help us further our collaboration initially. . . . But it helped because it told our people that the national agency leaders were behind us."

Dave Radloff, head of the Forest Service's reinvention efforts at the time, notes that it was controversial to simply get the chief's and director's statement on a joint letterhead. "This joint letter, on joint agency letterhead, was symbolically important. That letter, and the later ones sent out, became 'safe conduct passes' to the people in

Exhibit 8.2. Using Symbols to Support Collaboration.

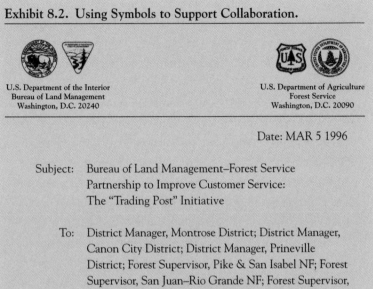

U.S. Department of the Interior
Bureau of Land Management
Washington, D.C. 20240

U.S. Department of Agriculture
Forest Service
Washington, D.C. 20090

Date: MAR 5 1996

Subject:    Bureau of Land Management–Forest Service
Partnership to Improve Customer Service:
The "Trading Post" Initiative

To:    District Manager, Montrose District; District Manager,
Canon City District; District Manager, Prineville
District; Forest Supervisor, Pike & San Isabel NF; Forest
Supervisor, San Juan–Rio Grande NF; Forest Supervisor,
Deschutes NF; and Forest Supervisor, Ochoco NF

The Bureau of Land Management and the Forest Service share
common customers and a desire to meet the needs of the public more
cost-effectively. Both agencies are promoting customer service and
have worked together over the past year to develop common service
standards and to measure customer satisfaction. The first returns from
our customer surveys highlight common themes and suggest joint
strategies for better serving customers of both BLM and the Forest
Service. There are real opportunities for our agencies to be partners
in providing better and more convenient service. . . .

the field. It encouraged them to push the envelope further and take
some risks. . . . But the idea of a joint letterhead created opposition.
Some in the headquarters told us, 'That's illegal, you can't do that!'
It took almost two years to finally get formal approval for a joint letterhead. Now, it can be used at any level, in the field, regional and
state offices, or at headquarters. And it helps."

Radloff adds an astute observation about the power of symbols: people often assume small acts have symbolic meaning, even when that's not intended. Example: which agency's name is listed first on the joint letterhead? You may be chuckling, but when employees are nervous, it's amazing the significance they can attach to such things. So the Forest Service is listed first on some joint letters, and BLM takes that spot on others.

The Trading Post later became known as Service First, and it continues to spread as more Forest Service and BLM units find ways to co-locate staff; share managers, staff, and other resources; and integrate some operations. For more, see http//www.fs.fed.us/servicefirst.

## Involve Stakeholders at Each Step

It's an old and accepted management maxim: people support what they help to create. The partnering workshop method discussed at the end of Chapter Five is entirely based on the notion of active stakeholder involvement. Nothing new here. So why do we often forget this insight?

Sometimes we don't forget, we simply choose to ignore it because it seems too costly or risky. First, actively involving stakeholders can slow things down, at least initially. Also, some stakeholders may use the initiative to further their own personal (or political) agendas. And personal antagonism and political conflicts often prevent parties from inviting others to the table. As any legislator can tell you, personality conflicts can derail an effort to pass good legislation as surely as policy differences can.

So keeping the stakeholders involved at every step has potential risks, without question. But ignoring this principle also incurs big risks. The EPA regional leader took a risk in stating the goal of a swimmable Lower Charles River by 2005, but he actually lowered his risks when he invited key stakeholders to join the effort and take meaningful roles. When this involvement is planned well it creates a powerful constituency for collaboration.

## Connect Collaboration and Self-Interest

In addition to involving stakeholders, it's effective to educate them and show them the connection between a collaborative initiative and the benefits they receive from it. "WIIFM?"—the old question, What's in it for me?—isn't necessarily selfish. Even if it is, the question must be addressed. The key parties in collaborative efforts can't be expected to invest large amounts of time, energy, and perhaps resources in their work together if their stakeholders don't see a tangible product or result that meets some important need. That's what some enlightened leaders in Arlington County, Virginia, discovered.

### Arlington County, Virginia, and Washington, D.C.

In the early 1990s the Arlington County Board of Supervisors held a planning retreat. One of the discussion topics might strike you as odd: How could Arlington County support the public schools across the river in Washington, D.C.? In fact it was anything but odd. The Arlington supervisors were discussing something that was in their self-interest.

Tony Gardner, Arlington's former county executive, describes the situation as follows:

Only about one-third of the county workforce lived in Arlington. It was just too expensive for many of our employees to live there. But the two-thirds who lived in adjoining counties had a very long drive [northern Virginia's traffic problems rival those of Los Angeles and Atlanta]. Some of our workers left for jobs in their own counties, to shorten their commute. In addition, the county had more jobs than the number of adults in their working years. The Board had an important issue: Where are we going to find good workers?

The closest source for workers was Washington. So we worked with some local businesses and they created partnerships with D.C. schools by offering mentoring, money, internships, and technology assistance to those schools. At that time the County Board was being asked to encourage the local businesses to form partnerships with our own county schools, but the Board ended up encouraging these business-school partnerships with D.C.

We also found ways to make transportation between D.C. and Arlington easier by adding some busses between the two jurisdictions. This was all done informally; we couldn't do it in a very visible, public way or the Arlington Schools would have objected.

As Tip O'Neill proclaimed, "All politics is local." We first want to know what a program or budget expenditure will do for us and our own community. The challenge facing the Arlington Board was to see, and show others, the connection between supporting the D.C. schools and the benefits back home in Arlington—which in this instance was a cadre of trained young people able to work in the county. Educating people about the *connection* between a partnership and its impact on them helps create a constituency for collaboration.

### Think Politically Without Becoming Political

Harlan Cleveland, former ambassador and retired dean of the Humphrey Institute of Public Affairs at the University of Minnesota, emphasizes this point. Managers and leaders in the public sector gain most of their credibility from their professional skills. But they must also understand the political world that drives their elected and appointed officials. The same is true for nonprofit leaders; they have to grasp the politics of their boards, funders, and local communities to get and keep the support they need. The most successful leaders use their political insights without appearing to be especially political.

Several of the collaborative leaders I've described have solid political skills. Mark Thomas recognizes and involves local elected officials whenever the Chautauqua County CPP experiences success. Few of his legislators have management backgrounds, few of them were actively involved in getting the CPP started, but Thomas understands the old saying, "Success has a hundred parents, and failure is an orphan." When there is a CPP success, Thomas shares credit with the elected officials (and with employees).

The New England EPA regional administrator understands the importance of timing and good media skills, which are critical in a political environment. The leaders of the Service First initiative understand the political concerns of the Bureau of Land Management. Being the smaller of Service First's two partners, BLM's leaders worry that their organization could be swallowed up by the much larger Forest Service. So BLM is given equal representation on the Service First national steering team, it receives the same funding when incentive grants are given to field units, and it gets equal billing on joint letterheads.

These are just a few examples of "thinking politically." Exhibit 8.3 lists some other useful approaches. Whatever steps you use, the main point is this: collaborative efforts can be undone quickly by political forces. It's in your interest to learn about the pressures and opportunities experienced by each of the parties, and to deal with those that threaten the initiative.

One final thought about thinking politically. Most of the examples and approaches listed here have this common theme: they widen the arena of engagement (see Lucy, 1988, who discusses "widening the arena of conflict," p. 32). That is, they create subtle pressures on the principals trying to collaborate by engaging additional stakeholders in the effort. For example, some regional collaboratives keep their local elected officials focused on the region's interests (and away from grandstanding) by including civic, nonprofit, academic, and corporate leaders on the initiative's governance board. Other regional efforts bring in respected outside authorities who study the region and issue well-publicized reports. Neal Peirce, one of the country's foremost experts on regionalism, has done this in many localities to good effect.

---

**Exhibit 8.3. Questions That Can Help You Think Politically.**

- Are any of the agencies rivals in some sense (same mission, same customers, struggling for the same scarce resources)? Related to that, are some of the principals rivals?

- Do the parties' major stakeholders have conflicts, low trust, or other reasons that lead them to distance themselves from one another?

- Is there a pecking order that reduces the willingness of some parties to come to the table? (Many state and local agencies and nonprofits resent the treatment they've received by federal agencies that came across as arrogant and unwilling to work as equals.)

- What do the *veto point occupants*—the people whose support is essential to progress—think about the collaboration? (For more on "veto point occupants," see Lucy, 1988, p. 30.)

---

"Widening the arena of engagement" raises the stakes involved. It can make the work much more challenging. It's counterproductive if done in ways that reduce trust among the principals (say, if one of them leaks information to the press to keep a certain proposal from moving forward). But when the arena is widened in an open manner, with the goal of focusing on the initiative's larger, shared purpose, the result is often politics at its best.

Many collaborators get so caught up in their internal planning and processes that they forget they have a larger audience that needs to know and needs to be convinced. Your challenge is to identify the key groups who can help (or sink) your efforts, and then use any strategy that will hook them. Creating this broader constituency keeps the parties at the table and the stakes high.

---

And what about constituencies that feel threatened by collaboration? Collaboration scholar Eugene Bardach raises this interesting point about constituencies: "From a narrow, constituency standpoint, collaboration is distinctly undesirable, because it threatens to blur an agency's mission and the agency's political accountability for pursuing it" (1998, p. 13). The quote at the start of this chapter (from Chrislip and Larson, 1994) is always hovering overhead: "There is no 'constituency for the whole.'"

There's no simple answer to this. Collaborative leaders need to remember that collaboration (like any change) will threaten some. The best advice is to appreciate that if no constituency for the whole exists, you need to *create* one. Collaboration involves helping people to think holistically and see larger possibilities. That's a major leadership challenge. It's also our next topic.

# 9

# Building Collaborative Leadership

*What is needed is for leaders of all institutions to
take responsibility beyond the walls. They have
to lead their own institutions and lead them to
performance. . . . But at the same time the members
of the institution—and not just the people at the
top—have to take community responsibility beyond
the walls of their own institution.*

*Peter Drucker*

W hen it comes to collaboration, leadership makes a huge difference. That's the experience of almost all collaboration veterans. And that is my conclusion from my study of over twenty instances of collaboration in government and nonprofit agencies.

But how to "lead as a peer rather than as a superior," as author David D. Chrislip (2000, p. 23) puts it? What are the key approaches employed by the individuals who work together on a collaborative project? In this chapter I'll describe an impressive collaborative effort to meet the needs of young children, and then explore four qualities of effective collaborative leaders and identify their key tasks.

### The Montgomery County Early Childhood Initiative

In the summer of 1999, the Montgomery County, Maryland, school district hired a new superintendent, Jerry Weast. The county was very proud of its schools, with good reason, but it expected Dr. Weast to bring new initiatives to deal with the community's growing diversity. One of Weast's early moves was to propose a new, $4 million program to serve the needs of children up through age five. County Council President Mike Subin, a strong proponent of such programs, surprised some people by objecting. According to one person at the meeting, Subin said, "The schools can't do this by themselves. You've got to talk with others and bring back a collaborative solution."

He challenged Weast to consult with the other agencies serving very young children. It was an enormous task: thirty-nine public and nonprofit agencies in the county provide services to young children and their families. These agencies respond to different funders with different expectations and performance measures, and they weren't used to working together.

A huge coalition of the thirty-nine agencies, involving almost a hundred people, was pulled together under the joint leadership of Associate Superintendent Ray Bryant, Lorraine Rogstad (director of the nonprofit Collaboration Council, which helps support collaborative efforts in the county), and Chuck Short (director of the county's

Health and Human Services Department, or HHS). This task force developed a comprehensive three-year plan and presented it to the County Council in less than six months. More astonishing, the task force also met the challenge issued by County Executive Doug Duncan to provide him with a budget for new or expanded services for very young kids in *three months!* Talk about high stakes. To prepare the budget required the task force members to share budget information that had never been shared before. They did it, and submitted a budget request on time.

## How They Did It

The chairs of the initiative, Short, Rogstad, and Bryant, met to identify the key agencies that had to be involved in the planning effort, and invited them to be part of the Montgomery County Early Childhood Initiative. Short drafted a memorandum of understanding and asked each of those organizations to sign it. All of them did.

The members drew on the recommendations in *The Children's Agenda,* a 1998 report written by a coalition of community groups that called for collaborative action to achieve seven outcomes for all children in the county. They agreed to use the eight principles for collaborative governance identified in that report (presented in Exhibit 9.1).

The task force members agreed to study and use the lessons learned from successful early childhood efforts in other communities. They organized into six task groups: planning, structure, program and budget, standards, comprehensive services, and data and evaluation committees. The program and budget committee included staff from the county's Office of Management and Budget (OMB) in its meetings. "Getting the providers to share their budget figures and the amount each proposed to spend on early childhood, that had never been done before," Rogstad notes. "We agreed to keep those figures confidential, and people honored that." Bennett Connelly, a service chief at HHS who played a major role in leading the task force, also emphasizes the importance of including OMB in these discussions. "Instead of having to convince OMB of our budget needs, they actually became *advocates* for the

**Exhibit 9.1. Montgomery County's Principles for Collaborative Governance.**

- Use collaboration as a vehicle for joint planning, policy development, and resource allocation.

- Recognize the interdependence of each agency's mission, and respect each one's autonomy, diversity, and cultural values.

- Initiate programs that are outcome-based, comprehensive, and preventive.

- Diminish or eliminate categorical, narrowly defined programs.

- Support replication of programs and strategies that demonstrate measurable positive outcomes.

- Use collaborative resource allocation strategies, including pooling of funds and development of joint budgets.

- Use accountability measures and benchmarks to track client well-being.

- Foster creativity, mutual trust, and respect among all partners and the community.

budget we put together! And OMB presented our budget to the council, which was most unusual."

Rogstad hired a full-time staff member to support the initiative. "That was a real key," she reflects. "This person was the 'glue' once we started meeting."

Ray Bryant organized a trip to visit North Carolina's Smart Start initiative, which is a model statewide program for children through age five and their parents. Its goal is similar to that of the Montgomery County effort: every child will enter school healthy and ready to learn. Ray brought Maryland Delegate Mark Shriver and his aides on the trip. Shriver was later successful in getting legislation passed at the state level to fund early childhood programs.

The coalition presented a budget to the county executive in April. The County Council agreed to fund almost 70 percent of the budget request. Connelly noted that the task force's entire plan wasn't even completed at the time the budget was presented. "The council primarily funded the items that we already had agreed to put into our plan."

The task force completed and presented its comprehensive plan to the County Council in June 2000, barely six months after the huge coalition began meeting. The plan puts forth several major recommendations. Among them:

- Integrate all current efforts to collect and track data on children and families into a *single data and evaluation group,* under the Collaboration Council's direction.

- Convene a "home visiting consortium" comprising programs currently offering home visiting services in the county.

- Develop an ongoing public engagement campaign. Based on the belief that parents are the first and best teachers of their children but often lack current information that would help them develop their kids, this strategy pulls together the fragmented public information efforts already in existence.

The task force's plan includes a matrix listing key strategies and activities for every major recommendation. The matrix identifies the group with lead responsibility for each task, and an evaluation criterion for each.

One of the key objectives in the plan was the creation of a new senior position for an early childhood coordinator. This position is formally part of HHS but also serves as a member of the public schools' executive team. The job was filled in January 2001, barely one year after the County Council's challenge. This dual appointment was a first for the schools and HHS, and is rare in the public and nonprofit sectors.

"Council wanted various programs to work seamlessly, and one way to do that was to make the new coordinator position a top management role in both HHS and the public schools," Short says. "The coordinator position is helping to create this seamless relationship. It's also a visible and important symbol of the special partnership that is growing among this large group of agencies." With thirty-nine agencies involved, it was difficult to see who was responsible for implementing the plan. This position focuses some accountability for the large county investment.

## Results

It's too early to know if the comprehensive programs are improving the outcomes for young children, although studies of similar programs elsewhere give reason for optimism. The results thus far are internal to the coalition. The thirteen agencies that do home visiting (some of which didn't even know of one another's existence before) now have a joint assessment process, which will help families receive appropriate services and avoid duplication. Also, a new level of trust exists among these agencies' personnel. For the schools and agencies to share budget requests with one another prior to submission is an important step in building trust and managing resources wisely. The huge amount of community input during the planning process helps ensure that there will be a constituency for the services that the council is asked to fund. And the dual appointment of an early childhood coordinator creates the capability for the community to address young children's needs in a seamless fashion, with real accountability for results.

## Challenges

In addition to the obvious challenges of creating and maintaining such a huge coalition, there were some interesting hurdles along the way. One could be termed "returning to role." When the task force completed its report, the real work (of greater collaboration around children's needs) was just getting started. But people had to put their home agency hat on again to focus on their agency's needs. Chuck Short had to work confidentially with the county executive to make some budget decisions. OMB staff switched back from being team players to their more traditional analytical (and sometimes adversarial) role. As Short notes, "This return to institutional roles was required because the larger organizations weren't in the same collaborative mode as the early childhood task force."

Some task force partners, especially private providers, had a hard time understanding the sudden change in roles. And, Short notes, when County Council staff "began reviewing the task force's budget request with their analyst hats on, many felt somewhat betrayed. We needed to work through this." Short says he learned from this "return to role" issue, and in subsequent collaborative efforts he's made sure that the group spends time discussing roles and develops what he calls an "extraction strategy."

Another major challenge involved policy-level staff, legislative analysts, advocates for children, and evaluators of the effort. They became so invested in the collaborative effort that they sometimes started micromanaging the process. That's a "good problem" reflecting these staff members' commitment to the effort, but it caused difficulties that needed to be addressed.

## Analysis

This case has several important aspects. It demonstrates that collaboration can move quickly when the basics are in place. The parties had a common goal (the development of very young kids) that none could achieve on its own. They wanted to meet and were ready to invest some effort in the process. They got the right people to the table (almost a hundred of them!). Through the use of a memorandum of understanding and an agreement to use previously developed principles for collaborative governance, they put an open and credible process into place. And three well-regarded leaders were champions for the task force.

Three of the other key ingredients were also present here. The stakes were high, created in part by the political pressure from county leaders to work collaboratively on a specific product in a very short time frame. The opportunity to quickly gain funding in the coming year's budget also increased the stakes. And the initiative's leaders did an excellent job of creating a constituency for their effort. They attracted and kept all thirty-nine stakeholder agencies involved throughout, they used their political smarts by involving elected officials and budget office personnel, they generated some quick and visible wins (the budget) and shared credit widely.

The three leaders also invested effort in their work relationships. Ray Bryant notes, "All of us were up front with each other . . . there were no hidden agendas. I've heard it said that '*collaboration is when you put your money on the table and your hands behind your back!*' That's what we did. Our relationships were built on shared respect and shared understanding."

## Four Qualities of Collaborative Leaders

Many collaborative leaders have appeared in the stories presented thus far. When you meet people like Lorraine Rogstad, Chuck Short, and Ray Bryant, their diversity is striking. I've also discovered the four shared qualities listed in Exhibit 9.2, and they intrigue me. First, these leaders strike me as being driven people; they pursue collaborative efforts with extraordinary determination. Second, and paradoxically, they are usually very modest, even humble at times. Third, they pull people into collaboration rather than pushing them. And finally, they have what I call a "collaborative mind-set." The following sections will take up each in turn.

---

**Exhibit 9.2.  Four Qualities of Collaborative Leaders.**

- Resolute and driven—especially about collaboration
- Modest—a strong but measured ego
- Inclusive—uses "pull" much more than "push"
- Collaborative mind-set—sees connections to something larger

---

### Driven, Determined Resolve

The first similarity relates to energy and sense of focus. These leaders are clearly driven people, especially when they are engaged in working across boundaries. Chuck Short is a case in point. He has a widespread reputation for integrity, competence, and commitment to clients. But these aren't the things that most energize him. Chuck Short gets absolutely passionate when he talks about collaboration.

"Collaboration has driven me for years. Maybe it comes from four years teaching at a Catholic school. It was very poor; if we needed desks we'd drive to a rummage sale and find some used desks for the classroom. We were always scrounging for the basics. So, when I got to county government, I naturally thought about partnerships. I'd say to someone, 'Well, you've got this, we have something different, let's share.'" Notice his choice of words: "naturally thought about partnerships," and, "collaboration has driven me." For the collaborative leaders I've met, nothing could be more natural than to partner with others.

Mayor Brent Coles of Boise, Idaho, comes across the same way. He's the informal leader of the Treasure Valley Partnership, a formal coalition of ten local governments that work to manage growth and transportation alternatives, maintain community identities, and protect open space in the region. The partnership has been successful in large part because of his understated but driven leadership. One colleague describes Coles as "quiet, soft-spoken, incredibly focused and driven . . . forceful but not bombastic . . . he doesn't let his ego go to his head, he treats people very well, and he just won't take no for an answer."

For collaborative leaders like Chuck Short and Brent Coles, collaboration becomes a crusade. Such leaders get increasingly energized by the work and its rewards. Fair enough, you might say, collaborative leaders are driven and focused people. But isn't that true of most leaders, collaborative or Lone Ranger types? No question about it. There's a big difference in the way many collaborative leaders demonstrate passion and drive, however, and that brings us to the second shared quality.

### Strong but Measured Ego

The leaders who succeed at collaboration have an unusual combination that seems to be central to their effectiveness. In addition to their drive and resolve, they are modest, even humble people. They combine a fierce commitment to their goals with an ego that allows plenty of space for different viewpoints. They excite but don't overwhelm others.

Having a "measured ego" means that they don't have to grab the headlines for every success. Quite the opposite, they seem to take great satisfaction when they can share credit for accomplishments with many others. Their ambitions are directed more toward organizational success than personal glory.

When asked about the roles they play in multiagency collaboration, these leaders use words like *servant leader, convener, facilitator, catalyst.* These aren't the classic roles played by a General Patton–type leader. These *are* the roles that collaborative leaders must play, and play well, to overcome the forces pulling people away from one another. As Dave Radloff of the U.S. Forest Service notes, "Some collaborative efforts fail because of the leaders' hubris . . . they have to be in charge, always. Those who have trouble collaborating are more likely to be arrogant. They can't give up control." Collaborative leadership is about a shared leadership style that we're only recently starting to understand and define.

As I was doing research on the nature of collaborative leadership, I came across Jim Collins's new book, *Good to Great* (2001). Collins has studied many world-class organizations and leaders over the past decade. In the mid-1990s he and his research team looked at a group of eleven companies that were transformed from "good to great" performance (measured by certain financial indicators) and sustained that extraordinary performance for a period of fifteen years or more. I was surprised to learn that Collins discovered something about the leaders of these exceptional companies that reflects the first two characteristics of collaborative leaders: each of the eleven good-to-great companies was led by someone who combined fierce resolve with personal humility. As Collins puts it, this type of leader is a "study in duality: modest and willful, shy and fearless." This leader combines an "unwavering resolve" with a "compelling modesty."

Collins and his team developed a hierarchy of leadership levels, each one appropriate in certain situations. The five levels are shown in Exhibit 9.3.

The collaborative leaders I've observed share the characteristics Collins identifies as "Level 5." They know how to influence others, and by always focusing on the group's goal, not personal or organizational power, they elicit the trust that's essential for collaboration. Others don't worry that these leaders are in it for their ego. Their resolve and passion is for the larger purpose, and their desire to include others and acknowledge their contributions is genuine. These leaders create plenty of space for others to contribute.

**Exhibit 9.3. Collins's Hierarchy of Leadership Capabilities.**

Level 5: *Level 5 Executive*—helps make good companies into great ones through combination of fierce resolve and humility

Level 4: *Effective Leader*—stimulates commitment into a compelling vision, resulting in high performance

Level 3: *Competent Manager*—helps clarify objectives and organizes people and resources toward meeting those objectives

Level 2: *Contributing Team Member*—contributes to team objectives, works well in a team environment

Level 1: *Highly Capable Individual*—contributes through technical competence, knowledge, attitudes, and skills

*Source:* Jim Collins, *Good to Great: Why Some Companies Make the Leap and Others Don't,* 2001, p. 20. Copyright © 2001 by Jim Collins. Reprinted by permission of HarperCollins Publishers Inc.

### "Pull" Rather Than "Push"

When the Early Childhood Initiative was in the planning phase, one of the leaders' key decisions was to invite a Maryland state delegate to join them when they visited North Carolina's Smart Start program. The delegate was extremely impressed, and came back and sponsored legislation funding early childhood services in Maryland. This is an example of the third shared characteristic: collaborative leaders use "pull" more than "push" to include others and create a shared agenda.

Push is direct, sometimes forceful, and sometimes necessary. It uses the authority that comes with a leader's formal role. But in collaborative efforts, leaders don't have any formal authority over the other parties, and push typically turns them off. Pull, on the other hand, gives people the space and time to come to their own decision about collaboration. When they opt to join, it's a conscious and voluntary act, which means it's a commitment.

So, just what is *pull?* Exhibit 9.4 presents some examples.

Compared to push, pull is less directive and confrontational. In martial arts terms, pull is aikido, channeling the other's energy and drive. Pull taps some inner need or motivation: a competitive spirit, a desire to build things, a desire to be part of an elite group. Many of the strategies for creating a constituency for collaboration discussed in Chapter Eight involve pull: the use of symbols, involving stakeholders at every step, thinking politically without becoming political.

Collaborative leaders use pull to engage people in collaboration in a variety of ways:

- They give others control, autonomy, and an invitation.

- They make use of personal commitment and belief.

- They make use of strategic thinking.

## Exhibit 9.4.  Push and Pull.

*Push:* Army ad—"Uncle Sam Wants You."

*Pull:* Marine ad—"We need a few good men."

*Push:* A boss or colleague says that you need to change your management style.

*Pull:* Anonymous, 360-degree feedback on your management style from colleagues and subordinates allows you to learn how others see you, and to review it in a supportive setting with peers.

*Push:* You tell staff their quality is down.

*Pull:* You take staff to visit customers and ask for direct customer feedback.

*Push:* You advertise a new retail development primarily through promotions in the media.

*Pull:* You advertise a new development by throwing a huge party on its premises a few days before it opens, and invite thousands of cab drivers and their families. (This is what the Rouse Company did when it opened the South Street Seaport in New York City in the early 1980s!)

*Push:* You teach geometry to kids who hate math.

*Pull:* You offer kids who hate math the opportunity to build a house (which requires significant geometry skills that they'll need to learn).

*Push:* I tell my son Josh he needs to read every day on vacation to keep his skills up.

*Pull:* I invite Josh's friend Zach (who loves to read) on vacation with my family. Because Josh is very competitive, he starts reading each day to keep up with Zach.

## Control, Autonomy, and an Invitation

One of the hurdles to collaboration is the fear of loss: of control, of autonomy, of quality. Assuring all parties that they'll retain the control and autonomy they need is a powerful way to pull them in. The JNET information-sharing network in Pennsylvania does this well by helping criminal justice agencies share information; each member agency decides what information to put into the network. The Early Childhood Initiative assured agencies that their autonomy would be respected. It was, and that helped.

## Personal Commitment and Belief

Another way to use pull is to speak personally and from the heart about your beliefs and commitments (as discussed toward the end of Chapter Seven). When Chuck Short talks about his personal commitment to partnerships and the critical importance of improving the lives of young children, others see his conviction and that pulls them in.

It's absolutely fascinating to watch collaborative leaders do this. They let go of their professional face, their eyes sparkle, they talk from their hearts and show extraordinary enthusiasm for the cause that's driving them. Because their commitment is so obvious and sincere, because they're not trying to convince anyone, their effectiveness increases.

## Strategic Thinking

Many collaborative leaders pull others into collaboration by thinking strategically. One of my favorite examples comes from academia, where collaboration can be especially difficult to achieve.

### Collaboration at the University of Virginia

It was the winter of 2001, and Bob Sweeney was looking for a strategy. As senior vice president for development and public affairs at the University of Virginia, he was expected to focus on just that—raising money for the university. Having just led the second-largest capital campaign at any American public university, he could have been excused for relaxing a bit. But Sweeney was already thinking of the next campaign, and he wasn't focused mainly on the money. Sweeney sees his role in much broader terms than fundraising. He has an intense devotion to the values of the university's founder, Thomas Jefferson, and truly believes he's in the business of *spreading Jeffersonian principles to succeeding generations.* If the deans of all ten (very autonomous) schools at the University could come together and agree that they were all in the same business, if they could commit to collaborating actively on some major initiatives, the next campaign could have a clear and inspiring theme. The problem was, the development leader isn't the person to pull the academic deans together in search of a vision.

Sweeney waited for the right time, and the right person. He knew there was a search for a new provost (who is usually the academic leader on university campuses), and when Gene Block was named provost, Sweeney saw an opening. Block was very well suited for the job. He'd been at the university for years, was well regarded, and appreciates the importance of collaboration. Sweeney met with Block and suggested an intriguing idea. They would cohost a series of "envision" sessions for the individual schools. At each session, the dean and a selected group of faculty from one school would be asked to discuss their hopes, aspirations, concerns, and goals for the school. These conversations would give the new provost a great way to learn about the schools in depth, and the development director would have a chance to see if there were some common aspirations that might translate into themes and projects for the next capital campaign. Fortunately, Block liked the idea.

The ten sessions were held during the fall of 2001, and they were remarkably successful. Deans and faculty talked openly about their hopes, about the tough issues they faced, about the help they needed from other schools or senior administrators. Block and Sweeney listened and probed, asked questions, and looked for common themes.

The process created quite a buzz; three other units asked for their own envision sessions, faculty and deans discovered a number of shared interests they didn't know existed, and Block identified several collaborative opportunities to pursue, including the creation of four centers that would meet critical needs of the state by tapping expertise found across the university. Despite a cut in higher education funding caused by the recession of 2001–2002, the provost was ready to move forward with an agenda that included participation from all ten schools, and none of the schools felt it was imposed on them. Quite the contrary, they helped create the agenda.

Sweeney was astute enough to think politically. He appreciated the fact that, symbolically, he wasn't the person to lead ten academic schools in a common direction (even if he did have a major role in something they all wanted—funding). He needed a champion with solid academic credentials and with clout. Block was the right person by position and by temperament. But they couldn't force a vision on these academics, so they tried a creative approach to pull the academics together. The deans and faculty had never been invited to an open, three-hour discussion with the provost to talk exclusively about their schools, their problems, their hopes. None of them would have missed it. Some of them began their own strategic planning efforts because of it. (For more on the envision process used at the University of Virginia, see Resource A.)

### Seeing Connections

When Bob O'Neill was county executive of Fairfax County, Virginia, he loaned one of his staff to a town in the county while the town's manager was away completing an MBA degree. "It seemed like the obvious thing to do," O'Neill later reflected. "The Town of Herndon had a need, I had some resources . . . of course we'd help." But not everyone saw it that way. Some asked why he did it, what was in it for the county. O'Neill's response? "Herndon's still part of Fairfax County, isn't it?"

The fourth commonality of collaborative leaders is a certain mind-set, a way of thinking. "They see across boundaries," as Harvard's Rosabeth Moss Kanter describes it (1996, p. 97). Like O'Neill, like most creative thinkers, these leaders have a natural or trained tendency to see *connections and possibilities* where others might see barriers or limitations. And the connections are usually to a larger purpose, one that gives them energy and hope.

People like Bob O'Neill, Bob Sweeney, and Chuck Short have a natural tendency to think holistically. They don't assume that collaboration is the solution for every problem. Rather, they assume that most complex issues are connected to other issues, that no one person or profession is likely to deal well with the problem in isolation, and that the opportunity to explore a problem with people from other units is almost always worth the effort. When the Montgomery County Early Childhood Initiative was first suggested, Short and his two colleagues started by asking questions such as these: Who else is invested in this goal? What's already being done, and how can we pool those efforts for greater good? If we can pull this off with all stakeholders, what other opportunities will we find to work together? That's how a collaborative mind-set works.

Terry Newell, faculty coordinator at the Federal Executive Institute, describes the same dynamic from a different point of view. As he points out, "The higher you go in an organization, the more stakeholders you must pay attention to. And dealing with many stakeholders requires an ability to think systemically. Collaboration requires leaders to use systems thinking, to identify and keep in touch with the stakeholders. If you can't think systemically you'll have a very hard time collaborating."

## Finding Meaning by Connecting to Something Larger

Collaborative leaders, like most human beings, have a hunger for connection to something larger than themselves. Unlike many of us, these leaders see possible connections to a larger purpose in their everyday activities (which, by the way, is one definition of spirituality). The Early Childhood Initiative is a good example. A new superintendent proposed a major new school system program to the County Council for financial support. But to Mike Subin, the leader of that council (and a natural collaborative leader), this was about more than a new school program. He told the superintendent to come back with a collaborative proposal, because the county was moving toward a collaborative model and away from go-it-alone programs. Chuck Short also looked beyond the immediate goal of setting up new programs for young kids. Short saw this initiative as an opportunity to break down barriers with the schools and with other agencies. He saw it as a chance to work seamlessly across boundaries with partners who brought wonderful and differing talents to the table. He also envisioned a process that would engage parents and other community members, to build strong support for the new proposal. And that's exactly what happened.

Bob Sweeney thinks in the same way. Most development professionals are totally focused on financial goals. After all, that's largely how they're measured. At the University of Virginia, Bob Sweeney raises the bar much higher. Not that he's out of touch with reality; the university's future financial health depends primarily on private philanthropy, and his officers must meet their financial targets. But for Sweeney the work is about more than money.

The purpose of development for Sweeney is to help the university achieve a state of national preeminence. It is to imbue in future generations a set of timeless principles articulated by Thomas Jefferson. He imagines his university to be a uniquely American expression linking education and democracy, where students would learn by experiencing a system of self-responsibility, by practicing leadership, and by living according to certain values. When Sweeney looks his staff in the eye and tells them that their work is about much more than the dollars, he gets through. He isn't afraid to show his zeal for the cause. He demonstrates his passionate commitment to the larger purpose, and shows others the connections between their everyday toil and a higher vision.

To recap, collaborative leaders share four desirable qualities—they are resolute and driven, have a measured ego, use pull more than push, and see connections to something larger. At their core these qualities come to this:

**Collaborative leaders are passionate to achieve a higher good, with others, and don't need to get the credit.**

## The Key Tasks of Collaborative Leaders

This is a short section, because most of the collaborative leader's tasks have already been discussed. The essence of a collaborative leader's work is to ensure that the elements in the framework described in Chapters Five through Eight are working well. These elements include the following:

### *The Basics*

- Helping identify the group's shared purpose or goal

- Demonstrating the desire to pursue a collaborative solution now, and a willingness to contribute something to achieve it

- Helping to identify the "right people" for the initiative (including both the obvious stakeholders and others whose voices are not always heard), bringing them to the table, and helping to keep them there during times of frustration

- Emphasizing the importance of an open, credible process (not for its own sake, but to build trust and engage all parties in the endeavor)

- Being a champion for the initiative, which means: using personal credibility to bring others together and validate the initiative's importance, reminding others what they have in common, anticipating hurdles, celebrating small successes, supporting group norms and ground rules, helping the parties negotiate differences and do joint problem solving, taking appropriate risks, and providing confidence and hope

*Other Keys to Collaboration*

- Modeling the behaviors that support open and trusting relationships

- Emphasizing the high stakes involved in the initiative

- Helping to build a broader constituency for collaboration among other stakeholders

These form the *substance* of a collaborative leader's work. The four qualities of collaborative leaders described earlier in this chapter suggest *how* such leaders do this work.

## And What About Your Own Collaborative Leadership?

Two obvious questions at this point are, How does my own leadership compare to these collaborative leaders' styles? And, Can I learn each of these collaborative leadership characteristics? At one level, these are questions only you can answer for yourself. At another level, you can get some help by discussing them with trusted colleagues and friends. Ask them how they see you in terms of your leadership in the areas addressed in Exhibit 9.5.

Some managers and leaders prefer to get feedback on such questions through anonymous 360-degree feedback systems. There's much to be said for that. It gives peers, those you report to, and sub-

**Exhibit 9.5. Questions on Your Collaborative Leadership.**

- Do you come across as someone who prefers to be the source of all new ideas?

- Do others see you as someone who typically wants to find the answers to problems and challenges on your own?

- How do you react when others' perspective on an issue is very different from yours? Is that an irritation to be avoided? An inconvenience to be overcome? An asset to be used?

- When you're working on an issue with others, how likely are you to ask if there's anyone else with a stake in the issue?

- When you're trying to influence others, how much do you tend to push your own ideas, and to what extent do you use pull to invite others into the discussion?

ordinates a chance to honestly assess your leadership skills. But it's also powerful to ask colleagues to give you direct, verbal feedback on these and related questions. These conversations need to be done in the right spirit—to help one another learn and grow. When that occurs, it can deepen and strengthen a collaborative venture and build collaborative leadership skills.

Can these collaborative leadership qualities be learned? The first one—a driven resolve—is probably inborn. The other three are clearly learnable. I've seen people develop them by getting feedback from trusted associates, through coaching, and by observing informal mentors who model these qualities. Once exposed to this collaborative leadership style, you don't need more information. As the authors of *The Knowing-Doing Gap* (Pfeffer and Sutton, 2000) demonstrate, most managers and leaders have a lot of information about effective leadership. They don't need more knowledge. True learning occurs in the context of action and reflection. What managers and leaders need to do is turn knowledge into change through practice, getting feedback, reflecting on their successes and mistakes, and trying again. We usually learn what's most important to us. How important is collaborative leadership to you?

---

In "The Dry Salvages" section of T. S. Eliot's last poem, *Four Quartets*, he wrote, "We had the experience, but missed the meaning." Eliot scholar Randy Malamud says that this poem is Eliot's farewell to poetry. He was looking back on his life and work, reflecting on some relationships he had with several people in which he failed to reciprocate, didn't realize the potential for deeper connection, missed the meaning. Collaborative leaders don't make this mistake as often as others. They tend to see multiple opportunities for meaning in their work and relationships, connecting to something larger than themselves. Whether due to enlightened self-interest, altruism, or something else, they very quickly see and make connections to a larger purpose.

Our organizations and communities are filled with people yearning to find meaning and to connect their everyday lives to a larger purpose. That's the main reason why the work of collaborative leaders is so powerful—and so essential.

# Part III

# Key Collaboration Issues and Tasks

# 10

# Phases in the Collaboration Journey

H ow do we get started? What should we expect? Are there predictable phases in collaborative efforts? These are understandable questions; they're also difficult to answer because there is so much variation in collaborative efforts. Some run smoothly, some get sidetracked by other priorities. Sometimes a core group quickly coalesces and works beautifully together, and sometimes past problems and low trust make it very slow going. It's also true that the external environment can impose deadlines and create high stakes that motivate people to action far faster than they thought possible, literally leapfrogging over the phases that most collaborative leaders must carefully negotiate.

## Phases of Collaboration

This chapter addresses four phases that reflect the experience of many collaborative efforts. These phases also mirror the phases couples often go through as they move from a first date to a long-term relationship. My research on public and nonprofit collaboration parallels that of Rosabeth Moss Kanter, the Harvard Business School professor who studied the experiences of thirty-seven private firms that engage in business alliances. Kanter writes that "relationships between companies begin, grow, and develop—or fail—much like relationships between people" (1994, p. 99). Since I'm using the metaphor of dating, I'll use language that fits that experience: courtship, getting serious, commitment, and leaving a legacy.

## Phase I. Courtship

At the beginning of any relationship, people are testing the chemistry and the potential for collaboration. Most of us can remember what this is like. We're excited and nervous, hopeful and apprehensive. How much to reveal, and how much to conceal? We want to put our best foot forward, which of course means that the early time together doesn't bring out our full selves. We're testing the waters at this point. When agencies consider whether to collaborate, the parties get acquainted and their senior leaders get to know one another and determine whether the personal chemistry and organizational values appear to be a good match.

*Some questions that arise in the courtship phase:* Collaborative efforts usually start with many more questions than answers. People come to early meetings wondering: Why am I here? What (if anything) do we have in common? What are we trying to create? What are the other parties' agendas? Do we have the right people at the table? Is this thing already wired? Will this be useful, or a waste of time? Can this alliance meet some of our important business needs?

*Some tasks during the courtship phase:* In the early meetings people need time together and information about each other and the project. They need to learn what the goal is, why it's important, why they have been asked to join. And they need to start forming relationships based on candor and trust. Exhibit 10.1 lists a few tasks in the courtship phase of your collaborative. Note that many of these tasks can be handled in Partnering Workshops, which were described briefly in Chapter Five. They are detailed in Resource A.

*Some indicators that this phase is going well:* The courtship phase is progressing well when there's a sense of momentum, when can-

**Exhibit 10.1. Courtship Phase Tasks.**

- Focus on the basics (described in Chapter Four). That includes determining if there is a good fit between the parties on their values and goals.

- Make efforts to create an open environment; talk about what's in it for each party, the concerns and risks each sees, the benefits for each and for the customers.

- Begin work on relationships—model openness through your use of self-disclosure.

- Identify the boundaries; what's on the table, what isn't.

- Develop the outlines of a game plan for the coming year, but keep it fairly general.

- Try one or a few small projects.

did statements begin to replace the initial reserved behavior, when the early politeness gives way to mutual searches for solutions, when respectful and direct disagreements on some issues are voiced.

**Phase II: Getting Serious**

Groups that fit together move from "Should We?" to "How Do We . . . ?" Many of the initial questions have been answered by now, and (like a couple) the partners are trying to figure out how to make the relationship mutually beneficial. The tentative, perhaps skeptical behaviors of the first phase are diminished; now the partners are trying to get on with the work that drew them together.

*Some questions that arise in the getting serious phase:* What, specifically, are we going to do together? How are we going to do it? How will we know when we get there? (That is, What success measures will we use?) Do we have common interests and complementary strengths? Is there a long-term potential to this relationship? Can we be open enough to disclose what we don't know, what we don't do well? How should the collaborative be governed? What about the politics of this initiative; who's going to be glad, who will be mad, and how influential are the groups that will be mad? How do we involve key stakeholders to learn their concerns and interests? Should we bring them in at all?

*Some tasks during the getting serious phase:* Now is the time to chart the course, to get some specific projects under way, and create a governance structure for the initiative. Exhibit 10.2 lays out the things that need to be done in this phase.

*Some indicators that this phase is going well:* The energy is now focused on getting work done (not on testing whether the initiative makes sense). There is some healthy impatience for results. In general, the parties have shifted from thinking in terms of "Should I

---

**Exhibit 10.2. Getting Serious Phase Tasks.**

- Form stronger relationships by gaining a deeper knowledge of the core group members.
- Develop a more detailed road map for the initiative: set some specific objectives for the year, with tasks, roles, and timetables.
- Start several short-term projects that require collaboration by the parties.
- Publicize the results of the early projects, and recognize those who contributed.
- Start to meet the rest of the family: identify other key staffers in each agency, inform them of the initiative's goals and impact on them, invite them to take on active roles in these projects.
- Identify stakeholder groups of each agency, meet with their leaders to get their views of the effort, and invite some of them to bring concerns and hopes to the core group.
- Design and create a governance structure for the partnership.
- Deal with any emerging signs that some people in the collaborating agencies are feeling threatened by the effort.
- Set some initial performance metrics to determine progress.

join?" to "How do we do this?" The chemistry and trust among the core partners is growing, and there's a desire for some visible results.

More people from each agency are getting involved, which brings both good news and bad. The good: collaboration is spreading beyond the initial group, and more people are invested in it. The bad: some people will see the effort as a threat and resistance to it will grow. Ironically, this is also good news, in that it demonstrates that many people are taking the collaborative seriously. If nobody's threatened, it's probably not viewed as an important change. Interpersonal integration is occurring; now integration is needed at the operational level.

### Phase III: Commitment

A relationship needs to move from "you and me" to "us." That means forming a new entity, integrating systems and operations, and adding real value. Your initiative is in the commitment phase when it's had some initial successes and clearly developed momentum and enthusiasm; the partners want to capture the early lessons learned, and have agreed to institutionalize the relationship into an ongoing entity.

*Some questions that arise in the commitment phase:* Are we ready to make a long-term commitment to each other? How do we ensure the future of this effort? And are we moving from "you and me" to "us," creating an entity that is larger than our individual agencies, something that will endure for our stakeholders and ourselves?

*Some tasks during the commitment phase:* Now is the time to build the formal structures to support the relationship and develop a constituency to support it. Exhibit 10.3 lays out the things that need to be done in this phase.

*Some indicators that this phase is going well:* The collaboration is clearly generating value for the parties and their customers or clients. Results are tangible, and people show genuine pride in the initiative. The parties see it as in their interest to be associated with it. There is a strong desire to institutionalize the initiative so that

---

**Exhibit 10.3. Commitment Phase Tasks.**

- Make changes in key human resources policies to support collaboration.

- Assign some people part- or full-time to the initiative.

- Integrate information systems among the agencies, where possible.

- Base promotions, in part, on collaborative behavior.

- Develop flexible budgeting systems so resources can be allocated as needed.

- Measure, track, and publicize the initiative and its results; recognize those who are contributing.

- Take active steps to grow an external and internal constituency for the initiative.

- Create a *brand*, an identity for the collaborative and its products and services.

---

it will outlast the current leaders. New members who join the core group are aware of and committed to its purpose. Stakeholders are seeing results and pressing the parties to maintain the initiative. The collaborative's leaders are focused on measuring results and ensuring that future leaders are selected with an eye toward their collaborative abilities. The leaders are also engaged in growing a constituency for collaboration.

## Phase IV: Leaving a Legacy

Internal learning, growth, and change characterize all strong and healthy relationships. Just as couples in such relationships learn from each other and leave a legacy through their children and their good deeds, agencies in long-term relationships can learn from one another and leave a legacy through the internal and external changes that result. I have seen such change occur primarily within the individual people involved in multiagency collaboration. When staff work closely with those from another agency, especially if they are co-located, they have opportunities to grow from the experience, and many do.

And what about the agencies themselves? They, too, have opportunities to grow by learning from the other parties: about their human resource and financial systems, their customer relationships, their methods for accumulating and sharing knowledge, and the like. However, internal change at the agency level seems to be less common than change and growth at the individual level. This may simply reflect the fact that cultural change takes time. It may also reflect the human desire to retain autonomy and a sense of identity: people think, "If we change some of our operations and culture, does that mean we become just like them?" For whatever reasons, many agencies (even in long-term, successful alliances) seem to miss the opportunity to learn from the other parties and make internal changes. It is an opportunity that collaborative leaders should seek out and exploit if they're serious about collaboration and organizational growth.

This phase can involve leaving an external legacy as well as learning among the participating individuals and groups. Collaborative efforts usually change over time, and some of their offspring may take on a life of their own. The Joint Venture: Silicon Valley Network (in Chapter Five) is a good example. JVSV frequently creates initiatives that, when successful, often spin off and become independent organizations. The Comprehensive Performance Partnership (CPP) created to help Chautauqua County improve organizational performance is another example. As the county started to internalize the changes initiated by the CPP, the CPP members began developing other projects that had countywide impact.

## After the Legacy

And sometimes, the collaboration ends. This leads to one final point about the phases of collaboration: the last phase may be its dissolution. It's not written anywhere that collaboration, once begun, must become permanent. Remember: *collaboration is a means, not an end*. When it creates an entity that yields significant improvement in customer service and performance, like the JNET information-sharing example among criminal justice agencies, it can and should continue indefinitely (or until some better approach comes along). But if collaborative efforts are used to address a specific problem or meet a need, and the effort succeeds, there may be no reason to continue the formal initiative.

Declaring victory and going home may be difficult for some, especially those who took the risk and invested the energy to get it started. But it's necessary to do at times, if only to avoid the bureaucratic trap of maintaining something simply for its own needs. Terminating a marriage is usually seen as an indication of failure. Ending a formal interagency alliance may be just the opposite.

### Collaboration Phases in Action: Home Health Care

JABA, the Jefferson Area Board for Aging, was created in 1975 as a joint exercise of power by the city of Charlottesville, Virginia, and the five rural counties in the regional planning district. Its mission is to "add dignity, security, independence, and fulfillment to the lives of older adults and their families." It was formed with a sixteen-member board of directors, appointed by the jurisdictions served. Its financial support came primarily from government; in addition to funding from the six local governments, JABA received financial support from the federal Older Americans Act and the Virginia Department for Aging. JABA staff and board members saw it as an agency that responded to the needs of its clients. That is, JABA started out as the classic nonprofit, doing good for those in need. And it had a fine reputation for accomplishing just that.

Despite the organization's well-earned reputation, JABA's leaders started to change its business model in the 1980s. "During the Reagan era, it became clear that federal funding was declining," notes Mark Reisler, a JABA board member since 1985 and former board chair. "Our CEO, Gordon Walker, helped us develop new revenue streams. We started an annual giving program. All of this helped but, given the fact that the great majority of our clients were indigent or near indigent, we knew we needed additional funding sources."

In 1986, JABA Inc. was formed. Its purpose was to enable JABA to increase its income and expand services. Unlike JABA, JABA Inc. is a corporation certified by the IRS with 501(c)(3) status. As a result, contributions to JABA Inc. are tax deductible. JABA, as a quasi-governmental entity, doesn't have the same status, which reduced its fundraising abilities. JABA Inc.'s board includes those on the JABA board, plus an additional six to nine community members elected by the board. Through JABA Inc., JABA has initiated several new programs. One of the most creative is its home health care partnership, Care Advantage Plus.

By the 1990s JABA Inc. had been running a fairly large home health program for several years. The program had about sixty staff who provided a variety of home health services to elderly individuals, including meal preparation, travel to the store to get their medications, and laundry help. The program cost over $1 million a year to run, about 70 percent of that coming from Medicaid, a little under 20 percent from a Medicare home health agency, and the rest from clients who could afford to pay.

Home health care was doing reasonably well in terms of client numbers and quality. But revenues were barely meeting expenses. The target client group was almost entirely low income, and few could contribute to their care. Gordon Walker and Leonard Lohman, JABA's CFO, started talking about the need for better financing. They sought a way to make money on the home health care program in order to expand services to more people, both private pay and indigent. That need triggered JABA's search for a new model.

## 1. Courtship: Looking for Partners

"We'd had a relationship with the University of Virginia since 1995," said Lohman. "UVa Continuum (a university-held corporation) had been purchasing our home health care services for some of its outpatients. Continuum told us they needed better backup when one of our home health aides was sick or couldn't come for some other reason. So in 1996, we started talking with Continuum about creating a new entity that would provide home health services to these clients." Lohman wrote a business plan to create a for-profit organization, and the UVa Continuum officials liked it. "But they weren't sure that JABA knew how to run a profit-making organization."

Through UVa, JABA officials met Debbie Johnston, a nurse who had started her own home health company, Care Advantage, which had a reputation for both quality and profitability. UVa wanted to form a partnership with Johnston's company and JABA. Gordon Walker met Debbie Johnston and they started learning about each other's organizations. They got along well from the start; she was very taken with him and his businesslike approach, and he respected her track record of success; each of her seven offices in Virginia was operating in the black. Johnston was also very attracted to JABA's proactive strategy, and appreciated its diversified funding and entrepreneurial style.

After a few discussions, the most promising option seemed to be the formation of a limited liability company (LLC) to provide expanded home health services. LLCs have the corporate attribute of leaving very little liability to their owners and members. They differ from other corporations in that LLCs are pass-throughs. That is, they don't pay state or federal taxes on their profits. All net earnings can be invested back into the business, paid to stockholders, or used for related purposes. JABA leaders met with university representatives and after some negotiations they developed a draft operating agreement. That agreement went to the UVa board, but then things slowed down. Lohman reflects, "It seemed like we had an agreement from the parties on the overall concept, but couldn't get UVa to give a final yes or no on the specifics." Walker was more graphic: "The marriage was never consummated; UVa got cold feet at the altar!"

Johnston had quickly approved the proposed agreement. Lohman worked on a phase-in plan that detailed the change from JABA Inc.'s current home health program to the new entity. But the UVa board couldn't seem to make a commitment. "We never got a definite 'no,' we just couldn't seem to get a 'yes' from the university board," Lohman recalls. "We asked UVa for a decision within six weeks. When they told us they couldn't respond in that time frame, we got tired of waiting."

## 2. Getting Serious: Negotiating an Agreement

In late 1996, JABA decided to go ahead without UVa. After informing the university of this decision, Lohman wrote a business plan for a home health partnership between JABA and Care Advantage. The plan showed the new organization getting to break-even within eighteen months. Johnston liked it. It reflected her kind of thinking, and gave her a high level of comfort in terms of working with JABA.

Johnston wrote a management plan showing what she and her company would provide, and the amount they would charge for their management services. Walker and Lohman were comfortable with it and took it to JABA Inc.'s board. Some of its members had difficulty with the notion of creating a for-profit entity; they saw JABA as a social service agency whose mission was to do good for those in need, not to make a buck. But the majority liked the concept, and urged Walker to move forward with the deal. Walker, Lohman, and Johnston decided to formalize their alliance through a detailed operating agreement.

### The Agreement

JABA Inc. and Care Advantage would each put up $50,000 in cash. They would create a board for the new entity, half appointed by JABA Inc. and half by Care Advantage. Under the proposed agreement, Johnston's company received a management fee for managing the new company, called Care Advantage Plus (CAP). It continued serving elderly people from the same six jurisdictions that JABA Inc.'s program had been reaching. Existing JABA Inc. home health staff would automatically transfer to CAP, and would be retained for at least four months. After that, their continued employment was up to the new company. Because of a shortage of home health aides in the planning district, it seemed unlikely that the new company would fire the JABA staff and go looking for new people. It looked like a win-win all the way around.

### The Resistance

Not everyone on JABA's board saw it that way. Board member Mark Reisler recalls, "Some of our board members were still asking, 'Why do this?' They worried that a for-profit organization would have different motives than ours, that we'd be seen as competing with others in the private sector, which could harm our funding. These members thought it was a radical departure from our core mission." There was no rebellion or organized opposition on the board, but several members needed time to get more comfortable with the concept. After some educational sessions with the board, the opposition lessened considerably.

Dealing with staff concerns took more time. Meetings were held with the home health nursing staff to explain the concept and how it would affect them. Debbie Johnston's management team met with the affected staff to discuss the benefits, bonuses, overtime, and other opportunities to increase earnings in CAP. JABA's leaders sent formal letters to these staff members, explaining the vision for the partnership and inviting comments. They explained the four-month transition period to CAP. Most of the nursing staff were satisfied with JABA's rationale for making this major change. Some employees said they'd been with JABA for years and thought it should continue providing the service. All decided to give CAP a try, however.

### 3. Commitment: Starting the Company

The JABA Inc. board approved the terms of the operating agreement. In early 1997, JABA Inc. and Care Advantage tied the knot and created CAP, which came into being in April of the same year. In almost every way, the joint venture has been a tremendous success. Some results:

- It reached break-even in fourteen months, four months earlier than anticipated.

- Services have expandeu. For instance, CAP began providing temporary health care personnel to health care offices (such as physicians' offices and nursing homes) to fill in for nurses who were out sick or on leave. This met a real need in the community, and it also provided useful revenue to the company. "It's been a real cash cow to us, frankly," Lohman notes.

- The client base has expanded. In addition to the low-income clients already served, CAP also serves a number of elderly who are able to purchase home care services.

- CAP is generating about $200,000 a year in profits. Half of that goes to JABA Inc. Those funds have expanded JABA's services to the community, primarily through increased services to indigent elderly individuals.

- Some of those profits fund a geriatric intervention assessment team. This team provides nursing clinic services to rural elderly individuals at JABA centers. The geriatric team is now providing over seven thousand hours of services to elderly people each year.

- The CAP board members are learning to work well with each other. They bring different perspectives; JABA's two representatives are more service oriented, the CAP reps focus largely on the bottom line. These differences are real; how many indigent clients can CAP afford to serve, for instance, given the "paltry" levels that Medicaid reimburses for such clients? "We understand each other's positions on this," says Reisler, "and we've learned to deal with the issue, but it remains an issue."

- All of the direct-care staff seemed satisfied with CAP and stayed with it. However, most of the former JABA home health managers left CAP during or after the four-month transition period (more on this later).

Debbie Johnston believes that CAP is meeting the needs of its clients and partner agency, and more: "This partnership has . . . taught both parties something. I've learned a great deal about low-income elder care. Hopefully JABA has inherited some of Care Advantage's entrepreneurial spirit. . . . Although working with a non-profit can be challenging due to the bureaucratic levels of decision making, this partnership has been win-win."

## Analysis

This example is different from most public and nonprofit alliances in two respects. First, it is a profit-making initiative. When there's a bottom line, it clarifies and speeds up the courtship and getting serious phases. If the financials look solid, that answers many initial questions. The other difference is that CAP is its own entity, separate from either of the partners, much like joint ventures in the private sector. This can be a powerful model for generating collaboration. The board and staff reflect the various constituencies, but they are part of an independent organization with its own goals, customers, and expectations. The collaborative venture isn't something they do when they finish their other work; the collaborative venture *is* their work.

That said, the parties still went through the same phases that many collaboratives experience.

### 1. Courtship

There was a courting period during which relationships formed and were very important. Part of forming relationships is learning about each other's personal and organizational values. Board member Reisler notes, "If our partner wasn't socially conscious, this partnership wouldn't have gotten very far."

The principals not only sized each other up, they tested the waters to see if a joint effort was conceptually feasible. Lohman wrote a business plan when UVa was still in the picture, and the principals determined that an LLC was the most attractive kind of corporation to create. As often happens, the nonprofit agency (JABA Inc.) was able to move much more quickly than the government agency (UVa). When UVa couldn't respond in a timely fashion, JABA Inc. officials chose to go with the suitor that seemed most attractive. They made some judgments about their potential strategic fit: which relationship seemed promising, and which didn't.

## 2. Getting Serious

Here, the principals had three major tasks: to determine if the new venture met each party's needs and the needs of the clients; to help the JABA Inc. board and staff get comfortable with the proposed agreement; and to create a governance structure. As is often the case at this point, the energy level and pace picked up considerably once the principals had a joint project to work on.

There was a marked difference in the pace of the different parties. After negotiating with one another and dealing with some JABA board members' discomfort, the principals were ready to commit and get the venture started. Some board members weren't initially taken with the concept. Even though they were a minority of the board, their concerns had to be taken seriously.

Board members are critical links to the community, and nonprofit managers sometimes make the mistake I once made when running an agency for the handicapped. I "got out in front" of the board in terms of my enthusiasm for committing resources to a prevention program, and didn't take the time to explain how this initiative would relate to their concerns. As a result, I never got the board's support or sufficient resources to make the program effective. JABA's leaders understood the need to bring all board members along, and invested the time to do so.

The staff weren't ready to act quickly, and many meetings were required to help them understand the new program, why the move was being made, and how it would affect them. Timing and pace is an important and sometimes difficult issue: each stakeholder must come along at its own speed, but those ready to move more quickly can't always wait until the slowest group is ready. In this case, they were able to strike a balance by developing the four-month phase-in period, giving JABA staff time to try out the new entity and make up their minds as they experienced it.

The getting serious phase also involved creating a governance structure for the new entity, a board with 50-50 representation from each partner. This was a critical step. The parties were taking a risk by creating a joint venture that would soon take on a life of its own. It takes care and candor to develop a governance arrangement that addresses the needs of the parties while giving the new organization the flexibility to meet the needs of its clients. There may be a temptation to move through these details quickly, but the parties are wise to think them through carefully. In this case, they did.

One more point to note: relationship building continued during this phase, as did the testing. In working through the details of complicated management and operating agreements, the principals gleaned important information about each other: does he understand the business we're about to enter? Is she good at follow-through? Can he bring his board and staff along? Does she have the flexibility to work with an agency that's always been nonprofit and is just now entering the profit-making world? The best way to answer such questions is by doing real work together. Learning how the other deals with various pressures and challenges can build the confidence and trust that a joint venture requires.

### 3. Commitment

This phase primarily involved the legal formalities of executing the agreement and making the transition to CAP. It included helping clients to understand the change, ensuring that their needs would continue to be met, and monitoring the results during the early months.

During this phase the CAP board members learned that they have some differences on key issues. One has to do with the number of Medicaid clients that CAP subsidizes. The two JABA representatives on its board argue that such clients must continue to form a large part of the customer base. The more business-oriented board members, of course, worry about the financial impact of accepting patients who don't cover their costs as well as others do.

Dealing with important differences can be a test for any new joint venture. One factor that helped was CAP's overall success. The former JABA staff are happy with CAP, as are the clients. And CAP is making money, which helps both partners (and allows JABA to increase services). This success helps create a constituency for CAP and makes it easier to deal with their differences. But nobody is in denial. As Reisler notes, "It remains an issue."

The former JABA home health managers had a difficult time working for CAP, and all but one left by the end of the transition period. They left for three related reasons:

- They kept their social services mind-set, wanting to do everything possible for those in need. From CAP's point of view, services cannot be delivered without taking costs into account.

- Productivity is important at CAP; each manager had certain goals to reach. When they didn't reach them, CAP managers weren't pleased. This was a change for the JABA managers.

- One former JABA manager felt she didn't fit in with the CAP administration. She had been the lead manager of the program under JABA, but no longer ran the show once it became CAP.

For most of the former JABA managers, the key issue was the cultural and mind-set change. A businesslike environment that emphasizes quantitative goals, measures, productivity, and profit is far different from the human services culture of JABA. It's very unfortunate when some people cannot make this transition, but it shouldn't come as a surprise. When it's possible to give managers a choice—stay in your home agency or try the new one—that's the wisest course. In this case that wasn't an option.

### 4. Learning and Legacy

Earlier I suggested that mature collaboratives have the opportunity for a fourth phase, one in which individual and institutional learning takes place. CAP seems to be at that level now. Debbie Johnston notes that she has learned a good deal about caring for low-income elderly individuals. The JABA board and staff are finding out what entrepreneurial ventures require, and are developing more business-like management practices within JABA and JABA Inc. And both are exploring each other's mind-sets and values as they negotiate their differences. Further, JABA has initiated programs to non-CAP clients through CAP's revenues.

When the parties learn from their collaboration, their chances of success and growth increase. Their clients are benefiting, but so are they and their respective organizations. In the case of CAP, the parties see that their collaboration is helping to make them better managers with broader perspectives. This growth gets them more invested in the alliance. Such benefits give the parties additional commitment and energy to deal with the opportunities that await them.

---

When a collaborative effort follows the phases I've described here, the parties are better able to plan their initiative. Even when that happens, other factors can help or derail the effort, and effective leaders need to be ready to manage them. I describe some of those factors in the next chapter.

# 11

# More Keys to Successful Collaboration

Necessary but not sufficient." That's the phrase academics and other researchers often use to indicate that a certain factor contributes to a given result, but that there's more to the story. It's a polite way of saying, "Not so fast, bud!" And that is precisely where I am in describing collaboration. The framework in Chapters Four through Nine contains the necessary conditions for most collaborative efforts to work. The phases described in Chapter Ten apply to many though certainly not all joint initiatives. But there are other items to put on your mental or written checklist, factors that can make a difference when the initiative is going slowly, when you're trying to figure out what's missing, or when you're just plain stumped. In this chapter, I'll discuss six important factors that affect collaboration:

- Maintain continuity of leadership among the parties.

- Help each party play to its strengths.

- Keep collaborative efforts voluntary, not mandatory.

- Acquire flexible resources.

- Measure and post results of the collaborative effort.

- Balance the need to plan with the requirement for results.

## Continuity of Leadership

Trainers who help develop teams sometimes say that when the team composition changes, you're starting over with a new team. Someone joins, someone else leaves, and the dynamics shift. Teams need to go back to the start, however briefly, and go through the phases of team development (such as forming, storming, norming, and performing) taught by many team-building consultants (Weber, 1982).

Collaborative groups sometimes have to start over as well. One of their big challenges occurs when a core group member is added or replaced. It's a challenge in two respects. First, the group needs to take time to revisit the team development phases. More important, the group is challenged because the new person wasn't a founding member of the collaborative. Few entrants have the same passion and commitment that a creator has to a cause. Even more challenging is the situation in which the new member doesn't share a commitment to collaboration.

What to do when founding members are replaced by others who lack the same level of commitment, or simply don't have a history with the initiative? There are at least two responses. One is to commit time to orienting the newcomers. Rather than assuming that things will go on as before, recognize that this is both a challenge and an opportunity to build new support. New members need time to learn, to find a role, to become convinced that the collaborative is in their agencies' interest. The core group can also use the transition time to step back and learn—how do the new members view the collaboration? What seems positive? What questions do they pose? The new members can offer fresh perspectives that help the core group to grow.

For instance, Joint Venture: Silicon Valley Network (discussed in Chapter Five) frequently has to orient new board members to its purpose and programs. Business leaders come and go in Silicon Valley, and JVSV struggles with this question of changing leadership. It uses its strategic plan, and its Index of Silicon Valley (which tracks twenty-six indicators of economic vitality and quality of life in the region) to bring new leaders up to speed with its challenges and initiatives. JVSV leaders also think carefully about how new members can be offered a meaningful role, one that helps them make a difference.

A more powerful approach to the challenge of changing leadership is to prepare for it in advance. If the collaborative involves a city, county, community college, nonprofit agency, and employees' union, what happens when the top executive in one of those organizations leaves? The collaborative group can influence the selection of a new executive by ensuring that it continually educates leaders of each member agency about the payoffs generated by the effort and the importance of hiring people in vacant positions who are supportive of collaboration. I described some methods for doing this in Chapter Eight, on creating a constituency for collaboration.

## Different Strengths from Everyone

Economists call it the "principle of comparative advantage." Barbara Gradet from the Baltimore County Department of Social Services refers to it as "differentiated assets." Management consultants sometimes call it "playing to your strengths." Whatever term you use, collaboratives are more likely to thrive when the members all bring some different assets to the table.

Several good things happen when the parties play to their distinctive strengths. First, obviously, the group is getting the best from its members; whoever has the best technology or the most effective team-building method or the most flexible funding contributes that strength and everyone benefits. Second, groups start on firm and comfortable ground. Remember: many forces act to pull people back to their home agencies, and one of those is fear of the unknown. When you can contribute a strength to a joint effort, you're on known ground. Another positive is that parties will learn from one another when each contributes a distinctive asset.

One of the most creative, simple, and effective examples of playing to each party's strengths is going on now in Pennsylvania's Department of Transportation (PENNDOT).

### PENNDOT's Agility Program

The program's title—"Agility"—turns out to be very apt. Agility has been a key strategy at PENNDOT ever since director Brad Mallory learned about the concept while reading *Agile Competitors and Virtual Organizations* (Goldman, Nagel, and Preiss, 1997). Agility is an approach that helps organizations become more nimble and proactive. It combines four principles:

- Enriching the customer
- Organizing to master change and uncertainty
- Leveraging people, skills, information, and technology
- Cooperating in virtual relationships

PENNDOT is working on all four agility principles. It is using the fourth principle in a most creative way to manage road maintenance.

Agility's partnership method boils down to bartering; it's an exchange of services of relatively equal value between the state and localities. PENNDOT county maintenance managers meet with the managers of the localities within that county (the state has sixty-seven counties and over 2,500 localities—cities, towns, school districts, boroughs, townships, and the like). They discuss their respective needs and resources, and find simple and quick ways to exchange what each does well, to keep the roads maintained.

They aren't constrained by formal responsibilities (here's where it gets interesting). PENNDOT is responsible by state law for certain maintenance functions on state roads, but if a locality can perform a state function on its portion of the state road in exchange for some service PENNDOT can provide on its local roads, they cut a deal and get on with it. For instance, in Hampton Township, PENNDOT widened a township road. In exchange, the township swept various state roads. In Lackawanna County, PENNDOT crews painted lines on more than twenty intersections, and lined the parking lots at the municipal building. The township did its share by clearing snow on two miles of state roads within the borough. Now, snow clearing is a state responsibility. But it's a very time-consuming task on state roads going through small boroughs. PENNDOT managers would prefer to focus on main roads with high levels of traffic. This agreement not only saves money and time, it also benefits the public in terms of safety: when local crews clear snow on state roads, the public gets faster service because the crews are close at hand and able to respond quickly when bad weather hits.

Another public benefit has to do with accountability. "Say there's a drainage problem at an intersection of a township road and a PENNDOT road," says Rick Hogg, a PENNDOT district engineer. "Before Agility, there might have been an argument between the two agencies, each saying 'it's their problem, let them fix it.' Now there's no finger pointing. See, the customer doesn't care who owns the problem, customers just want it fixed . . . so we work it out. We find out what each agency can contribute, and we estimate the value of their contribution (in terms of employee time and financial cost), and look for ways to keep it equitable. It really comes down to relationships—that's a major part of how we'll sustain delivery of government services in the future."

And what about bureaucracy? There isn't any. The deal is formalized in a three-page agreement. "What used to take months of haggling and legalistic memos of understanding now is decided in weeks or days," says Jim Slaughter, chief of application development for PENNDOT. "The one issue is, how do we determine what's 'equal value?' Is washing fifteen bridges the same as painting lines on five miles of roads? That's important to determine, but the managers work it out locally; there's no state office micromanaging the process."

Then there's the question of liability. Who is responsible for the work done when one party is working on the other party's roadways?

The answer is, all parties continue to be responsible for the quality and safety of roads assigned to them by law. Think of it as a formal contractual relationship: the owner has liability for the premises, regardless of who worked on them. Thus, each party must ensure that the other has done work at an appropriate quality level. Sometimes, that means saying no to a proposed exchange, if one agency doesn't think the other is up to doing its part well.

Sherri Zimmerman, director of PENNDOT's Bureau of Municipal Services, oversees the Agility effort. She estimates that Agility saved the state over $8 million in its first three years. More important, it helps state and local governments use their resources and strengths to maintain and keep roads safe. For more on Agility and its method for playing to each partner's strengths, check http://www.dot.state.pa.us (click on Special Interest Areas, then scroll down to Municipal Services, where you'll find a link to the Agility program).

## Voluntary Rather Than Mandatory Efforts

When people are forced to collaborate, when a funding body or legislative group mandates it, the result is more likely to resemble "malicious compliance" than committed collaboration. People go through the motions when forced to collaborate. They don't start with the energy and enthusiasm that is needed for collaboration, and they probably won't have a committed champion to help bust the barriers. When a team from the U.S. Forest Service wrote a report on collaborative stewardship, it described what collaboration isn't as well as what it is. One of the team's conclusions: "Collaboration is not a process that can be forced" (U.S. Forest Service National Collaborative Stewardship Team, 2000, p. 3). It's a logical conclusion; collaboration rests on a foundation of trust, and it's hard to establish trust if you're told you have no choice.

Fair enough, you may be thinking, but what can you do when collaboration is being forced on you? The best answer is, encourage the parties to come together before that happens. And sometimes the threat that collaboration will be mandated (or that a central governing body will make the decisions for the organizations and take away all of their control) is enough to bring the parties to the table. That may be one reason why more than forty states are working together on the Streamlined Sales Tax Project. This is an effort created by state governments and the private sector to simplify sales and use tax collection. Businesses like insurance companies that work across the country have a terrible time keeping up with fifty different state application processes and fifty sets of rules in each state. The project aims to both simplify and create consistent standards for state taxes, and the states want to do so before the feds mandate the answers.

"If the states don't make their regulatory systems more uniform, the business lobbies in Washington will push Congress to preempt the states and pass federal legislation requiring uniformity," warns Peter Harkness, publisher of *Governing Magazine*. "Business wants a 'frictionless economy' to succeed in the global economy, and the states have a real challenge now: will they embrace this change and thrive, or have it thrust on them?" Utah's Governor Mike Leavitt sums it up simply: "It's going to take real statesmanship" (Walters, 2001, p. 24).

## Flexible Resources

"You'll need some 'glue money,' " says Con Hogan. He's talking about flexible resources for small things like food at meetings, rental of space and equipment, brochures. And, as a collaborative gains strength, many leaders find they need consultants or part- or full-time coordinators. One major factor in the success of the Montgomery County Early Childhood Initiative (discussed in Chapter Nine) was the full-time staffer the Collaboration Council hired to support the effort.

In my experience, the challenge isn't finding the money. The challenge here is to *realize* the need and to meet it appropriately. I've seen several groups insist during their first year that they wouldn't need extra help or additional funding; they would handle it all themselves. There's something very positive in that, because it can reflect a sense of determination and pride.

Most large collaborative efforts, however, do run into a need for additional help and resources. The core group makes a mistake when it tries to support all new activities with existing funds. Most organizations don't hesitate to seek additional resources when starting a new program. If the collaborative effort is a priority and requires new resources, the parties need to step up and seek the funding.

## Measurement and Publicity for Results

There are two important quotes to memorize when dealing with the important issue of performance measures. One comes from Vince Lombardi, perhaps the greatest pro football coach ever:

**"If you aren't keeping score, you're only practicing."**

The other statement, interestingly enough, was made by the preeminent physicist of the twentieth century, Albert Einstein:

**"Not everything that can be counted, counts; and not everything that counts can be counted."**

Two seemingly conflicting assertions. And the problem is, they're both valid! When we keep score of a program's outputs and outcomes, the staff pay more attention and work hard to achieve the desired numbers. But some of life's most important moments aren't countable. If a public library collaborates with a city museum, as happens regularly in Chicago, we can count the number of kids and families who attend. We could measure how well the kids retain certain facts about the exhibits. But would you try to quantify the delight they experience when seeing a dinosaur for the first time?

The sense of wonder when shown how a flower opens and closes with the sunlight? If you believe that things don't exist unless they can be quantified, what does that say about love? Joy? Patriotism?

Some collaboration veterans are strong believers in the importance of measuring and posting results, and I agree with them, with two caveats. First, *measurement doesn't always mean quantification.* Many professionals perform peer reviews on the quality of their colleagues' work without reducing it to numbers. They have certain agreed-upon standards that guide them in conducting peer review. Second, timing makes a big difference when it comes to instituting measures. As John Gardner has pointed out, we can do more harm than good if we emphasize rigorous measurement of results early in a creative project. It may take two years or more to learn how to make the collaborative effort work. An emphasis on measurement and quantification in the early stages can lead to more game playing (to make the numbers look good) than value, and can distract the principals from moving the work forward.

Measurement and evaluation efforts can be initiated at the start of a collaborative effort and provide excellent feedback, however, if the resources are sufficient support an independent evaluation effort. That's how the Smart Start program in North Carolina began. Launched in 1993 by Governor Jim Hunt, Smart Start is a state-local community partnership that provides services to kids up through age five, with the goal of helping all children enter school healthy and ready to learn. The state included significant funds at the outset for an evaluation component of Smart Start, and contracted with a respected center at the University of North Carolina to conduct ongoing assessments. This has added to the program's credibility, as well as its quality.

Nonetheless, all professionals worthy of the name want to know whether what they're doing is working, and that requires some sort of assessment and measurement. Moreover, measuring and publicizing results can build confidence in the initiative's effectiveness, and that helps create a broader constituency for collaboration.

Many academics and practitioners are studying the important but difficult issue of performance measures. My own experience and review of the research leads to these conclusions:

• *Use a few measures for a given work unit or program area.* No one can focus on twenty or thirty measures; keep the number in the single digits and it will get employees' attention.

• *The measures that matter most to your external constituents relate to outcomes.* Are there fewer fires? Is the incidence of low-birth-weight babies going down? These are the kinds of outcomes that our agencies were created to achieve. Nonetheless, collaboratives can and should track internal measures of inputs and outputs, *if* such measures are related to the desired outcomes. If the desired outcome is a reduction in the incidence of low-birth-weight babies, then an effective output measure is the percentage of pregnant females receiving quality and regular prenatal care.

Bob Behn, at Harvard's Kennedy School of Government, argues persuasively that outputs can be much more motivating to employees than outcome measures, because employees can quickly see their impact on producing an output. It can take years or decades to determine how well an outcome (teaching children, improving water quality) was achieved. Providing employees with near-real-time feedback on their output production compared to their targets can be highly motivating (Behn, forthcoming). But keep in mind that the outside world cares primarily about outcomes. And, as Behn and others point out, a focus on outcomes can push staff to collaborate with other agencies, since most important outcomes are only achieved through a coalition effort.

An intriguing example of using measures to foster collaboration is going on in Iowa. The state's twenty-five agencies are now organized into six "enterprise planning teams," groups of agencies with similar missions (health, environment, education, and the like). Agency leaders within each team set three to five teamwide goals that cross agency boundaries. They track and post results quarterly on a state Web site. And, perhaps most important, Governor Vilsack and Lieutenant Governor Pederson meet with the agency heads of each team on a quarterly basis to review progress within each goal area. The governor and lieutenant governor try to ask "Why?" when the numbers look bad, to take the fear out. Jim Chrisinger, who is responsible for accountability systems for the state, notes, "We are working hard to create an environment in which data are used to drive change, not blame. The goal is to break down silos and silo-type thinking, and get agencies within an enterprise planning team to focus on common goals."

- *Make measures visible, and capture them frequently.* Measuring performance once a year may satisfy certain funders, but that won't help you improve performance. Posting results on certain measures can be done as often as biweekly or monthly. Doing so, and having staff meet to discuss and take action on the measures, helps to create high stakes.

- *Identify a manager responsible for each performance area being measured.* It makes no sense to rigorously measure performance if nobody is given the responsibility of overseeing that performance area. Identifying a person (or team) focuses accountability, and gives the goal managers the credibility to take needed actions. When the New England EPA office gave a respected staffer the job of being a goal manager for the Charles River cleanup described in Chapter Eight, it took a big step in the right direction.

- *Don't assume you'll get it right the first time.* This is far more art than science. Be forgiving at the start, use the first two or three years to learn which measures are most useful.

- *Don't tie performance on measures to financial consequences.* This is controversial. Some believe that performance must be related to agency funding or individual bonuses if the measures are to be taken seriously. But if that's the case, should we reduce the number of cops on the street when crime goes up? Crime often rises during recessions; are you sure you want to cut the police department at such times? Should we cut the funding to our country's intelligence and law enforcement agencies because some of them failed to share important information prior to September 11, 2001, about the terrorists who brought down the World Trade Center?

If we tie measured performance directly to financial consequences, only one thing is perfectly predictable: employees will find
a way to game the system. Still, there do need to be consequences
for performance. And some of the most effective consequences are
the immediate feedback from peers, customers, boss, and others.
That's one reason why the CitiStat method is so powerful. The performance is made visible by comparing measured performance with
certain targets; important people pay careful attention to it and ask
lots of questions, and the clear expectation is for performance
improvement. That builds what I call a culture of performance and
accountability, and it's a very strong motivator.

• *Ask staff to use the information gleaned from measures to learn
and improve.* Assume that most professionals care strongly about
their effectiveness, and that appropriate measures can help them
learn. Doing so will decrease staff members' defensiveness and
increase their focus on the measures and their meaning.

• *Finally, involve the staff who do the work in determining the appropriate measures.* If you do, and if those staff members believe that the
measures are meant to provide useful feedback, they can be powerful indeed. Peter Block has sound advice on this point: "The test for
useful measures is whether the partners would choose these measures
for each other, if the business were their own" (Block, 1993, p. 208).

For an excellent discussion of performance measures, check the
Kennedy School of Government's Web site: http://www.ksg.harvard.
edu/visions/performance_management.

## Planning Balanced with Results

Many collaboratives confront an apparent dilemma: they need a
good deal of time to plan their project, yet the more time given to
planning, the less the sense of high stakes and the greater the feelings of frustration at "endless meetings with no results." What to do?

This is an *apparent* dilemma, not a necessary one. The problem
exists if we get into an either/or way of thinking, what the authors

of the wonderful book *Built to Last* call the "tyranny of the Or" (Collins and Porras, 1994, p. 43). Either/or thinking limits our range of options. For instance, did Bill Clinton do many positive things for the country, *or* was he guilty of grossly immoral acts as president? I believe many historians will answer yes. It's possible that a leader can be seriously flawed *and* make important, positive changes.

For partnerships the question should be phrased, *How do we achieve the necessary level of planning while at the same time maintaining a bias for action?* And the most powerful response to that question is to integrate planning with action. You needn't spend six to nine months doing detailed planning, with the intention of acting later once the plan is finished. Rather, realize that the plan must be flexible and dynamic, that it shouldn't be highly detailed at the start, and further refine it in an iterative fashion as actions are implemented.

Some military planners understand this concept well. Dwight Eisenhower used to quote Helmuth von Moltke, a nineteenth-century Prussian field marshal: "Plans are nothing; planning is everything." Von Moltke knew whereof he spoke. His army defeated a larger and better-equipped French force in 1870 that everyone "knew" would win. But von Moltke knew something else: "No plan survives contact with the enemy." The idea is to get a general strategy, and continue to modify and add to it through the course of acting.

## Do Planning and Knowledge Lead to Action and Change?

The question of balancing planning and action rests on a certain assumption, one widely taught in the behavioral sciences: the idea that behavioral change follows attitudinal change:

**Attitude change → Behavioral change**

It seems only natural that insight leads to action and change: if I understand, I will do.

And not only that. It also assumes that behavioral change *only* comes after attitudes change. You know the phrase: "*first* we need to get people to buy in—" This seems to make sense, and when attitudes do change they produce powerful behavioral change. But, sad to say, the assumption doesn't work out often enough. Try turning it on its head, and see what you think. Consider the following quotations:

- "If you do it, then you will know it."—David Sun, Kingston Technology (Pfeffer and Sutton, 2000, p. 249)

- "We will do it and we will understand."—Exodus 24:7

- "It is easier to act ourselves into a better mode of thinking than to think ourselves into a better mode of acting."—Richard Pascale (1990)

The assumption underlying these statements may appear counterintuitive, but I've seen many people and organizations gain from this wonderful insight. Figure 11.1 sketches it graphically.

**Figure 11.1. Behavior and Expectation.**

**Begin by Expecting Different Behaviors**

The notion is that we try a new behavior. We (and others) observe the results. How well does the new behavior work? If it's positive, we have an opportunity to alter our attitudes about that behavior. We may, or may not, see it differently. And the cycle continues. We change a little more in that direction, observe the results, and have another chance to change attitudes. . . .

For instance, if your manager asks you to take a team approach to a task you've done individually in the past, and if the manager gives a plausible reason for doing so, you'll probably give it a try. Moving around the circle in Figure 11.1, you and others will observe the results. Was the task done better or faster using the team? Was the customer more pleased with the results? Was quality improved? If the answers are yes, you (and others) have an opportunity to alter your attitudes toward the team approach. You may decide teams make sense, or you may think the success was a fluke. The next time you use a team approach you'll again observe the results, again have a chance to alter (or not alter) attitudes toward it.

There are many examples of this phenomenon. Most adults getting started with computers don't get over their jitters by listening to a sparkling lecture on the wonders of technology. Instead they learn a few functions, try them out, succeed and make mistakes, get past some of the fear and try some more. Slowly—as behaviors improve—attitudes follow suit. The same with a young child getting on a bike for the first time, or an adult getting into a rigorous exercise regime. The behavior changes, and people have an opportunity to alter their attitudes as they see the results.

It's useful to take this back to the issue of planning and acting in collaboration. My bias is for action in the start-up phases. Rather than spending month after month planning and seeking consensus on vision statements, detailed operational plans, and governance structures (hoping to get buy-in), I prefer early action. Create an initial plan, then find opportunities for joint projects that move toward the overall goal. As you work on activities like joint training for staff, pilot projects, and customer surveys, it gives the initiative energy. Relationships can be strengthened as people learn with and from each other. Equally important, the results of these early actions are fed back into the plan, which gets modified in an iterative fashion.

So the apparent problem of balancing the need to plan your collaboration with the necessity for results turns out to be an opportunity, not a problem.

———

Maintaining continuity of leadership, helping the parties play to their strengths, keeping the initiative voluntary, measuring and posting results—when collaborative leaders pay attention to these factors (as well as the key elements noted in Chapters Four through Nine), they greatly improve the prospects for interagency collaboration. And that has been the major focus of this book, helping managers and leaders learn how to work across the boundaries that separate their agencies from others. But many people are struggling with the more immediate challenge of working across the boundaries that exist *within* their organizations. It's to that topic that we now turn.

# 12

# Collaboration Within a Single Organization

*You can't force collaboration, but you can expect it.*
*Chuck Short*

Most of the examples in this book pertain to collaboration across organizational lines, and the challenges of getting several government or nonprofit agencies to work together on a common cause. Collaboration is also a challenge *within* many organizations, and the hurdles tend to be similar: turf, different goals, lack of trust and respect, worries about losing autonomy and control, and few incentives. What's known about successful collaboration across divisions and departments within one agency? Do the same basic factors that promote alliances across organizational lines also work within individual organizations? Are the leadership issues different?

Almost all middle and senior managers face this dilemma. Whether you're trying to manage cross-agency collaboration or not, you probably have wondered why it seems difficult to get division and department heads to play together. This chapter presents a powerful example of an agency that addressed that problem, with impressive results.

## Transformation at the Financial Management Service

The Financial Management Service (FMS) is fairly small by federal standards, with about eighteen hundred full-time equivalent employees. But its mission and impact are huge. FMS serves as the banker for the government's civilian agencies. It makes over 800 million payments to the American people each year, sending Americans their Social Security checks, paying contractors, and paying federal workers. It also acts as a collection agency for the government, taking in over $2 trillion annually in taxes and $2.7 billion annually in debts owed to the government. FMS handles all claims for lost, forged, and stolen checks. With such a vital mission, FMS employees have to be able to work well together across its eight functions. Unfortunately, for many years that wasn't happening.

## A Balkanized Agency, an Angry Congress

In December 1997, Bureau of Public Debt Director Dick Gregg was asked by Treasury Secretary Robert Rubin to take over FMS. Gregg quickly learned that the agency was in serious trouble on many fronts.

### Behind the Curve with the Debt Collection Act

FMS has the lead role in implementing a major federal law called the Debt Collection Improvement Act of 1996. Prior to the Act, citizens who were delinquent in paying money they owed to one agency could still collect money owed to them by a different agency. FMS had to develop systems that would enable it to offset payments to individuals by the amount of money they owed the government. Two years after the Act was passed, none of its seven major provisions had been implemented, and Congress wasn't amused. Connie Craig, an FMS assistant commissioner (an "AC," in agency parlance), put it bluntly: "Debt collection was in disarray."

The office charged with managing the Debt Collection Act operated without cohesion or direction. To track progress on the Debt

Collection Act, FMS produced a monthly report showing the growth in electronic payments. Two different FMS units produced this report. Why two reports? Because *there was no expectation* from senior management to produce *one* report.

### No Single Agency Voice

A project team from FMS would go to an agency and give it certain information. A while later, another FMS project team would go to the same agency and give conflicting information. Often, neither of the two teams even knew the other was meeting with the same agency!

### Division at the Top

There was a strong perception within FMS that the previous com-missioner and deputy commissioner were frequently at odds with each other over major policy issues. Many staff members seemed to shop between the two for the answer they wanted to hear, and the split at the top was felt throughout the agency.

Relationships among associate commissioners and other senior managers were very strained all down the line. As Craig put it, "In the old days you could feel the tension in the air at executive board meetings. I didn't want to go to those meetings—nobody wanted to go to them!"

## First Steps

On his first day at FMS, Gregg made clear to the ACs how he oper-ated: "I said that our first priority was to make the FMS culture one of teamwork. I gave them examples of thinking and acting with a broad perspective. I said that we would speak with one voice, not several, that information would be shared widely, and issues would be dealt with early and directly. I emphasized that we would have a few common objectives, and that we'd do business from an agency-wide perspective."

Gregg brought his former deputy, Ken Papaj (pronounced "Pop-eye") with him. Unlike the two people they replaced, they worked closely together to clarify expectations and give managers feedback on what they were doing well and what had to change. Most of the managers welcomed this more collaborative approach.

Most, but not all. After Gregg's first month, two ACs announced their retirements. They weren't asked to go, but apparently decided that they didn't want to work in the changing environment. After one year, several other senior managers had left; some retired, others were asked to make lateral transfers. Nobody was fired. Gregg replaced them with people who could work collaboratively and could generate results. As one senior manager said, "It seemed pretty abrupt to some folks. . . . But Dick was very consistent with both words and actions. He told us what he wanted, why he wanted it, and that he expected us to do our part. . . . He made his expectations very clear."

## Other Actions That Led to Change

Several other moves made an impact on the culture. Gregg made particularly sure that the agency's formal and informal systems were aligned with his new direction and priorities.

### Emphasizing Values in Performance Appraisals

The first behavioral element in the appraisal now is collaboration. It spells out in some detail what collaboration means and what's expected of the managers: to support overall agency priorities, support critical needs of other offices, to share information and ideas openly. Performance appraisals aren't taken seriously in many agencies. Gregg believes they should mean something, and should reflect the principles he believes in.

### Use of Matrix Teams

FMS puts people from different offices and disciplines together on teams that deal with important cross-cutting issues. According to John Newell, AC for regional operations, "These teams meet weekly or more often to keep on top of operational issues. They're especially important at the lower levels of the organization."

## Modeling the Desired Behavior

During Dick Gregg's first year as commissioner, a study revealed the need to close one of the agency's regional offices. It was done in a way that reflected Gregg's values and expectations. He clarified up front the process and criteria that would be used to identify the office to be closed. The day after it was announced that the Chicago office would be closed, an AC met with all of the affected employees to explain what was happening. Ken Papaj also visited the office later and reiterated FMS's commitment to do what it could to support the employees.

An outplacement firm provided extensive training and retraining for the employees there, and also received authority for buy-outs for employees who wished to retire early. And senior managers worked closely with the union. Only one formal complaint was filed; employees knew the management team tried hard to make the transition work for them.

## Communicating to Engage People

Gregg and Papaj understand one of the fundamental principles of organizational communications: if you want to make an impact on people's minds, you have to engage them in a two-way dialogue, and that requires *small group face-to-face experiences.* As Gregg puts it, "The biggest challenge I've faced here has been to get our message out to the rest of the organization. . . . It's the culture that has to change, and to change it you can't rely on lots of formal mechanisms and processes."

Gregg and Papaj meet with small groups of employees in the employees' office space. They talk about FMS priorities and discuss them in terms that relate to that unit. They also spend time listening to the staff's questions and suggestions, which keeps them in touch with employee concerns.

## Indicators of Success

Several success indicators have appeared since Dick Gregg became commissioner. In one of the most vivid examples of collaboration, two ACs got together on their own and identified a function done in one unit that belonged more appropriately in the other. They met and discussed the change, agreed on the approach, and then made a joint proposal to Gregg and Papaj. It is rare for executives to "give up" some of their responsibility and resources unless it's a real disaster. This wasn't a disaster. Rather, two ACs made a decision for the good of FMS.

The two offices that used to duplicate each other's work producing the same report on the transition to electronic payments now produce just one. Gregg gave them one month to figure out how to eliminate the redundancy, or he would do it for them. They figured it out. The report in and of itself was not that important. What was important was the fact that there had been no expectation to work together to develop one chart in the past. Today, there is much greater collaboration and much less distrust between those two organizations.

The conversion of FMS's automated systems prior to the Y2K date change was a major test of collaboration in FMS. In this effort, all eight FMS AC areas were heavily involved and needed to work closely together. And in many areas, the visibility and interest from the public and Congress was immense. For example, FMS's readiness for making Social Security payments sparked great concern and interest. In addition, because some decisions on information technology infrastructure had not been made earlier, FMS got a late start on Y2K. Even though the pressure was immense, all offices worked well together and when 2000 arrived FMS programs performed without any problems.

Perhaps the most dramatic turnaround in collaboration occurred in 1998 between the Debt Collection Office, Regional Operations, and Information Resources. These offices hadn't worked together in implementing the Debt Collection Act. Nevertheless, in 1998 they worked tirelessly and cohesively to transfer responsibility from the IRS to FMS for collecting debts by offsetting tax refund payments. This was a huge success, accomplished under tight deadlines with all three offices pulling together. And since the transfer collections have increased $600 million each year.

### Challenging Assumptions

Dick Gregg is a fascinating individual. His personal and leadership style challenge some deeply held assumptions many of us have about organizations, leaders, and change. Exhibit 12.1 sets them out side by side to point up the contrast.

Gregg emphasizes that the turnaround at FMS wasn't a one-person job. "What Ken and I have done is set high expectations for collaboration and performance, and put together a good team of ACs that understand and welcome this way of doing business. Those ACs in turn are reinforcing this culture of teamwork with their peers, within their own organization and with other agencies. So, together, FMS senior management is moving in the same direction. . . . We're all responsible for the change that has occurred and is still occurring at FMS."

# Analysis: Internal Collaboration in Action

What fosters collaboration within one organization? How does this compare to collaboration across several organizations?

FMS is just one example of collaboration within a single organization. But the themes evident in this case are consistent with other positive examples of collaboration within one organization I've studied, including four cities—Chicago, Baltimore, Hampton (Virginia), and Charlotte (North Carolina), one state agency—the Virginia Retirement System, and one private sector example, General Electric under former CEO Jack Welch's leadership. The common themes that emerge are at once powerful and simple.

**Exhibit 12.1. Assumptions About Organizations, Leaders, and Change.**

| Widely Held Beliefs | Dick Gregg's Beliefs |
|---|---|
| Major organizational change takes at least five to seven years. | FMS culture could make major changes within two years. |
| When making and implementing decisions, you can involve lots of people (which slows things down) or decide yourself in order to act quickly. You can't do both. | Decisions must be *both* quick *and* inclusive. You do that by clarifying at the outset what's needed, getting input from lots of staff, then deciding and moving forward. You don't need to seek consensus. You need clarity, openness to input, a decision and an explanation afterward. |
| In the public service, visible mistakes will kill you, so reduce risk by being very thorough and taking your time to get it right the first time. | Make your decision and go forward. If, months later, you realize it isn't working well, you refine it then. |
| With multiple (often conflicting) stakeholders, and a chaotic environment, it's very difficult for organizations to control their agendas; they must become very nimble at responding to change continuously. | Leaders should articulate a small number of priorities and expectations, keep the message simple and reinforce it at every opportunity, and fiercely guard that agenda. |
| Comprehensive change methods like TQM are needed to get everyone aligned with an overall direction and with customer needs. | TQM was too complicated for FMS. The agency went ahead successfully without it. |

## Clear Expectations

First, these examples demonstrate the power of expectations. I heard it over and over in these organizations: "He *expects* us to collaborate." An observer of Chicago government put the same sentiment into different words: "Mayor Richard Daley makes sure his managers understand they aren't just in the business of running their individual departments; they're really in the *Chicago* business." Those who observe GE know that its managers never, *never* went to Jack Welch to tell him about *their* new idea. No, they talked about the idea they'd learned from another unit that seemed worth trying. They knew Welch expected them to steal proven practices from others because he drilled that expectation into them over and over.

Another approach to making expectations for collaboration very clear is through the use of performance contracts. When Bob O'Neill was city manager of Hampton, Virginia, he wrote performance contracts with his department heads to help them understand and focus on key priorities. "I told the directors, 'we're paying you a lot of money, we expect you to build cooperative relationships with those people you need to support your department's mission'" (quoted in Osborne and Plastrik, 1997, p. 247). The performance contracts outlined the results each department was expected to achieve. O'Neill did other things that helped foster collaboration, but he credits the performance contracts with sending a clear and important message about his expectations. For more on the advantages and potential challenges of performance contracts, see Resource A.

## Few High Priorities

Second, these leaders have a small number of major priorities, they make those priorities clear, and they expect each department to contribute to them. Recall Gregg's comments on his first FMS senior management meeting: "I emphasized that we would have a few common objectives, and that we'd do business from an agency-wide perspective." In Baltimore, Mayor O'Malley's major priorities are reflected in specific performance targets that he emphasizes persistently through the CitiStat method. His priorities include several that can only be achieved through the combined efforts of multiple departments.

Charlotte, North Carolina, uses a different approach to clarify high priorities.

### Charlotte

Since 1992 the Charlotte City Council has emphasized major themes (called "focus areas"), which drive Charlotte's policy and administrative decisions. The focus areas are community safety, neighborhoods, economic development, transportation, and restructuring government. To reinforce the importance of these priorities, the City Council structures its committee system around the five focus areas. Each focus area has a strategic plan that includes a small number of goals; the committees see themselves as policy implementers for their focus area strategic plan. The city manager created four "focus area cabinets," groups of city departments that each work on a particular focus area (two of the focus areas, with overlapping issues, are served by one cabinet), as shown in Figure 12.1. Each cabinet is chaired by an assistant city manager, and only department heads serve on cabinets, ensuring that the city's top managers are accountable for its key priorities.

Charlotte uses a customized version of the balanced scorecard performance management and measurement system, to translate its mission and focus areas into tangible, measurable objectives and measure progress. Each focus area cabinet is accountable for one or more of the eighteen corporate objectives. For instance, the Transportation cabinet includes five departments: planning, transportation, police, aviation, and engineering. Each of these departments also supports at least one other cabinet.

Charlotte's emphasis on focus areas and its alignment around them has led to significant improvements in city services. Del Borgsdorf, city

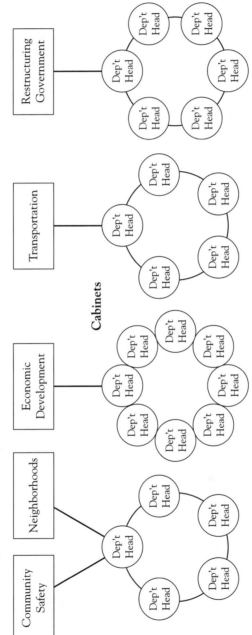

**Figure 12.1. City Council Focus Areas.**

manager of San Jose and former deputy city manager in Charlotte, says, "Most cities are really just confederations of operating units. The focus area cabinets and our balanced scorecard measurement system have helped us to integrate across business units."

The city's emphasis on a few high priorities is also having a positive impact on the use of management time. In 1996, as the focus areas were starting to take hold, senior managers spent fully 70 percent of their monthly executive team meeting time on operational matters. By 2000 they had reduced that to 30 percent, freeing up time for strategic thinking and learning. Figure 12.2 gives the numbers.

Nobody's declaring total victory in Charlotte's efforts to get employees, council members, and citizens to focus on a few citywide priorities. But the city's progress is impressive. Its structured emphasis on focus areas and focus area cabinets has been maintained for over a decade, surviving political shifts in the composition of City Council. For a detailed history and description of Charlotte's comprehensive approach to setting and managing priorities, go to http://www.ci.charlotte.nc.us/cibudget/publications.htm, and click on "The Charlotte Story."

**Figure 12.2. Time Use of Executive Team.**

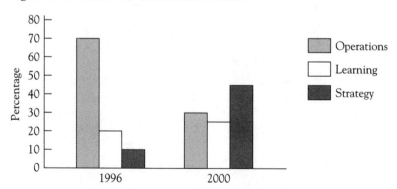

## Open Communications

In addition to their very clear expectations and priorities, these collaborative leaders are praised for their open communications and emphasis on shared information. Dick Gregg's utter consistency helps his associates understand what's needed and why. A political consultant would say that Gregg is always "on message." But he's more than that; he's also very intent on learning what employees think, what they need to do their jobs well, and what gets in the way of improving performance. Indeed, he usually prefers to listen rather than talk. Other leaders who foster collaboration, like former Virginia Retirement system director Bill Leighty, ensure that all employees understand their agency's and unit's business objectives along with performance to date on those objectives.

## Key, Early Personnel Decisions

Another similarity involves the selection of senior managers. At FMS, Dick Gregg wanted his assistant commissioners to collaborate with one another and to model collaboration for the employees. Those who couldn't, or wouldn't, either left on their own or were transferred. Mayor O'Malley did the same in Baltimore, as did Jack Welch at GE. Some might see this as cold or unfair. Strong leaders who insist on collaboration would answer that it would be unfair *not* to move managers who refuse to share information and resources with others.

In Jim Collins's fine book about companies that went from "good to great," he describes the same emphasis on early personnel decisions. Collins writes, "The executives who ignited the transformations from good to great did not first figure out where to drive the bus and then get people to take it there [which was what Collins had expected to find]. No, they *first* got the right people on the bus (and the wrong people off the bus) and *then* figured out where to drive it" (Collins, 2001, p. 41; emphasis in original). This approach, which Collins calls "first who . . . then what," is counterintuitive. Most management gurus teach the importance of first establishing clear mission, vision, and strategies, and then filling key positions with people who are aligned with the overall direction. Collins found just the opposite.

To be clear, leaders who foster collaboration within their organizations don't begin by cleaning house and automatically replacing the senior management team with a new one. Typically, a new leader interviews and observes the existing managers, makes clear the challenges ahead (even if the new direction isn't entirely clear), and gives people the choice of working in some very different ways or finding work opportunities elsewhere. That's just what Dick Gregg did at FMS. Did it create some anxieties during the early months? Absolutely. Given how much trouble the agency was in, some anxiety was appropriate, even important. It may seem ironic, but this can be the most humane approach when a new leader takes over a struggling organization.

### Focus, Follow-Through, Accountability

Finally, these leaders are extraordinarily focused and determined human beings. Nobody doubts that they mean what they say; nobody suggests that they are guilty of "management du jour." And how do they demonstrate their determination? *Through relentless follow-through*. They don't see a single reason why it should take five to seven years to significantly improve performance, as many management theorists preach these days. Indeed, each of them saw significant change within their first two years at the helm. They insist on clear goals, give reasons for those goals, communicate them consistently, and follow through by insisting on frequent accountability and recognition for accomplishments.

It's useful to reflect on these themes. Fostering collaboration within a single organization seems to involve the activities outlined in Exhibit 12.2.

---

**Exhibit 12.2.  Leadership Tasks to Foster Internal Collaboration.**

- Set clear expectations to collaborate.

- Articulate a few high priorities to which all units are expected to contribute (some of which require collaboration).

- Emphasize open, two-way communications and information sharing.

- Select managers who willingly collaborate with their associates.

- Maintain persistent follow-through and accountability (recognizing outstanding performance, dealing directly with low performers).

---

Three things strike me about these common themes. First, these are basic, Management 101–level principles. Absolutely nothing new here. It's almost too elementary to put these in writing. Which raises the question, if these are basic management approaches, if they get people to work across internal agency boundaries, why aren't they used more often? Put differently, why is collaboration still a challenge within so many agencies?

That leads to my second reaction. Internal collaboration is more the exception than the rule because of a problem in most people's minds. We often succumb to the belief that people just seem to have a lot of difficulty working together, and there's not much we can do about it except hold team-building sessions led by talented consultants (which is a way of signaling our own inability and unwillingness to deal with it). When others see such attitudes, they know that they're free to go their own way. Contrast that with the attitudes of leaders who clearly expect collaboration and act continuously on that expectation. For instance, Mary Dempsey, commissioner of libraries for Chicago, describes working for Mayor Daley this way:

> He cares passionately about this city, and he's constantly thinking, "What will make this city better?" He keeps

focusing on bigger questions, like how do we help all kids learn to read, how do we build strong neighborhoods. . . . He's always sending department heads articles and newspaper clippings with notes for us to follow up on various ideas. *It's expected* that we look broadly at the city, that we think broadly about how our own departments (and other organizations) can contribute to the city. His love for the city raises the level of our thoughts and actions. . . . It would shame a department head to be seen as thinking narrowly about "their" unit.

Daley has the fourth collaborative leadership quality discussed in Chapter Nine—a collaborative mind-set. He sees connections that some others don't, and helps people see a higher purpose in their work. When a neighborhood needs city assistance, it's provided in an integrated way. Several departments work closely with the residents, local merchants, and one another to begin the renewal effort. Where others see an abandoned building and signs of crime, Daley and Dempsey see an opportunity to build a library, create a park, invite a local developer to build a community center that spurs neighborhood development. Then they get other departments, nonprofits, and neighborhood groups and business leaders involved. Soon a declining area has been transformed; there's a renewed sense of community, purpose, and pride.

This has happened in many Chicago neighborhoods. It's not primarily a story of smart urban redevelopment. It's much more about collaborative leadership, one that sees the potential in a neighborhood, expects others to work across boundaries to achieve that potential, and focuses on a higher purpose in the work. Daley and the other leaders described here don't assume that working across boundaries is too hard. They assume the opposite, they expect the opposite, and gradually a culture of collaboration builds within the organization.

### The In-House Difference

A final observation. The leadership style of those who achieve collaboration across internal boundaries differs in one significant respect from the leadership styles that promote collaboration between agencies where nobody is in charge. As noted in Chapter Nine, that type of leadership relies on "pull" more than "push." When nobody is in charge, when peers try to collaborate, it's the rare leader who can successfully push everyone in a given direction. Rather, peers lead through pull and persuasion; when they lead it is because others freely give them permission to do so.

But when someone is in charge, when one person has formal authority to lead an organization, that person must use a good deal of push to lower the walls between units. Those walls exist for good reasons; they're wired into the organization chart, they define where money flows and who reports to whom, they define the lines of accountability, they're sometimes legislatively mandated. And they will continue to play a role, albeit a diminished one, in the new information economy.

But when people in an agency don't tend to work together across internal lines, when hoarding is more common than sharing, they need much more than inspiring vision and values statements, more than nifty technology that makes information sharing easy. To overcome the forces pulling them back to their home units, employees need to know that their leaders are resolutely determined to get units working together. They need to have confidence that hoarding behavior isn't accepted, that sharing is the norm, and that there are consequences for both. Steve Kerr, when he was chief learning officer at GE, put the issue in stark terms: "At GE, *hoarding of information is considered an ethical violation.*" Leaders who give these messages sometimes must use push in humane but resolute ways.

As Table 12.1 shows, collaboration within a single organization shares many of the key elements that support collaboration across agencies, but not all of them.

**Table 12.1. Comparison: Collaboration Across Agencies, Collaboration Within One Agency.**

| Factors | Across Agencies | Within One Agency |
|---|---|---|
| The Basics | Necessary. | Helpful, not critical. |
| Open, Trusting Relationships | Almost always essential. | Helpful. |
| High Stakes | Very important, especially at the start. | Very important, sometimes created by the leader's expectations and insistence on accountability. |
| Constituency for Collaboration | Very useful for sustaining collaboration once it's begun. | The biggest challenge for strong leaders; will there be a constituency to maintain collaboration once the leader departs? |
| Collaborative Leadership | Essential; involves "pull" more than "push." | Essential; involves at least as much "push" as "pull." Also includes clear expectations, a few high priorities that require collaboration. |

## This Is Not Beyond You

At this point, it might be tempting for some readers to look at the very strong personas of people like Dick Gregg and conclude, "If that's what it takes to get people to play together, this belongs in the 'too hard' category." An understandable response, but not a necessary one. There's nothing at all overwhelming about Dick Gregg or his deputy Ken Papaj, about Chuck Short in Montgomery County or Bob Sweeney at the University of Virginia or a number of others who are finding ways to ensure collaboration within their organizations. They aren't genetically programmed differently from the rest of us.

What these leaders really have in common is their commitment to some fundamental leadership methods and their passion for results. It's a matter of some age-old practices more than personality types. If you employ these practices in your own way, you will get collaboration and more. You will see greatly improved results that touch customers in meaningful ways. You will be amazed to see the internal walls start to crumble, and your constituents will be delighted as the services improve. And when you connect collaboration to "something higher," as these leaders do, the results will be inspiring. The citizens' lives are improved. The community benefits. And the people within the organizations find greater meaning, value, and purpose in their work.

These approaches are not beyond any of us. Why would you want anything less? It's waiting to happen.

---

"But did the change have 'legs'? Did it survive the leader's tenure?" Such questions are asked about every strong leader's impact. Collaboration prospers when committed leaders like Richard M. Daley and Dick Gregg make it abundantly clear that they expect employees to work across boundaries. Determined leaders can generate considerable collaboration on their watch, but do such leaders leave a legacy of collaboration, one that's cemented in the culture, or can the next leader easily undo their good work?

Finding ways to institutionalize the collaborative changes driven by one leader into the organization's culture is an enormous topic. Indeed, it merits an entire book of its own. I offer some ways to approach this central issue in the final chapter.

# 13

# Toward a Collaborative Culture

*There's no one thing and there's no short-term thing.*
*The only thing I know that works is total commitment*
*and unbelievable patience. It just takes time. . . .*
*Sustained change only comes with patience and*
*determination.*

Joe Thompson, former undersecretary,
Department of Veterans Affairs

In 1982, an eight-year-old antitrust suit against AT&T was settled, breaking up AT&T's monopoly in telecommunications. Soon after, an AT&T executive approached Tim Gallwey, author of *The Inner Game of Tennis* (1974), and asked an unlikely question. The executive was impressed with Gallwey's approach to the mental side of the sport, and he asked if Gallwey could use some of his insights to help AT&T change its corporate culture. Gallwey was surprised. He knew little about corporate life and very little about AT&T, but he spent some time listening and learning about the company's culture. For seventy years, AT&T had been a place where safety, security, and loyalty were highly valued. As employees told him, "The deal is, if we come to work on time, do what is expected of us, and keep our noses clean, we are part of the family and will have a job for life" (Gallwey, 2000, p. 31). Clearly, this culture had to change if AT&T was to succeed in its new, highly competitive and market-driven environment. But how to do that?

Gallwey's first assignment was to work with some AT&T operators. In one experiment, he helped them learn to listen carefully to their customers' voices in order to detect their emotional state—friendly, hurried, irritated, and so on. Then he helped the operators become more aware of the quality of their own voices, focusing on such aspects as the amount of warmth they were projecting. Soon the operators were responding with increased warmth when they detected a high level of stress in the caller. It worked very well; the operators very quickly realized how much impact they could have on a caller, even in a few seconds. That led to a significant reduction in the operators' stress level, and their customers perceived them as being much more courteous. And as their attitudes and assumptions about their work changed, the culture of their unit also began to change.

## The Problems with "Changing the Corporate Culture"

I've heard it many times: "Before we can become a high-performing organization (or change to deal with our new environment), we must change the culture around here." On the surface, this sentiment makes sense. Corporate culture, defined by Schein as the deep level of "basic assumptions and beliefs" shared by employees (1985, p. 6), is a powerful force on employees' behavior. People learn fairly quickly in a new job what it takes to get ahead—show enthusiasm, keep your mouth closed and your eyes open, or (at the old AT&T) be loyal, work hard, and come to work on time. When an organization faces the need to make major changes and the old culture holds it back, people naturally start talking about changing the culture.

I have two problems with the notion that "we've got to change the culture." First, I don't believe that an organization's culture changes because managers and leaders set out to change it. To use an economic term, culture is usually a "lagging indicator"—it changes *after* certain work practices change and prove successful. Consider the AT&T example. Gallwey didn't sit down with the operators and ask them to develop a set of corporate values that should guide them in the future. He didn't discuss attitudes and values at all. Rather, he started by discussing an experiment intended to make their work more interesting and less stressful. He then taught them some *skills* that they found useful in their daily work and nonwork lives, and those skills were effective. Attitudes weren't mentioned, but attitudes started to change as the new behaviors delivered positive results. Recall the quote from Pascale in Chapter Eleven: "It is easier to act ourselves into a better mode of thinking than think ourselves into a better mode of acting."

My second problem with the notion of changing the culture is that it betrays a misunderstanding of the strength and origins of organizational cultures. Cultures exist for very good reasons. As Schein notes, employees' assumptions and beliefs "are *learned* responses to a group's problems of survival. . . . [Assumptions and beliefs] come to be taken for granted because they solve those problems repeatedly and reliably" (1985, p. 6). AT&T's culture had served its employees extremely well since 1913, when its president, Theodore Vail, cut a deal with the government to become a regulated monopoly. Do you really think that its employees would be eager to change their assumptions and beliefs because its leaders began a campaign to "change AT&T's culture"?

All that being said, an agency's culture *must* change if collaboration is to become the norm. If you can't change the culture by dealing with it directly, and if cultures are notoriously resistant to change, what options do you have?

## Three Strategies for Jump-Starting Major Organizational Change

I have observed three strategies that help people let go of their current assumptions and beliefs when faced with the need to make major changes. None of these strategies focuses explicitly on the culture; rather, all are ways to jump-start major change by helping people recognize the problems of the old approaches and gain experience with new organizational practices and behaviors. When these changes produce positive results, cultural change usually follows. Note that these are not mutually exclusive strategies; some leaders use more than one of them at different times during their change efforts.

Each of these strategies is premised on a truism about personal and organizational change: "Before you can begin something new, you have to end what used to be," as change expert William Bridges puts it (1991, p. 19). Bridges calls the first change phase "endings." Social scientist Kurt Lewin (1951) termed this phase "unfreezing." Whatever you call it, leaders need to prepare people for change by explaining the reasons change is needed, the cost of continuing to do business in the old way, and the benefits of adopting new practices.

### 1. "Shock Therapy": Top-Down Change

When James Lee Witt took over the Federal Emergency Management Agency (FEMA) in April 1993, he inherited a truly dysfunctional organization. Its detractors called it rigid, not customer-friendly, unable to communicate across its internal stovepipes, terrible in relations with state and local emergency management agencies, and very poor at delivering its mission (other than that, everything was going swimmingly!). Senator Fritz Hollings of South Carolina famously complained that it was "the biggest group of bureaucratic jackasses ever assembled in one place at one time in the history of America!"

By the time Witt left office almost eight years later, the agency had gone through a true transformation. It had formed excellent relations with external stakeholders, its employees were collaborating well internally, and its overall performance was excellent. Witt had instituted a new business model he called "all hazards": every FEMA employee would be deployed to any natural hazard that occurred (in the old FEMA, some people specialized on hurricanes, others on floods or earthquakes or tornadoes; such narrow jobs reinforced the employees' failure to collaborate across boundaries). The work practices and culture changed profoundly under Witt, and the new approaches continued when a new administration took over in 2001.

Witt made a number of major changes in FEMA; some involved shock therapy. For instance, one Friday afternoon in 1994, Witt called all of FEMA's Senior Executive Service (SES) employees to his office for a long meeting. He explained why they needed to change the way they did business and the importance of moving to the "all hazards" model. Then he delivered the shocker: *every one of them would be rotated.* Some were moved to offices that they had publicly bad-mouthed in the past, and a few were given lower-level assignments. Moreover, certain middle managers were given jobs formerly held by SESers. The actions had an enormous impact on the agency. Nobody was in denial: FEMA was going to change.

Shock therapy is difficult (and sometimes risky) to administer, but there are times when it is necessary. As Exhibit 13.1 shows, shock therapy is effective when the agency is in serious trouble and other efforts to change have proved futile and when agency leaders have strong support from their key stakeholders to pull it off. Witt's close relationships with key congressional members and with President Clinton were necessary for his actions to work.

### 2. Let a Thousand Flowers Bloom: Bottom-Up Change

When an agency is very decentralized and power is diffused among many managers and external stakeholders, shock therapy is almost impossible to use. It may make more sense to focus on bottom-up change, what I call the "let a thousand flowers bloom" strategy. We saw an example of this in the Service First initiative used by the Forest Service and Bureau of Land Management in Chapter Eight. The original idea to collaborate across the two agencies began in the field and was inspired by serious budget cuts; the agencies simply didn't have the resources to achieve their missions acting alone. When local units started to improve service by co-locating offices and sharing staff and equipment, the concept spread. Soon the agencies' two leaders made Service First a priority, announced it in

Exhibit 13.1. Three Strategies to Jump-Start Major Corporate Cultural Change.

| Strategy | Definition | Examples | When to Use | Requirements |
|---|---|---|---|---|
| **Shock Therapy** (top-down change) | Senior leader creates sudden, destabilizing changes to organization systems, structure, and staffing. | Reduce the number of organization levels by half; change the basic business model; move all senior managers to new positions. | Organization is in serious trouble with customers, funders, other stakeholders; the problems are long-standing; other attempts to help didn't work. | Leaders make clear why the changes are occurring; senior leader is a strong individual with support from key stakeholders; there is a political consensus on the agency's mission and on need for big change. |
| **Let a Thousand Flowers Bloom** (bottom-up change) | Leaders invite employees to make certain kinds of changes (use of teams, customer service initiatives, and so on) at their level. | Encourage local units to co-locate similar functions; cross-train staff to integrate services; form pilot teams to demonstrate innovative practices. | Agency is decentralized, power is diffused; staff see the need for change; there is no emergency requiring sudden change. | Headquarters acts to reduce internal barriers to change; customers' reactions to change are captured and shared internally; informal leaders become champions for certain changes. |
| **Multiplier Mechanism** (inside-out change) | Leaders institute a new method across the agency that leads to many associated changes. | CitiStat; emphasize collaboration in all promotion decisions; require all mid-level and senior managers to rotate every two to three years. | Major change is needed quickly; informal leaders have considerable power. | Relentless follow-up by senior champion; just-in-time training for those using the new mechanism; alignment of key human resource policies and practices with new mechanism. |

joint letters to the field, and encouraged all managers to use the Service First approach wherever it made sense.

This strategy doesn't have the kind of sudden, attention-getting impact of shock therapy, but it does assist in the "unfreezing" phase: it can help many employees open up to new ways of thinking and acting and start letting go of past practices. The leader's role is to clarify the reasons for change, highlight the successful changes that occur, act as a "downfield blocker" to reduce internal barriers to change, and ensure rapid communication of the results each unit is achieving.

### 3. Create a "Multiplier Mechanism": Inside-Out Change

When Baltimore Mayor Martin O'Malley initiated the CitiStat program, he created what I call a multiplier mechanism: a new method was introduced, it was used relentlessly, and over time it led to a number of other positive changes that moved city government forward. When Iowa organized its twenty-five state agencies into enterprise planning teams and the agency leaders in each team set shared goals that could only be achieved through multiagency collaboration, it set in motion a multiplier mechanism that created positive ripples throughout those agencies. The same "virtuous cycle" is occurring in Charlotte since the city council adopted five "focus area" priorities, organized council committees and departments around those priorities, and started measuring results that required the departments within each focus area to collaborate.

There are no silver bullets in terms of large-scale organization change. Recall Joe Thompson's quote at the start of this chapter: "There's no one thing and there's no short-term thing. The only thing I know that works is total commitment and unbelievable patience." But some changes can produce what economists call a multiplier effect. This strategy works well when agency leaders have communicated very clearly the reasons for change, when they implement the new mechanism persistently, when just-in-time training is provided to staff using the new mechanism, and when key human resource policies and practices are aligned with the mechanism.

One of the most powerful ways to create a multiplier mechanism is to change the criteria for promotion in an organization. The best example I know is happening at the Department of Defense (DoD). Since it was formed by President Truman in 1947, DoD has been plagued by interservice rivalries. The Army, Navy, Air Force, and Marines each have strong and proud cultures; they're not exactly known for graciously sharing resources, information, or parts of missions with one another. In recent years, however, that has been changing. The Goldwater-Nichols Act, passed by Congress in 1986, requires all staff officers to rotate through one or more "joint" positions in order to be eligible for promotion beyond colonel and get their first star. Joint positions can be filled by personnel from any of the four services. These positions involve working for two to three years with members of the other services at certain commands, including the National War College, NATO offices, and Special Operations Command. Most officers who rise to three or four stars have held many joint commands.

Rotating through several joint positions has become the norm for officers who want to move up, and the program is producing a number of positive ripples. It is increasing communication among the four services. It leads to better understanding of the roles and missions of each service. It helps officers develop relationships in all four services. Ultimately, it is helping the four services perform as a single, integrated force. Some of the benefits of this integration were demonstrated during the war against terrorism in Afghanistan in 2001 (Jordan, 2002).

## From Initial Successes to Long-Term Change

These three strategies for jump-starting change get people's attention. They can help employees start to let go of the past work practices. When the new practices work well, attitudes and values begin to shift. But more is needed for the positive start to become "the way we work around here." Any major change will produce a good deal of "pushback" by employees and others; a move toward collaboration creates more than the usual level of resistance, for all of the reasons discussed in Chapter Three. There are many ways to transform initial change into long-term cultural change. I've seen the approaches identified in Exhibit 13.2 work well. Let's examine each in turn.

### Benefits Experienced by Many

At some point, large numbers of employees must *experience* the benefits of collaborating in their everyday work for an extended period of time. Among the collaboration hurdles discussed in Chapter Three, several relate to rewards and costs. The organizational benefits for collaborating are usually unclear at the start, but the costs are very evident and are borne up front. Further, employees often see no personal reward for collaborative behavior. But when collaborative practices persist for several years and many employees experience real benefits, it makes believers out of skeptics.

Joint Venture: Silicon Valley, described in Chapter Five, is committed to this approach. JVSV is a nonprofit representing business, government, education and community groups. Its vision is "to build a community collaborating to compete globally." After a rocky start, it expanded its board to represent all key community elements. It hired a well-respected individual who provided half a decade of

---

**Exhibit 13.2.  Toward a Collaborative Culture: Some Strategies.**

- See that the benefits are experienced by many.
- Hold people accountable for outcomes that can be achieved only through collaboration.
- Ensure constancy of purpose.

excellent leadership during its formative years. But I think the main reason that JVSV has had excellent success in creating a more collaborative ethic among Silicon Valley organizations has to do with a very conscious strategy: it *involves hundreds of community leaders in collaborative initiatives that create tangible benefits*.

For instance, it started the Enterprise Network, which provides teams of experienced business executives to mentor new start-up companies. JVSV also spearheaded SmartSchools, an initiative involving business, nonprofits, and thousands of volunteers who worked to connect more than a hundred schools to the Internet. JVSV publishes the annual *Index of Silicon Valley*, which tracks more than twenty-five indicators of quality of life and economic conditions in the Valley. It provides a credible database helping thousands of area residents and organizations understand the emerging issues and trends affecting them. You can access the *Index* through the JVSV Web site, http://www.jointventure.org.

JVSV also led an enormous effort to develop the Silicon Valley Uniform Building Code, which created a standardized building code for twenty-seven localities and reduced local building code amendments (exceptions) from four hundred to eleven. This change has radically simplified the building process for both the private sector and local governments. It sponsored another huge project to streamline important local government permitting and licensing processes. The effort has reduced processing time for construction and other permits by 50 to 75 percent. And it finds creative ways to develop "civic entrepreneurs." More than two hundred people are active on JVSV boards and advisory groups at any given time.

When large numbers of people around you begin doing things differently and they benefit in some concrete way from the change, it influences their behavior and attitudes, which influence your own. Ultimately, it affects the organization's culture. That's one of the key lessons from Joint Venture: Silicon Valley, and it's confirmed in a fascinating book called *The Tipping Point* (Gladwell, 2000). The author describes the factors leading to "social epidemics," trends that hit a take-off (or tipping) point. For instance, the first low-priced fax machine was introduced in the United States in 1984; eighty thousand were sold. Business increased slowly until 1987 when sales mushroomed to a million. There were two million fax machines in operation by 1989. Suddenly, many people stopped asking, "Do you have a fax?" and started asking, "What's your fax number?" Cell phones showed the same "tip" around 1998 (p. 12). Fashion trends, sales of new products, even political movements (such as the fall of Communism in Eastern Europe in 1989–1991) often hit such tipping points.

Gladwell found that one of the major ingredients in social epidemics is what he calls the "power of context": we are exquisitely sensitive to changes in our immediate social surroundings. Robert Cialdini, an expert on sources of social influence, documented the same phenomenon; he calls it the power of "social proof" (Cialdini, 1984). As Cialdini writes, "We will use the actions of others to decide on the proper behavior for ourselves, *especially when we view those others as similar to ourselves*" (emphasis in original, p. 142).

The point, then, is to find ways to engage large numbers of people in collaborative activities that make a difference in their work lives. The benefits may be improved customer service, simplified work, or improved career advancement prospects. Whatever the payoff, when people experience the benefits of a new approach they talk to their peers, they show their enthusiasm, and they don't need twelve-step organizational change programs to convince them. They start influencing others for the best of reasons: they've found a better way to do the work.

To help large numbers of people (both employees and external stakeholders) experience the benefits of collaboration over an extended time period, consider the steps listed in Exhibit 13.3.

The last approach listed in Exhibit 13.3—assembling groups of people who can describe the benefits of collaborative efforts—was one of the key methods used by the Department of Veterans Affairs when it began its *"One VA"* initiative in 1998. The goal of *One VA*

**Exhibit 13.3. Some Methods to Help Many Experience the Benefits of Collaboration.**

- Provide structured projects that allow dozens or even hundreds of employees to be involved in well-planned, collaborative projects.

- See that these projects are designed to create early, visible successes.

- Develop a cadre of employees (and retirees and customers if appropriate) trained in collaborative skills, who assist the various project teams with their work.

- Ensure that employees who contribute time to collaborative projects are recognized, not punished (which often happens because of the time required to do this work).

- Create joint task forces of employees from different units or organizations to work on important tasks. Provide training and support.

- Offer employees many opportunities for rotational assignments in other units (or other organizations), to expand their perspectives.

- Convene meetings with a large number of employees and other stakeholders, where the participants bring examples of collaboration already going on in their organizations.

is to improve customer service to veterans by getting employees in the department's three separate functions to share information, streamline processes, and work as one to provide customers with seamless service. Approximately 2,500 employees and external stakeholders participated in one of five regional conferences held during a one-year period. Participants included all levels of management, front-line employees, union officials, veterans, and other external groups.

Prior to the conferences, VA employees from across the country submitted over three hundred success stories demonstrating *One VA* results in terms of better service, more effective operations, and increased cooperation across organizational lines. At each conference approximately twenty success stories were showcased as exhibits and four success stories were shown on video, to help people see and understand concrete examples of building a more collaborative organization. Conference participants had been asked in advance to become "investigative reporters," with the task of interviewing other employees and veterans to discover examples of (and barriers to) working across boundaries.

Through these and other creative methods, VA leaders are engaging thousands of employees and customers in the daunting task of getting 220,000 employees in three separate functions to work seamlessly.

## Accountability for Collaboration Outcomes

It's critical to hold people accountable for some outcomes that can be achieved only through collaboration. Helpful as it is to engage large numbers in collaborative work, at some point certain people need to be accountable for results. When managers realize that they can't achieve the results expected of them by acting alone, they see collaboration as an important means to their desired ends. And when several units are given shared goals and must report regularly on progress toward those goals together, it creates an environment favoring collaboration.

I've already described examples of shared goals in Baltimore, Iowa, and Charlotte. There are many ways to use shared goals and measures to promote collaboration. One potent method is to write performance contracts with senior and middle managers, spelling out the goals they're responsible for, how progress will be measured, and the other agencies or units they need to work with to achieve those goals. (Performance contracts are described in Resource A.) What strikes me is the number of managers and leaders who have jumped on the performance measurement bandwagon, use measures to assess the performance of *individual units*, and then ask why people aren't working across boundaries more often! We know what gets measured usually gets done. It's time to use that insight intelligently, by measuring progress toward important outcomes that require collaboration. Doing so will often require the kind of changes in organizational structures and information flows described in the Charlotte, Baltimore, and Iowa examples.

### Constancy of Purpose

When quality management guru W. Edwards Deming articulated his fourteen points of quality, constancy of purpose was number one (Walton, 1990). Constancy of purpose is a powerful tool for any change, and it certainly makes a profound difference when it comes to collaboration. In many government and nonprofit agencies, managers are accustomed to seeing new leaders espouse beautiful visions and daring strategies, only to become "OBE"—overtaken by events. It's no wonder that many adopt a "wait 'em out" strategy; they've seen too many exciting change efforts come and go.

Constancy of purpose has been demonstrated in Charlotte, with impressive results. As described earlier, Charlotte's philosophy of learning and collaboration is being enacted in many ways and through several methods. But without question, much of the credit for Charlotte's success has to do with its long-term commitment to the same five priorities. Its elected officials have maintained those priorities for over a decade, which sends a strong signal throughout City Hall that they are real. In the political world, one month is short term, and three months is long term. Charlotte has maintained its focus area priorities and collaborative structures since 1992, through several council elections. This is not "management du jour." Rather, it's how they're doing business in Charlotte, and those who like working collaboratively do well in this culture. Those who don't appreciate this kind of work are having a tougher time, and some have retired early or left for other jobs.

One way to promote constancy of purpose during times of a change in leadership is to create a broad constituency for collaboration, as discussed in Chapter Eight. One of the major reasons why the VA's *One VA* initiative was supported by the new Bush administration in 2001 (it was initiated by a political appointee during the second Clinton term) is that it had a very broad constituency. Those promoting *One VA* made sure to seek active involvement from its various stakeholders from the outset. They brought representatives from the General Accounting Office and the Office of Management and Budget, as well as Capitol Hill staffers, to their large *One VA* conferences, and those external stakeholders often became ambassadors for the approach. This broad support made it far easier for a new political team to maintain it.

Constancy of purpose is powerful when moving toward a more collaborative culture, because the forces that pull people back to their individual units and individual mind-sets are always present and must be overcome. Constancy of purpose generates trust; employees start to believe that the change isn't going away—its leaders are sincere and its prospects are good. As the authors of a book on generating social capital in organizations put it, "One element of authenticity is persistence. As trust builds over time, so we prove our commitment over time; what we do day after day reveals what matters most to us" (Cohen and Prusak, 2001, p. 185).

That last line is worth repeating. "What we do day after day reveals what matters most to us." It's our daily actions that convey our true values, not the words we might write on an organizational values poster. We may judge ourselves by our intentions, but others judge us by our behavior. When we show through our behavior, day after day, that collaboration is important and valued and necessary for success, others believe us. Attitudes change. Informal leaders start to champion the effort. And work is transformed.

---

## A Final Thought

When the Berlin Wall came down in 1989, it was an extraordinary moment. The collapse of that historic symbol of repression and division heralded the end of seven decades of Soviet control. Many hoped it would also signal the beginning of something new, of an era in which walls were replaced by bridges, when the differences dividing people would be seen as less important than the common interests that could unite us. Now, as ethnic hatreds and terrorism pick up where the cold war left off, as technology allows us to retreat into separate, narrow niches of nonreality and entertainment, such thinking seems incredibly naive. And perhaps it is.

Or maybe, just maybe, this is precisely the time to rediscover that we human beings are far more alike than different, that the categories and lines we use to define and separate us are blurred to the point of irrelevance. We can find creative ways to build bridges to other groups and organizations, not to become better bridge builders, but for the purpose of creating better outcomes for those we serve.

And that's why I believe so fully in the promise of collaboration—it enables us to co-create with others what we cannot create (as well) by ourselves. The barriers separating us exist first and foremost in our minds. Our organizations have taught us, all too well, about hierarchical thinking and fragmented work processes and division of labor and power. Today's environment favors lateral and systemic thinking. It requires more partnerships, fewer rigid boundaries. It supports knowledge sharing, not knowledge hoarding. It requires leaders who connect their work to a higher purpose. The stakes are far too high today to put up with narrow-minded thinking and turf-oriented actions. Agencies that respond to these new realities are being rewarded; others are becoming less relevant.

If we can think about collaboration more, about separation and differences less, we can achieve the futures that we want and that our children and communities deserve. Once you have seen the promise of collaboration, as the many people described in this book have done, there is no reason to go back. The choice, and the challenge, are yours.

# Resources

# Resource A

# Four Methods That Promote Collaboration

In the text, I described several structured methods that foster collaboration. Here are some details and suggestions for using four of them: partnering workshops, Baltimore's CitiStat method, performance contracts, and the University of Virginia's envisioning process. Partnering workshops are a powerful tool for collaborating with external organizations; the other three methods are especially effective at promoting collaboration across internal boundaries.

## 1. Partnering Workshops

Colonel Charles E. Cowan, U.S. Army Corps of Engineers (ret.) and former director of the Arizona Department of Transportation, writes: "Partnering is a strategy for success. In over three years' experience we have (1) virtually eliminated time growth, (2) substantially reduced cost growth, (3) experienced no new litigation, (4) reduced paperwork by 2/3, (5) gained new respect for our industry partners, and (6) are having fun!"

Partnering workshops have been used by a variety of government and private sector organizations since the 1980s. This method helps organizations that are frequently in conflict, to develop common goals and win-win relationships. Its most frequent use is in the construction industry. Here's how the partnering process works:

1. Prepare for it—educate your organization. Since partnering aims to replace adversarial modes of operating, all levels of employees need to understand its purpose, method, and expected results.

2. Educate the other organization or organizations you plan to partner with. In a bid solicitation, for instance, the organization requesting the work should specify that the partnering process will be used with the winning contractor.

3. Gain commitment from senior management. The leaders of every involved organization need to understand the philosophy, methods, and results of the partnering approach.

4. Identify partnering champions (or leaders). The organizations' leaders usually identify one or two people to represent their agency when the partnering workshop is planned. The champion also helps with follow-through after the workshop. The Army Corps of Engineers recommends two champions for each participating organization. One is a senior management champion who educates people about partnering and instills the partnering ethic into the culture. The other is a "managing partner" champion, usually an operational manager, who carries out the partnering charter and nourishes the key relationships involved.

5. Prepare for the partnering workshop. This involves agreeing on the desired outcome for the workshop and the individuals to invite, finding a neutral facilitator, obtaining a site, and drawing up an agenda. (See Exhibit A.1 for a sample.)

6. Conduct the partnering workshop. This may last from one to three days. The deliverables from the workshop include the following items:

   *Partnering charter.* This is a formal agreement among the partners, in which they spell out their mutual goals, objectives,

**Exhibit A.1. Sample Partnering Workshop Agenda.**

**Day 1:**

A.M.

Introductions

Overview of partnering

Overview of the project

Experiential exercise: "Win as much as you can." This is a structured simulation in which teams win or lose points depending on their tendency to cooperate or compete.

P.M.

Debrief exercise

Discussion of win-win possibilities for the project

Identification of each organization's previous experiences in partnerships

Discussion of project goals

**Day 2:**

A.M.

Learning about individual differences: Myers-Briggs Type Indicator

Profile of each team's Myers-Briggs styles

Conflict management exercise

Discussion of interest-based negotiation; develop norms for dealing with conflicts in this project

P.M.

Develop project charter, including conflict-management norms and project goals, time line, roles, communications channels, evaluation methods, and the like

Have each participant sign the charter

Review the session, prepare for first steps

Adjourn

time lines, roles, and the like. These are some common partnering goals for construction projects:

- Complete the project so that it meets the design intent.

- Complete the project without litigation.

- Achieve savings of $ _____.

- Finish the project _____ days ahead of schedule.

- Avoid lost-time injuries by promoting a safe job site.

- Ensure fair treatment for all parties.

- Solve problems at the lowest possible management level.

*Conflict resolution process.* In the charter, or in a separate statement, the partners describe their process for dealing with differences (for example, alternative dispute resolution methods).

*Evaluation process.* How will we know when we've been successful? Who will determine success? What are the criteria to be used? Will it be an ongoing assessment process?

7. Conduct periodic evaluations. The partnering champions and agency leaders meet during the course of the project to compare "actual" with "planned." Are the goals, time lines, and other provisions of the charter being accomplished? If the charter needs to be revised, these are the times to do so.

8. Celebrate successes. This happens throughout, not just at the end. A good time to celebrate is at the completion of each project milestone.

For more on partnering, see *Partnering: A Concept for Success*, by the Associated General Contractors of America (1991). Also see *Partnering*, by Lester Edelman, Frank Carr, and Charles L. Lancaster (1991), of the U.S. Army Corps of Engineers (part of its *Alternative Dispute Resolution Series, Pamphlet 4*).

## 2. CitiStat

CitiStat is Baltimore's method for making performance visible and holding middle and senior managers accountable for performance on a frequent basis. Mayor Martin O'Malley instituted it in June 2000, six months after taking office.

**Format**

The CitiStat format is simple. It includes the following elements:

*Agency Reports*

All city agencies and departments submit reports every two weeks, using an assigned data template. CitiStat staff analyze the data, which forms the basis of the CitiStat session for the department or agency.

*CitiStat Team Memo and CitiStat Session*

The CitiStat staff analysis of the unit's data is sent to the mayor and his cabinet prior to the CitiStat session. The memo summarizes the unit's data, identifies key trends (positive and negative), and poses questions that are used at the session. For instance, the October 5, 2001, memo regarding the Baltimore Public Works Bureau of Solid Waste asks questions such as these:

- The projected overtime budget in the Motor Vehicle Fund is $2,894 (mostly for graffiti removal); it is currently projected to spend $68,000. What is driving the increased overtime in graffiti operations?

- What has the response been to the new leaf collection policy? Is the Bureau tracking the number of complaints in this category?

At the CitiStat meeting, the department and agency heads answer the questions that apply to their areas. The meetings conclude with agreements on follow-up action to be taken during the two-week period before the next session.

*Follow-Up Memo*

After each session, the CitiStat team prepares a follow-up memo that summarizes the key points made during the session, and follow-up steps that the agency or department head agreed to take by the next CitiStat meeting (for example, "track the number of leaf-collection related complaints" and "submit a quarterly statistical comparison of overtime, lost man-days, and complaints"). These follow-up memos reflect the driving rhythm of the mayor and the CitiStat system; they are produced and disseminated within twenty-four hours of each CitiStat meeting.

**Critical Success Factors**

A review of the program's performance indicates that the following aspects are most important to its success:

- *Measuring and posting key performance data.* Current performance and trend lines are continually captured and analyzed (examples: time to fill a pothole, number of thefts in a given neighborhood, percentage of kids who haven't been inoculated in a school area).

- *Holding regular and frequent meetings at which senior managers are held accountable.* The meetings, led by senior managers every two weeks, review the performance data for a department with its managers and focus on trends, causes, possible remedies.

- *Relentless follow-up and accountability.* The senior managers expect department managers to take agreed-upon steps between meetings to learn causes of problems, and to deal with those problems and report back on those results.

- *Focusing on a relatively small number of issues.* By targeting just a few items to track and measure, the priorities for that department become clear. This also focuses managers' and employees' attention on those priorities, and it creates an atmosphere that helps people in different units collaborate, because many of the problems and issues cross organizational lines.

- *Forming coalitions of agencies to deal with complex issues that cross departmental lines.* It doesn't work to say "that's beyond my control" in the CitiStat system, because the various units that have partial control are brought together to deal with complex issues. Again, data are captured, analyzed, displayed, and discussed bi-weekly, and individuals are accountable for follow-up.

Several medium and large cities in the United States are implementing their own versions of CitiStat.

## 3. Performance Contracts

For those who seek greater collaboration across boundaries within a single organization, performance contracts can be powerful tools. They are most effective when used in the context of an overall performance management system.

Performance management systems are comprehensive approaches to managing ongoing operations. They usually include the following elements:

- Annual agency goals and objectives.

- Balanced performance measures for the key goals. These are best expressed as outcomes—results—not outputs.

- Strategies and activities to meet each objective.

- Accountability for each objective (responsible person or unit, time lines, and the like).

- Tracking mechanism that informs all staff of the current status of the goals and outcomes.

- Consequences for achieving the goals and objectives.

For a good write-up on performance management, and on "flexible performance agreements," see Chapter Three of *The Reinventor's Fieldbook* (Osborne and Plastrik, 2000). Here are some elements found in good performance contracts:

- The department's or unit's mission

- Its key operational responsibilities

- Its current and requested budget

- The desired outcomes for the year

- Some measures for each outcome

- A means for changing or updating the contract

- How and when the manager and the manager's supervisor will communicate concerning the contents of the contract

Exhibit A.2 lists a set of sample contract provisions that can be used as a model. Note that the last item in the sample, "collaboration strategy," will be more powerful the more specific it is. That is, the manager and supervisor constructing the contract should identify some projects that this manager's unit is charged with completing, but that can only be completed by working with other units. Similarly, other units' projects that require this manager's assistance should be put on the contract.

## Exhibit A.2.  Performance Contract Example.

The items that Bob O'Neill (see Chapter Twelve) found most useful when using performance contracts with his Hampton, Virginia, department heads, were the following:

1. *Critical Success Factors.* What are the three or four major elements needed for your department to successfully meet its mission? [*Note:* These must be translated into performance measures.]

2. *New Initiatives.* What new initiatives will your department begin this year? [*Note:* These must be related to policies and priorities of the elected officials.]

3. *Change initiatives.* What are you doing today to ensure that the organization improves tomorrow? [*Note:* These are specific, concrete projects. An example might be a description of improving a specific business process that affects customer service.]

4. *Infrastructure improvements.* What are you doing to invest in the capacity of the organization to improve? [*Note:* This differs from item 3 in that it relates to organization-wide improvement efforts that affect the basic infrastructure of the agency, not one-time specific initiatives.]

5. *Cost-savings and redeployment strategy.* What are you doing to determine which activities should no longer be done, which should be done with less effort, which should be done by other organizations? [*Note:* This challenges the assumption that the organization should continue doing what it's already doing.]

6. *Collaboration strategy.* What are you doing to support the activities of other units within your organization, and to support other organizations?

When an organization establishes goals and measures for a group of departments or agencies, as happens in the state of Iowa (Chapter Eleven) and the city of Charlotte (Chapter Twelve), performance contracts for each department or agency head should reflect those goals and measures, and identify the other units that share responsibility for those goals. Performance contracts have the following advantages:

- They clarify senior leadership's expectations. When done well, they include both parties' input so that each understands what is needed by the other to achieve the stated results.

- They can strengthen alignment across an organization. If the senior leader of an agency puts elements such as collaboration in everyone's performance contract, the results can be powerful.

- The contract can provide a tool for results-based accountability.

- The contract can help make performance more visible. When everyone is looking at the same data on the unit's progress toward certain high-priority goals, it can be a powerful tool for learning and change.

- Perhaps most important, contracts can focus employees on the key results they're accountable for achieving.

Performance contracts are not without hazards and drawbacks. These are some of the potential challenges:

- Some internal administration units may be threatened by a perceived loss of influence over the units whose managers have contracts with the agency head.

- Some employees may think it politically foolish to publicly commit to certain results, believing they'll only be blamed if they fall short and will receive no recognition if they succeed.

- Some managers may try to game the system by suggesting easy-to-achieve results. That, of course, is a risk with any measurement system.

These are factors critical for success with performance contracts:

- Contracts work best when they involve a genuine conversation between the parties. If it's simply a top-down "lay on," the boss may be delighted but the subordinate has little if any stake in the contents of the contract.

- It's essential to emphasize results in the contract—real outcomes, not just outputs.

- "Less is more." Limit the contracts to a relatively small number of items. Five or six is plenty.

- The boss's priorities need to be reflected in the contract.

- Consider including one result that requires cross-unit collaboration; bring the heads of the collaborating units together periodically when that result is discussed.

- It adds great power to the contracts when managers at each level share what's in their own contracts with their direct reports and write performance contracts with the next lower level that reflect the same priorities.

- What's critical, of course, is *follow-through*. When senior leaders pay attention to contracts, call in their managers regularly, and focus on results to date, the contracts become important parts of those managers' daily work life. When that doesn't happen, the contracts lead to more *Dilbert* cartoons around the office coffee pot!

A *final note on alignment:* Performance contracts are especially powerful when they are reinforced by senior management's behavior. It does little good to write detailed performance contracts emphasizing specific outcomes without collecting data on the results. Nor does it help to put key priorities into the contracts, and then emphasize other priorities when talking with managers.

For an excellent write-up on the use of performance contracts, see "Results-Oriented Performance Agreements: A Key Tool for Setting Clear Expectations," by John Kamensky, available online at http://www.aspanet.org. The article is in the site archives, dated January 7, 2002.

## 4. The University of Virginia Envision Process

Collaborating across the units within a single organization can be difficult, especially if authority is widely diffused. That's usually the case in large agencies that have several regional and local offices. It's also the case in most universities; deans have great autonomy, and tenured faculty have enormous security. It's a challenge to get people with that much independence moving in a common direction.

Leaders at the University of Virginia found a way to gain an uncommon level of communication and collaboration among the ten academic schools by using a process they called "Envision." It worked as follows:

### Preparation

1. The provost discussed the envision process at a meeting of deans, so that they would all hear from him, at one time, the reasons and thinking behind the approach.

2. The provost then formally invited the dean of each school to host an envision session. The dean was also asked to select fifteen faculty to join in the discussion. The session was to be

an open conversation at which the faculty and dean would exchange views on the school's strengths, challenges, and future direction. They were also asked to discuss their own hopes, aspirations, and concerns about the school and the university.

3. Each school worked with the Development Office to create an information packet, listing the university's budget and recent budget history, the school's programs and national rankings, the results of the recent university capital campaign, and other related information. This gave all participants a common information base from which to begin the conversation.

4. All deans were notified about the schedule. The provost made it very clear that deans were welcome to observe other schools' sessions. They needed to inform the host dean in advance.

5. The consultant for the process met with the dean (and sometimes the faculty) of each school prior to its session. The consultant explained the purpose, format, and expectations for the session, and the faculty and dean discussed the issues they thought were important to raise. The consultant also presented the questions to be used, and invited the dean and faculty to help customize those questions to their school.

6. The sessions took place.

### The Envision Sessions

- The sessions were held from September 2001 through February 2002. Exhibit A.3 lists the questions that were used most frequently.

- Each session lasted about three hours. A summary of each session was produced and disseminated.

**Exhibit A.3. Envision Questions.**

1. What are the key factors, issues, and trends in the external environment affecting your school?

2. How is your school responding to these trends?

3. What's at the "core" of your school? What distinguishes it from others?

4. What are its major strengths?

5. What are some areas for growth?

6. What are the key issues confronting the school now and in the future?

7. What are your major goals for the next three to five years?

8. What's in place that will help you achieve these goals?

9. What else is needed (from the university, from outside) to achieve these goals?

10. What are some "transformational ideas" that your school, with others, would like to pursue (ideas that might attract significant outside funding)?

11. What haven't we asked you that we should be asking?

*Initial Follow-Up and Results*

- A summary of the key points and themes from all sessions was sent to the deans.

- Many deans and faculty reported that they found the discussions stimulating. They had never had an opportunity for such in-depth discussions with a provost and other deans.

- After the last session, the provost convened a meeting of the ten deans, reviewed the summaries of each session, and together they discussed a number of cross-cutting ideas and interests that had emerged from the Envision sessions.

- The provost announced four initiatives he wanted to pursue that came out of the Envision sessions. These initiatives were intended to deal with current and future statewide needs, and they would each require participation from several schools and departments.

- In addition to these specific plans, the Envision sessions led to increased communication and collaboration across schools. Many deans said they developed a better understanding of what other schools are doing and where their interests and needs intersect. Some of the ideas generated at the sessions are affecting the design of new facilities.

- Finally, three other units within the university have requested Envision sessions with the provost and vice president, because of their desire to be part of this unusual, university-wide planning effort.

# Resource B

# Some Questions and Answers Concerning Collaboration

1. *What are some conditions that don't call for collaboration?*
Collaboration is usually unwise in the following circumstances:

- Several parties care about an issue but only one is accountable for it, is under pressure to deal with it quickly, and has the ability to handle it competently.

- The individuals who would be responsible for meeting and working collaboratively are overwhelmed with pressing matters that cannot be delegated or delayed, and nobody else is available to represent and speak for their organizations.

- The senior organizational leaders assigning the task can't agree on the project's goals.

- The parties have a history of significant conflict and low trust.

- The likely costs (financial, political, time) are greater than the perceived benefits.

- Certain parties, whose involvement is critical to success, refuse to (or for other reasons cannot) participate.

*2. I often need to collaborate with others, but sometimes others aren't open to collaboration (and I have no formal authority over them). What are my options?*

One possibility is to avoid using the word *collaborate*. It makes some people uncomfortable. Instead, remember that collaboration is a means to an end. Ask yourself what end—what goal or outcome— it is that you're concerned about. Who else cares about that and is in a position to help achieve it? If others share your concern and have some ability to affect the outcome, it may make sense to focus on that and not talk about collaboration. Discuss the problem or goal that you both care about, discuss why it's important and how to deal with it, and see if others decide that collaboration is a useful option.

A second option is to approach those who don't seem interested and (if you have a reasonably good relationship) simply ask if they're interested in working on the joint effort together. Do it in an open, even curious way, not in a demanding or judgmental fashion. You may be incorrectly assuming the person isn't interested in collaboration.

If you learn that people really aren't interested in working together, it's time to do some "intelligence gathering." Is it a fear that they'll lose more than gain? If so, see question 4. Is it that they've tried collaboration before and it was a huge waste of time? Of that they simply don't see anything in it for themselves or their agency? Or that they have concerns that others in the core group don't meet their quality standards? Your response will depend on the reason that others are reluctant to engage. Many people get frustrated and try to apply pressure on others to collaborate. A far better response is to get into a learning mode and smoke out the reasons for their apparent lack of interest.

*3. We're working on a collaborative project and the basics are in place, but it's going very slowly. We make agreements, we follow up, but we're moving at glacial speed. What can we try?*

This is often a problem, especially in the early phases. Here are some ways to track down the cause of the problem:

- First, ask what's holding things up. Is it a trust problem, a lack of time because of other demands, a lack of support from senior leaders? See if you can determine the cause and deal with it directly.

- Also, see if the basics (as outlined in Chapter Five) are, in fact, fully in place. Perhaps the champion is distracted by other duties. Perhaps this project isn't a high priority for the agencies involved. Return to the basics to determine if something is missing.

- Consider two other possibilities. First, this project may not have a strong external constituency. Lacking that can reduce the pressure on the parties to contribute. In addition, the initiative may not have generated a sense of high stakes.

Here are some options: Put the initiative on hold until it becomes more important to the agencies involved, or find ways to raise the stakes (discussed in Chapter Seven). You can also generate momentum by setting some short-term, important goals that the group can meet, and inviting a few external stakeholders to assist in meeting those goals. Invite one of the core group members to be the initiative's champion. It also helps to measure your progress and celebrate successes.

4. *Some of the people in our group seem more interested in protecting their organizations than in contributing to our effort. How can we deal with this?*

You can address this either indirectly or directly. There are good reasons for each approach, depending on the specifics of your situation. Here is an indirect approach:

- Review the ground rules (or establish them if they don't yet exist). Do any of them talk about making a positive contribution (in terms of time, money, information, other resources)?

- Hold a retreat for the group, led by an outside facilitator. Use the retreat to build some trust and strengthen relationships, so that people feel safe in discussing questions such as these: What are the potential benefits we each see in this project? What are our major concerns? What would it take for each of us to be more fully committed to this project, or more enthusiastic about it? When discussing such questions, it's critical that everyone adopt a posture of curiosity, so that you truly explore each other's mind-sets and eliminate any criticism or judgment from the discussion.

- Widen the arena of engagement. That is, bring in some external stakeholders and others who care about the project you're working on, and whose presence may raise the level of energy and commitment in the group. External stakeholders could include special interest groups, the media if appropriate, academics, oversight groups, and the like.

- Invite those who seem defensive to take part in an important short-term project, one that requires active involvement and energy from each person working on it. Some people get less defensive and more motivated when they have a concrete task that needs to be done.

A more direct approach could include these options:

- Deal directly with those who seem to be in a defensive mode. Talk with them one-to-one, explain what you're observing, ask what they see as the pluses and minuses of the effort so far, and try to draw out the reasons why they may be "playing defense." They may not see themselves the way you do. If they do have a lot to lose, let them know it's in everyone's interest (including theirs) to put their concerns on the table.

- Bring up the issue in the group. This is far easier if the group agrees on ground rules for mutual respect, candor, and being open about what's on the table and off the table as far as the collaborative project goes.

- Hold a meeting with senior leaders from each participating organization, and identify what's working well and what (not who) is slowing the group down. Tell them that the group won't succeed if things don't change. Ask them to work with each other to determine if each agency is, in fact, committed to the project.

5. *There's low trust within the group. We've tried to talk about this, but people are uncomfortable discussing it together. How can we build some trust?*

The answer is, it depends. If the low trust reflects a history of bad blood among the *individuals* involved, that can be very difficult to resolve. If the trust problem is among the *participating agencies*, the individuals in the group may still be able to establish the trust necessary to work on this project.

If the problem is primarily a lack of interagency trust, here are some options:

- Develop ground rules that affirm the importance of developing trust and of acting in trustworthy ways.

- Periodically ask members, Have we been following our ground rules? Invite them to discuss what's working well and when they may have been disappointed by others' behavior.

- Realize that trust doesn't usually exist because we want it; it has to be *built*. Look for opportunities that allow members to follow through on assignments. Openly admit any mistakes you make. Listen carefully to others in order to determine their interests and values. Make your own values explicit insofar as they relate to the project. Take time to learn about each other.

- If the trust problem exists between some individuals in the group, reread the answer to the first question in this list. You may need a different set of participants; you may have to put the project on hold.

*Note:* For an excellent discussion of trust and related issues in collaborative groups, see *Collaboration: A Guide for Environmental Advocates*, by E. Franklin Dukes and his colleagues (2001), pp. 35–40.

6. *We're trying to make decisions by consensus. How can we avoid "lowest common denominator" decisions?*

This is a problem for many groups. The desire to reach consensus can result in relatively low-quality, uncreative decisions for several reasons. For one, some people believe that consensus means that everyone fully agrees. I think that's a huge mistake. And some people are so eager to reach agreement that they quickly come together on the first option presented; the desire for closure and for agreement may reduce the group's willingness to think carefully about the option being considered.

Consensus can be a powerful approach if it's understood and used properly. It's not a replacement for critical thinking. It needn't require unanimity, nor is it about being nice. Consensus means everyone has input, everyone feels heard, and the group comes up with a decision that all (or most) can support. Consensus works best under the following conditions:

- The group agrees to a ground rule that members won't hold out for 100 percent of what they want on each issue.

- The group agrees that consensus is most powerful when it results in decisions that have strong support from the group and are also of high quality. "High quality," of course, may be a very subjective term, but the point is to make explicit the desire to seek solutions that are *effective* in solving problems. The fact that everyone supports a decision isn't enough to make it a quality decision.

- It's sometimes OK to make a decision that some members dislike. Try hard for consensus first, listen carefully to the reasons why some oppose a given option, and see if those reasons can be addressed. If consensus isn't achieved, it may be more important to decide and move forward than to wait for a future option that everyone can support.

- The group can agree at the outset that, when there isn't 100 percent agreement but the group can't wait any longer, a "super majority" (65 percent, 75 percent) is enough to move ahead. In such cases, it's fine for those who strongly disagree to register their minority opinion in writing.

- In some cases, it helps to bring in a neutral outsider who has considerable subject matter expertise on the issue being discussed. The group can decide how to use such experts: to critique the options being considered, to offer their own options, to help the group move forward if it is stuck.

7. *How do we evaluate the work of our collaborative group?*
I see at least three ways to do this:

- *External:* Is the group developing options and initiatives that are moving toward the desired goal?

- *Internal:* Is the group working well together? Is it following through on stated ground rules and group norms? How well are members communicating, developing trust, making use of their time, following through on tasks, managing conflicts, and the like?

- *Serendipity:* Are the unforeseen consequences of the group's work favorable? Are spin-off projects being created? Are customers and other stakeholders showing increased confidence in the participating organizations? Is the group's work leading to increased creativity in the member organizations? Is learning and growth occurring in the participants and their home agencies? Is the group generating new knowledge that may help in other endeavors?

Unfortunately, the serendipity standard is not used often in evaluations, but it should be. Many potentially very important outcomes are left unstated in the initial write-up of objectives. Unexpected results, whether positive or negative, should be measured and reported in any evaluation of collaborative work.

8. *What can we do when politics puts our effort at risk?*
This large topic was touched on in Chapter Eight. Smart collaborative leaders keep their political antennae up; you can have everything going for you in terms of keeping a core group of partners focused and working well together, and suddenly the whole effort can be derailed by political forces that are (or seem to be) beyond your control.

One reason that happens is that some professionals don't think in political terms. That is, people often prefer to think in technical and rational terms about a given project: "here's the goal, here's why (we think) it makes sense, here's an action plan to achieve it, let's tell others why this makes sense and how they can help us succeed." Sometimes that kind of straight-line thinking works, but don't count on it. We need to think in much broader terms if we're serious about collaborative work.

Here are a few of the key elements involved in thinking, and acting, in politically smart ways:

- Look at politics as simply one other aspect of the environment affecting your project. It's not somebody else's concern, it's not an evil to be dreaded, it's a way of thinking systemically about others' interests.

- Realize that politics is largely about influence, perceptions, shifting coalitions, relationships, and egos; it's not necessarily about making a rational case for acting in a certain way based on "the facts." That is, politics is usually messy, but it can be managed.

- Thinking politically can start with the question, How do we build support for our initiative? Stories are usually much more persuasive than facts in building support. Facts are important, but work best when put in a context, which means you need to describe the need or problem you're addressing through the use of an easy-to-understand story.

- Once you have the story articulated, think about building a constituency that cares about that story and the problem it describes. How does your initiative address an important problem that large numbers of people care about? It's important to focus on the problems that preoccupy other groups, and show how your story addresses their problems.

- Your initiative needs legitimacy to gain a strong constituency. What, and who, can give it legitimacy? Whose support raises its visibility? Whose support will help you marshal resources for it? And whose support do you need in the early phases to help you gain others' support later?

- Who are the "veto point holders" whose opposition could kill the initiative? Why would they be opposed, and how can you deal with their concerns?

- All these ideas are based on the assumption that you don't react to political trends and pressures after they build up; rather, you think and act *from the outset* with political interests and issues in mind.

9. *We have one very large agency and three small ones represented in our collaborative effort. Why does this sometimes create problems? How do we avoid those problems?*

People in small organizations frequently worry about joint efforts with larger ones, for several reasons. They worry that the larger agency will try to call all of the shots, will take credit for all accomplishments, and won't respect the talents and capabilities of those from the smaller agencies. They worry that they'll lose their identity. And in some instances, they worry that the larger one will try a "hostile takeover" and seek support for a merger.

The larger agency's representatives may also have some concerns. If we put the lion's share of resources into this effort, will we get our share out of it? Will others put in the same amount of energy that we're expending? Will they relax and assume we're taking care of all the issues?

The people in the larger agency are in the best position to prevent these real or imagined problems. They can do so by doing the following:

- Rotating the location of the meetings.

- Rotating leadership or facilitation of the meetings.

- Offering some resources when needed but asking others to contribute their fair share as well so that all parties have a stake in the effort.

- Being appropriately modest. That's a characteristic of successful collaborative leaders, as we discussed in Chapter Nine. It's especially important when one party has a reputation of taking over or is much larger than the others.

- Being especially careful to ensure the existence of one of the basics, an open and credible process. Those who have some worries about the "800-pound gorilla" may be overly sensitive to the smallest signs that the larger agency is trying to throw its weight around, so the process used to support collaboration must be transparently open and owned by all parties.

- Agreeing to a ground rule (or putting out a memorandum of understanding or statement) that spells out how much the respective parties will contribute to the effort and how they'll reap any rewards.

10. *Our collaborative group works well together, and we've come up with a great option to deal with our shared concern. The problem is that one of the parties in our group won't be served well if we take this option. There's no way that this option is in the interest of this one party, and we all recognize that. What can we do?*

That's a very tough question, and such situations do arise. There aren't perfect win-win solutions to all problems. The most important thing to do is to be absolutely, brutally honest about the situation. In addition, see if there are ways in which the sacrifice can be shared by others. Most parties are willing to give up something if they see that everyone's in the same boat. Another approach is to look to the future and rotate the benefits. If this collaborative effort will go on for several years (as in a jointly sponsored program), then it's imperative that the party who's "losing" with the current approach be a winner in the next round.

11. *What do we do with people or agencies that only take and don't give back?*

Healthy relationships are reciprocal relationships. That's as true with organizations as it is with people. Smart negotiators know this. That's why they sometimes cut deals that involve a series of small steps, with periodic options to terminate or change the arrangement based on their experience together (thus if one party doesn't follow through, you learn it quickly and with relatively little loss).

If the parties don't know each other well, or if one has a reputation for all take and no give, you need to make your expectations clear (partnering workshops are excellent ways to do so) and to take a series of small steps together to allow the parties to demonstrate their willingness to contribute in an equitable way. If one party doesn't walk its talk and only takes from the others, your best options are the following:

- Quietly confront the problem in a one-to-one conversation

- Use the peer pressure of the core group by discussing the degree to which each party is contributing and following the established ground rules

- Make the one-sided nature of the relationship visible to others (such as external constituencies of the parties involved) so that there's a cost to the behavior

- Take the problem to a senior leader in the party's organization

- Get a mutually respected outsider to intervene and mediate a solution

Some military agencies have used retired generals and admirals to serve as mentors or coaches for teams trying to collaborate. Military retirees usually maintain their networks with their active-duty colleagues. That gives them access to the current leadership of the Defense Department agencies, which means they have some clout and can intervene to deal with problems like this one.

Some of the ideas presented here come from an insightful paper on the issue of politics and collaboration: "The Will and the Way: Local Partnerships, Political Strategy and the Well-Being of America's Children and Youth," by Xavier Briggs (2002).

# Resource C

# Collaborative Assessment Tool

You can use the elements in our collaborative framework to assess a current or proposed collaborative venture. It's especially useful to have all members of a collaborative group fill it out individually, then compare scores and comments. Doing so helps you learn what's working and what's needed.

I. To what extent are these elements in place?

|  | 1<br>Very little<br>or not<br>at all | 2<br><br><br>Somewhat | 3<br>To a<br>good<br>extent | 4<br>To a<br>great<br>extent |
|---|---|---|---|---|
| **The Basics: The parties have** | | | | |
| A shared purpose or goal that they cannot achieve on their own | ___ | ___ | ___ | ___ |
| A desire to pursue a collaborative solution now | ___ | ___ | ___ | ___ |
| The right people at the table | ___ | ___ | ___ | ___ |
| An open, credible process | ___ | ___ | ___ | ___ |
| A champion for the initiative | ___ | ___ | ___ | ___ |

| | 1<br>Very little<br>or not<br>at all | 2<br><br>Somewhat | 3<br>To a<br>good<br>extent | 4<br>To a<br>great<br>extent |
|---|---|---|---|---|
| Open, trusting relationships among the principals | ____ | ____ | ____ | ____ |
| High stakes | ____ | ____ | ____ | ____ |
| A constituency for collaboration | ____ | ____ | ____ | ____ |
| Collaborative leadership | ____ | ____ | ____ | ____ |
| **Other factors:**<br>Continuity of leadership | ____ | ____ | ____ | ____ |
| Each party plays to its strengths | ____ | ____ | ____ | ____ |
| Collaboration is voluntary, not mandatory | ____ | ____ | ____ | ____ |
| There are flexible resources | ____ | ____ | ____ | ____ |
| Results are measured and posted | ____ | ____ | ____ | ____ |
| There's a balance between planning and action | ____ | ____ | ____ | ____ |

II.  Look at the elements that received a 4 or 5.
   1. Which elements are most important to your initiative's success?

   2. How can you and others maintain or even strengthen the elements noted in answering the preceding question?

III. Look at the elements that received a 3 or lower.
    1. Which elements are most important to increase now?

    2. What are some steps you and your associates can take to increase them?

IV. Consider the major hurdles to effective collaboration (from Chapter Three).
    Which of them are creating problems for your initiative?

|  | Major Hurdle | Minor Hurdle | Not a Problem |
|---|---|---|---|
| **Individual:** | | | |
| The need for power | ____ | ____ | ____ |
| Self-serving bias | ____ | ____ | ____ |
| Fear of losing control, autonomy, quality, identity, resources | ____ | ____ | ____ |
| Lack of trust and confidence among the principals | ____ | ____ | ____ |
| Turf concerns | ____ | ____ | ____ |
| **Organizational:** | | | |
| Costs are clear, benefits are unclear | ____ | ____ | ____ |
| Different goals and measures among the parties | ____ | ____ | ____ |
| Little organizational credit or reward to those who collaborate | ____ | ____ | ____ |

|  | Major Hurdle | Minor Hurdle | Not a Problem |
|---|---|---|---|
| Individually oriented appraisal systems | ____ | ____ | ____ |
| Line-item budget systems | ____ | ____ | ____ |
| No clear answer to the WIIFM? question from the organization's viewpoint | ____ | ____ | ____ |
| Different rules, different cultures; which ones apply? | ____ | ____ | ____ |

**Societal:**

| | | | |
|---|---|---|---|
| Ethic of individualism | ____ | ____ | ____ |
| Bias toward competition | ____ | ____ | ____ |

**Systemic:**

| | | | |
|---|---|---|---|
| Constitutional separation of powers and fragmentation | ____ | ____ | ____ |
| Narrow, categorical funding programs | ____ | ____ | ____ |

V. Of the most troublesome, which are most important to address? List as many as three, and indicate ways you and others might address each of them.

1. _____

   _____

   _____

2. _____

   _____

   _____

3. _____

   _____

   _____

# Resource D

# The Research Base for This Book

The research for this book comes from four sources. One was a review of the collaboration literature. I won't detail that here; the references are listed in the Bibliography at the end of the book, and the ones I found most helpful are cited throughout. A second source came from interviews with more than eighty managers and others who have extensive collaboration experience. They are listed in the book's Preface.

The third source for this framework comes from the cases that I studied. I selected cases based on these criteria:

1. The underlying issue was so complex that it couldn't be handled by one agency alone; several units or agencies worked together on the issue.

2. The collaboration has been in operation for at least two years (all but two have been going for three or more years).

3. Internal and external stakeholders consider the collaboration partly or largely successful (in terms of meeting its objectives).

I studied more organizations than found space in these pages, but all added insights to the analysis. The following list provides a brief sketch of each of the cases (with a note as to the chapter where they're discussed in more detail, if applicable). Note that cases with an asterisk after the name are available in longer and more detailed form on the *Working Across Boundaries* page of the Jossey-Bass Web site at http://www.josseybass.com.

- *Agility Program.* The Pennsylvania Department of Transportation (PENNDOT) has formed road maintenance partnerships with hundreds of the state's local governments by means of a program called Agility. The managers barter an exchange of services; if the state has superior equipment for repair work, and the locality can clear snow off a state road faster than PENNDOT, then they swap services on those roads. (See Chapter Eleven.)

- *Baltimore Child Advocacy Center.* Two departments with extraordinarily different cultures—police and social services—jointly run a center whose mission is to prevent and treat victims of child sexual abuse and find the perpetrators. (See Chapter Two.)

- *Care Advantage Plus.** In 1997 a nonprofit agency serving the elderly in Central Virginia and a for-profit health care provider created a profit-making entity that delivers home health services to senior citizens of various income levels. (See Chapter Ten.)

- *City of Baltimore—CitiStat.** CitiStat is a tool borrowed from the New York City Police that holds managers strictly accountable for performance on a regular and frequent basis. It also fosters collaboration between city departments as well as with outside agencies. And the results are proving positive. (See Chapters Seven and Twelve.)

- *City of Charlotte, North Carolina.** The elected officials and managers of Charlotte do an exceptional job of maintaining a small number of high priorities, called "focus areas." City Council committees and city departments are organized according to these focus areas, and their performance is measured by area-wide metrics. (See Chapters Twelve and Thirteen.)

- *City of Chicago.*\* Mayor Richard M. Daley has made it absolutely clear that he expects his department and agency heads to work closely together to revitalize urban neighborhoods, improve kids' learning skills, and provide quality services to the citizens. Department heads know that *they're all in the Chicago business.* (See Chapter Twelve.)

- *Columbia River Regional Forum.*\* The Regional Forum is a collaborative effort among five states, six federal agencies, and thirteen Indian tribes. They share the goal of saving several species of salmon on the endangered species list. The agencies are making progress despite a lack of clarity on their roles, cultural and technical differences among the parties, and a long history of low trust. (See Chapter Three.)

- *Comprehensive Performance Partnership.*\* Five public and nonprofit organizations formed a partnership with the Chautauqua County (New York) government to help the county develop a performance-focused organization based on measurable outcomes. This represented an enormous change in county government culture, and the partners played critical roles in creating a framework for the change, providing hands-on training, developing performance measures, and giving the change effort political support. (See Chapter Eight.)

- *EARN.*\* In Southern Maryland, several social service and workforce development agencies, together with the local community college, have worked together since 1997 to streamline services to common clients. The agencies have pooled some resources for staff training, are sharing information that used to be hoarded, use common intake forms, and are jointly running a one-stop center that meets training and development needs for citizens in this three-county area. (See Chapters Three and Six.)

- *Export Assistance Centers.* * Spurred by the Export Enhancement Act of 1992, three federal agencies put aside their turf and differences to form one-stop Export Assistance Centers around the country. The centers serve small and medium-sized American firms doing business overseas. In the past, the federal government's assistance to American exporters was delivered through a maze of nineteen disconnected programs. The three agencies, Export-Import Bank, Department of Commerce, and Small Business Administration, are sometimes joined by state agencies to jointly run these centers in order to cut red tape and provide simple, integrated solutions to business customers. The cross-trained staff bring the strengths of each agency to their customers.

- *Fairfax County Central Registration.* A school-county partnership formed in 1999, when the Fairfax, Virginia, Board of Supervisors and School Board directed the staff to work together in the cause of serving school-children with special needs, many of whom come from other cultures. The school and county responded by getting their respective social work staff members to work together at the school's annual registration process, where they assess students' (and their families') unmet needs in the areas of health care, child care, and employment. Staff identify services for families, make referrals, and provide maps showing the service locations in the families' native languages if necessary.

- *Financial Management Services.\** This U.S. Treasury Department agency functions as the banker for most of the federal government, dispensing and receiving payments involving hundreds of billions of dollars. When a new commissioner took over in December 1997, he helped transform a group of fiefdoms into one agency, where managers and executives understand that collaboration is part of their job and a key to high performance. (See Chapter Twelve.)

- *JNET.\** Pennsylvania's law enforcement agencies are sharing information in novel and powerful ways. By leveraging advanced technology and allowing member agencies to determine what information they share and with whom, JNET is giving the state's citizens faster and more effective crime prevention and criminal justice services. (See Chapter Four.)

- *Joint Venture: Silicon Valley Network.\** This nonprofit regional collaborative was created in 1993 to enhance the economic vitality and quality of life for the 2.3 million residents of the high-tech region around San Jose and Palo Alto, California. It's a large and inclusive partnership, involving leaders from business, government, higher education, labor, and community groups. (See Chapters Five, Seven, Eleven, and Thirteen.)

- *Linkages to Learning.* This program allows parents in Montgomery County, Maryland, to obtain a variety of needed services for school-age children and their families through one-stop shopping at their neighborhood public school. Linkages staff work closely together and collaborate with a large number of public, nonprofit, and business organizations.

- *Montgomery County Early Childhood Initiative.*\* An intensive, multiparty effort including government, nonprofit, and public school agencies—in all, thirty-nine agencies and almost a hundred people— developed a comprehensive plan for improving the educational and health outcomes of young children in the county. Its accomplishments include the hiring of a senior manager for early childhood programs, who has a dual appointment with both the county schools and county social services department. (See Chapter Nine.)

- *One VA.*\* The Department of Veterans Affairs is trying to act like one organization in serving the veterans who are its customers. It is integrating information systems, collaborating across boundaries to respond much faster to veterans' claims for compensation, and helping its employees learn how their work connects to the larger goal of serving the country's veterans. (See Chapter Thirteen.)

- *Service First.*\* U.S. Forest Service and Bureau of Land Management offices in the western United States are forming impressive partnerships. They are sharing staff and other resources, co-locating some offices, even integrating certain operations. Many are achieving their goals of financial efficiency, better customer service, and improved land management. (See Chapters One, Six, Eight, and Thirteen.)

- *Smart Growth.*\* Several faculty members at the University of Maryland came together to design a curriculum for a "smart growth" program, which has to do with efforts to plan for growth in a way that balances the needs of the environment, the economy, and population growth. Despite an academic culture that emphasizes individual autonomy, the group succeeded in planning and delivering the program with positive results. Now a national smart growth center is functioning at the university, supported by four different academic schools.

- *Smart Start.* Smart Start is a state–local community–private sector partnership devoted to early childhood development. The state puts up most of the funds and sets certain standards in three core areas: child care, health, and family support. Local partnership boards are formed in each community to ensure that everyone is at the table. Evaluations done each year have demonstrated the program's effectiveness. (See Chapters Five and Eleven.)

- *Treasure Valley Partnership.*\* Urban sprawl in the Treasure Valley portion of Idaho convinced local leaders that they must think and plan as one community, even as they respect the autonomy of each locality. Nine cities and counties formed a partnership in 1997 to guide the area's development in a smart way and work together for the common good. And they have some solid accomplishments to their credit. (See Chapter Nine.)

- *Virtual teams in the intelligence community.* The thirteen U.S. intelligence agencies often get high marks for the quality of the work they do individually, but do much less well in terms of joint projects and information sharing. Congress is pressing them to learn how to collaborate. One approach: the use of "virtual teams" that collaborate using advanced technology. Some are doing well, others are struggling.

In addition to these cases, two additional examples were researched. One involves a research university, one of its largest schools, and a nonprofit foundation that raises money for that school. Despite several efforts to improve coordination and collaboration between the school and foundation over the years, the parties have managed little significant improvement.

The other example can only be called a failure to date, although it appeared to be successful at the time I did the research. This one involves efforts to share information and resources between the FBI and the CIA. These two agencies have a history of low trust and often disrespect, but in the mid-1990s they began efforts to share personnel, information, and other resources in their joint effort to combat terrorism. The deputy director of each agency's counterterrorism center is on loan from the other agency, they have had some successes in the use of joint teams, and working together they were able to prevent some large-scale terrorist attacks that were planned during the millennial celebration.

Then came September 11, 2001, and revelations that each agency had prior information on some of the terrorists who attacked the World Trade Center and Pentagon, information that wasn't shared. Given the horrific events of that day, the calamitous results and ongoing investigations, and the possibility that it could have been prevented or reduced in scope had these and other agencies shared what they knew, their efforts to collaborate certainly cannot be considered successful at this writing. I include references to this and the previous case because it is possible to learn from efforts that show mixed results and from failures as well as from successes (Hersh, 2001; Harris, 2002; Novak, 2001).

The fourth and last source that informed this framework was my own experience in consulting on partnership efforts. These experiences go back to the mid-1990s, when an increasing number of clients began asking for assistance in forming and sustaining partnerships. Some of these consultation efforts were short-term interventions lasting a few weeks to a couple of months. Some have lasted one to two years, and one has gone on since 1996.

# Bibliography

Arsenault, J. *Forging Nonprofit Alliances*. San Francisco: Jossey-Bass, 1998.

Associated General Contractors of America. *Partnering: A Concept for Success*. Washington, D.C.: Associated General Contractors of America, 1991.

Associated Press. "FedEx Begins Carrying Mail for Postal Service." *Washington Post*, Aug. 27, 2001, p. A5.

Austin, J. E. *The Collaboration Challenge: How Nonprofits and Businesses Succeed Through Strategic Alliances*. San Francisco: Jossey-Bass, 2000a.

Austin, J. E. "Principles for Partnership." *Leader to Leader*, 2000b, *18*, 44–50.

Axelrod, R. *The Evolution of Cooperation*. New York: Basic Books, 1984.

Axelrod, R. *Terms of Engagement: Changing the Way We Change Organizations*. San Francisco: Berrett-Koehler, 2000.

Bardach, E. *Getting Agencies to Work Together: The Practice and Theory of Managerial Craftsmanship*. Washington, D.C.: Brookings Institution, 1998.

Behn, R. D. "Why Measure Performance? Different Purposes Require Different Measures." *Public Administration Review*, forthcoming.

Bellah, R. N., Madsen, R., Sullivan, W. M., Swidler, A., and Tipton, S. N. *Habits of the Heart: Individualism and Commitment in American Life*. Berkeley: University of California Press, 1985.

Bennis, W. *Organizing Genius: The Secrets of Creative Collaboration*. Boston: Addison-Wesley, 1997.

Block, P. *The Empowered Manager: Positive Political Skills at Work*. San Francisco: Jossey-Bass, 1987.

Block, P. *Stewardship: Choosing Service over Self-Interest*. San Francisco: Berrett-Koehler, 1993.

Bolman, L. G., and Deal, T. E. *Reframing Organizations.* (2nd ed.) San Francisco: Jossey-Bass, 1997.

Bridges, W. *Managing Transitions: Making the Most of Change.* Boston: Addison-Wesley, 1991.

Briggs, X. "The Will and the Way: Local Partnerships, Political Strategy and the Well-Being of America's Children and Youth." Faculty Research Working Papers Series, Kennedy School of Government, Harvard University, Jan. 2002.

Bryson, J. M., and Crosby, B. C. *Leadership for the Common Good: Tackling Public Problems in a Shared-Power World.* San Francisco: Jossey-Bass, 1992.

Buckingham, M., and Coffman, C. *First, Break All the Rules: What the World's Greatest Managers Do Differently.* New York: Simon & Schuster, 1999.

Bunker, B. B., and Alban, B. T. *Large Group Interventions: Engaging the Whole System for Rapid Change.* San Francisco: Jossey-Bass, 1997.

Byrne, J. A. "The Horizontal Corporation." *Business Week,* Dec. 20, 1993, pp. 76–81.

Chea, T. "Proving the Value of Industry Partnerships." *Washington Post,* Jan. 30, 2001, p. E5.

Chrislip, D. D. "The New Civic Leadership." In B. Kellerman and L. R. Matusak (eds.), *Cutting Edge: Leadership 2000.* College Park, Md.: James McGregor Burns Academy of Leadership, 2000.

Chrislip, D. D., and Larson, C. E. *Collaborative Leadership: How Citizens and Civic Leaders Can Make a Difference.* San Francisco: Jossey-Bass, 1994.

Cialdini, R. B. *Influence: The New Psychology of Modern Persuasion.* New York: Quill, 1984.

Claiborne, W. "Agencies Pool Resources at National Fire Center." *Washington Post,* Sept. 6, 2000, p. A17.

Cleveland, H. *The Future Executive.* New York: HarperCollins, 1972.

Cleveland, H. *Nobody in Charge: Essays on the Future of Leadership.* San Francisco: Jossey-Bass, 2002.

Clines, F. X. "Baltimore Uses a Databank to Wake Up City Workers." *New York Times,* June 10, 2001, Sec. 1, p. 24.

Cohen, D., and Prusak, L. *In Good Company: How Social Capital Makes Organizations Work.* Boston: Harvard Business School Press, 2001.

Cohen, E., and Tichy, N. "Leadership Beyond the Walls Begins with Leadership Within." In F. Hesselbein, M. Goldsmith, and I. Somerville (eds.), *Leading Beyond the Walls: How High-Performing Organizations Collaborate for Shared Success.* San Francisco: Jossey-Bass, 1999.

Cole, E. "Partnering: A Quality Model for Contract Relations." *Public Manager,* Summer 1993, pp. 39–42.

Collins, J. *Good to Great: Why Some Companies Make the Leap and Others Don't.* New York: HarperCollins, 2001.

Collins, J. C., and Porras, J. I. *Built to Last.* New York: HarperCollins, 1994.

Covey, S. *The Seven Habits of Highly Effective People.* New York: Simon & Schuster, 1989.

Davis, S., and Meyer, C. *Blur: The Speed of Change in the Connected Economy.* New York: Warner Books, 1998.

Denise, L. "Collaboration vs. C-Three (Cooperation, Coordination, and Communication)." *Innovating,* 1999, *7*(3), 25–35.

DePree, M. *Leadership Jazz.* New York: Dell, 1992.

Dewar, T., Dodson, D., Paget, V., and Roberts, R. *Just Call It Effective.* Richmond, Va.: Pew Partnership and University of Richmond, 1998.

Drucker, P. F. *The Age of Discontinuity: Guidelines to Our Changing Society.* New York: HarperCollins, 1968.

Drucker, P. F. *Managing in Turbulent Times.* New York: HarperCollins, 1980.

Drucker, P. F. *Innovation and Entrepreneurship: Practices and Principles.* New York: HarperCollins, 1985.

Drucker, P. F. "The New Pluralism." In F. Hesselbein, M. Goldsmith, and I. Somerville (eds.), *Leading Beyond the Walls: How High-Performing Organizations Collaborate for Shared Success.* San Francisco: Jossey-Bass, 1999a.

Drucker, P. F. "Managing Oneself." *Harvard Business Review,* Mar.-Apr. 1999b, pp. 64–74.

Dukes, E. F., Firehock, K., Leahy, M., and Anderson, M. *Collaboration: A Guide for Environmental Advocates.* Charlottesville: Institute for Environmental Negotiation at the University of Virginia, Wilderness Society, and National Audubon Society, 2001.

Duncan, D. M., and Short, C. L. *Measuring Progress: A Strategy to Get Results.* Montgomery County, Md.: Department of Health and Human Services, 1999a.

Duncan, D. M., and Short, C. L. *Partnerships for People: A Plan for the Future.* Montgomery County, Md.: Department of Health and Human Services, 1999b.

Dwyer, J. "Before the Towers Fell, Fire Dept. Fought Chaos." *New York Times,* Jan. 30, 2002.

Edelman, L., Carr, F., and Lancaster, C. L. *Partnering: Pamphlet 4, Alternative Dispute Resolution Series.* Fort Belvoir, Va.: Army Corps of Engineers Institute for Water Resources, 1991.

Eisenhardt, K. M., and Galunic, D. C. "Coevolving: At Last, a Way to Make Synergies Work." *Harvard Business Review,* Jan.-Feb. 2000, pp. 91–101.

Foster, R. N. *Innovation: The Attacker's Advantage*. New York: Simon & Schuster, 1986.

Friedman, M., and others. "Results and Performance Accountability Implementation Guide." Available online: http://www.raguide.org/. Access date: May 6, 2002.

Frydman, B., Wilson, I., and Wyer, J. *The Power of Collaborative Leadership: Lessons for the Learning Organization*. Boston: Butterworth-Heinemann, 2000.

Fukiyama, F. *Trust: The Social Virtues and the Creation of Prosperity*. New York: Free Press, 1995.

Gallwey, W. T. *The Inner Game of Tennis*. New York: Random House, 1974.

Gallwey, W. T. *The Inner Game of Work*. New York: Random House, 2000.

Gardner, S. *Beyond Collaboration to Results: Hard Choices in the Future of Services to Children and Families*. Phoenix: Arizona Prevention Resource Center and the Center for Collaboration for Children, 1999.

Geyer, G. A. "Chicago Using Web of Libraries to Bind City." *Dallas Morning News*, June 19, 2000, p. 13A.

Gibbs, N. "Special Report/The Littleton Massacre." *Time*, May 3, 1999, pp. 25–36.

Gibbs, N. "Characters and Campaigns: The 2000 Election." Address given at the Chautauqua Institution, Chautauqua, New York, Aug. 8, 2000.

Gladwell, M. *The Tipping Point: How Little Things Can Make a Big Difference*. New York: Little, Brown, 2000.

Goldenkoff, R. N. "Opportunities and Challenges of Public/Private Partnerships." *Public Manager*, Fall 2001, pp. 31–35.

Goldman, S. L., Nagel, R. N., and Preiss, K. *Agile Competitors and Virtual Organizations*. New York: Wiley, 1997.

Gray, B. *Collaborating: Finding Common Ground for Multiparty Problems*. San Francisco: Jossey-Bass, 1991.

Hammer, M. *Beyond Reengineering*. New York: HarperCollins, 1996.

Hammer, M., and Champy, J. *Reengineering the Corporation*. New York: HarperCollins, 1993.

Harris, S. "Come Together." *Government Executive*, Mar. 2002, pp. 23–30.

Harwood Group. *Planned Serendipity*. Charlottesville, Va.: Pew Partnership for Civic Change, 1998.

Hennig, M., and Jardim, A. *The Managerial Woman*. New York: Pocket Books, 1976.

Hersh, S. "What Went Wrong: The C.I.A., and the Failure of American Intelligence." *New Yorker*, Oct. 8, 2001, pp. 34–40.

Hesselbein, F. "The Campaign for Leadership." *Leader to Leader*, 2000, *17*, 4–5.

Hesselbein, F., Goldsmith, M., and Somerville, I. (eds.). *Leading Beyond the Walls: How High-Performing Organizations Collaborate for Shared Success.* San Francisco: Jossey-Bass, 1999.

Higham, S. "DC Study Lambastes City's Child Protection: Report Cites Breakdown in Abuse Investigations." *Washington Post*, Aug. 19, 2000, p. B1.

Higham, S., and Horwitz, S. "Brianna, Buried in System's Mistakes." *Washington Post*, Dec. 16, 2000, p. A1.

Hogan, C. D. *Vermont Communities Count: Using Results to Strengthen Services for Families and Children.* Baltimore: Annie E. Casey Foundation, 1999.

Holdrege, M. A., Barnett, G., and Reid, S. G. "Models of Staffing Innovation Through Partnering." *Public Manager*, Winter 2000–2001, pp. 6–10.

Horn, M. "Managing Across: The Collaborative Leader." Address given at *Governing Magazine* Conference, "Managing in All Directions." Hershey, Pa., Dec. 10, 2001.

Howe, P. J. "Renaissance on the Charles." *Boston Globe*, Oct. 5, 1997, Sunday Magazine, p. 14.

Independent Sector. *Crossing the Borders: Collaboration and Competition Among Nonprofits, Business and Government.* Washington, D.C.: Independent Sector, 1999.

Joint Venture. *The Joint Venture Way: Lessons for Regional Rejuvenation*, Vols. 1 and 2. San Jose, Calif.: Joint Venture, 1995, 1999.

Jordan, K. "It Paid Off in Afghanistan: Eight Lessons from the U.S. Military That You Can Use." *Harvard Management Update*, 2002, 7(3), 1–4.

Kamensky, J. "Results-Oriented Performance Agreements: A Key Tool for Setting Clear Expectations." [http://www.aspanet.org]. Jan. 7, 2002.

Kamradt, B. "Wraparound Milwaukee: Aiding Youth with Mental Health Needs." *Juvenile Justice*, 2000, 7(1), 14–23.

Kanter, R. M. "Collaborative Advantage: The Art of Alliances." *Harvard Business Review*, July-Aug. 1994, pp. 96–108.

Kanter, R. M. "World-Class Leaders: The Power of Partnering." In F. Hesselbein, M. Goldsmith, and R. Beckhard (eds.), *The Leader of the Future: New Visions, Strategies, and Practices for the Next Era.* San Francisco: Jossey-Bass, 1996.

Katzenbach, J. R. *Teams at the Top.* Boston: Harvard Business School Press, 1998.

Katzenbach, J. R., and Smith, D. K. *The Wisdom of Teams.* New York: Harper-Collins, 1993.

Kayser, T. A. *Mining Group Gold: How to Cash In on the Collaborative Brain Power of a Group.* (2nd ed.) New York: McGraw-Hill, 1995.

Kemmis, D. *The Good City and the Good Life*. Boston: Houghton Mifflin, 1995.

Kennedy School of Government, Harvard University. "Get Results Through Performance Management: An Open Memorandum to Government Executives." Cambridge, Mass.: Visions of Governance in the 21st Century program, JFK School of Government, Harvard University, 2001.

Kettl, F. D. "What's Next." *Government Executive*, Jan. 2001, pp. 21–26.

Kitfield, J. "Covert Counterattack." *National Journal*, Sept. 16, 2000, pp. 2858–2865.

Kitfield, J. "Anti-Terror Alliance." *Government Executive*, Feb. 2001, pp. 51–59.

Kohn, A. *No Contest: The Case Against Competition*. Boston: Houghton Mifflin, 1986.

Kouzes, J. M., and Posner, B. Z. *The Leadership Challenge: How to Get Extraordinary Things Done in Organizations*. San Francisco: Jossey-Bass, 1987.

Kouzes, J. M., and Posner, B. Z. *Credibility: How Leaders Gain and Lose It, and Why People Demand It*. San Francisco: Jossey-Bass, 1993.

Labovitz, G., and Rosansky, V. *The Power of Alignment: How Great Companies Stay Centered and Accomplish Extraordinary Things*. New York: Wiley, 1997.

Lewin, K. *Field Theory in Social Science*. Chicago: University of Chicago Press, 1951.

Light, P. C. "Clout Is Key; Post Lacks It." *USA Today*, Oct. 9, 2001a, p. 14A.

Light, P. C. "Homeland Security." Interview on *Morning Edition*, National Public Radio, Oct. 2, 2001b.

Linden, R. M. *Seamless Government: A Practical Guide to Re-Engineering in the Public Sector*. San Francisco: Jossey-Bass, 1994.

Linden, R. M. *Workbook for Seamless Government: A Hands-On Guide to Implementing Organizational Change*. San Francisco: Jossey-Bass, 1998.

Lipman-Blumen, J. "The Age of Connective Leadership." *Leader to Leader*, 2000, *17*, 39–45.

Lipnack, J., and Stamps, J. *The Teamnet Factor: Bringing the Power of Boundary Crossing into the Heart of Your Business*. Essex Junction, Vt.: Wright, 1993.

Lipnack, J., and Stamps, J. *Virtual Teams: Reaching Across Space, Time and Organizations with Technology*. New York: Wiley, 1997.

Loeb, V. "USPS, FedEx in 'Alliance' Talks." *Washington Post*, Sept. 7, 2000, p. A23.

Loescher, M. S., Schroeder, C., and Thomas, C. W. *Proteus: Insights from 2020*. Hendersonville, N.C.: Copernicus Institute Press, 2000.

Lucy, W. *Close to Power: Setting Priorities with Elected Officials*. Chicago: American Planning Association, 1988.

Lucy, W., and Phillips, D. *Confronting Suburban Decline*. Washington, D.C.: Highland Press, 2000.

Marshall, T.S.T. "Partnering for Census 2000." *Public Manager,* Winter 2000–2001, pp. 11–13.

Martin, D. "Guys, Dolls and Winning the War on Crime." *New York Times,* Aug. 12, 2001, p. WK 4.

Mathis, J. "Oates: Local Police Underused in Intelligence." *Ann Arbor News,* Oct. 14, 2001, pp. B1–B2.

Mattesich, P. W., and Monsey, B. R. *Collaboration: What Makes It Work—A Review of Research Literature on Factors Influencing Successful Collaboration.* St. Paul, Minn.: Amherst H. Wilder Foundation, 1992.

McClelland, D. C. "Toward a Theory of Motive Acquisition." *American Psychologist,* 1965, *20*(5), 321–333.

McClelland, D. C. *Power: The Inner Experience.* New York: Irvington, 1975.

McClelland, D. C., and Burnham, D. H. "Power Is the Great Motivator." *Harvard Business Review,* Mar.-Apr. 1976, pp. 100–110.

McGee, J. "In Federal Law Enforcement, 'All the Walls Are Down.'" *Washington Post,* Oct. 14, 2001, p. A16.

McGehee, T. "The Changing Nature of Work." *Leader to Leader,* 2001, *21,* 45–55.

McKenna, R. *Real Time.* Boston: Harvard Business School Press, 1997.

Metzenbaum, S. H. "Measurement That Matters: Cleaning Up the Charles River." Regulatory Policy Program Working Paper RPP-2001–05. Cambridge, Mass.: Kennedy School of Government, Harvard University, 2001.

Montgomery County Collaboration Council for Children, Youth & Families. "The Children's Agenda: Boldly Fitting the Pieces Together." Montgomery County, Md.: Montgomery County Collaboration Council for Children, Youth & Families, 1998.

Morley, E., Vinson, E., and Hatry, H. P. *Outcome Measurement in Nonprofit Organizations: Current Practices and Recommendations.* Washington, D.C.: Independent Sector and Urban Institute, 2001.

Mosk, M. "Baltimore Mayor's Rising Profile." *Washington Post,* Oct. 15, 2001, pp. B1, B5.

Nock, S. L. "Turn-Taking as Rational Behavior." *Social Science Research,* 1998, *27,* 235–244.

Novak, R. D. "Same Old FBI." *Washington Post,* Oct. 25, 2001, p. A31.

O'Malley, M. "CitiStat." Presentation to *Governing Magazine* Conference in Baltimore, Oct. 11, 2001.

O'Neill, R. J., Jr. "Forces of Change in the Public Sector." *Public Manager,* Fall 2000, pp. 4–5.

"Orpheus Chamber Orchestra." *CBS-TV Sunday Morning,* Apr. 26, 1987.

Orthner, D., Cole, G., and Ehrlich, R. *Smart Start Collaboration Network Analysis Report*. Chapel Hill: School of Social Work, University of North Carolina, 1998.

Osborne, D., and Gaebler, T. *Reinventing Government: How the Entrepreneurial Spirit Is Transforming the Public Sector*. Boston: Addison-Wesley, 1992.

Osborne, D., and Plastrik, P. *Banishing Bureaucracy: The Five Strategies for Reinventing Government*. New York: Perseus, 1997.

Osborne, D., and Plastrik, P. *The Reinventor's Fieldbook: Tools for Transforming Your Government*. San Francisco: Jossey-Bass, 2000.

Owen, H. *Open Space Technology: A Users' Guide*. (2nd ed.) San Francisco: Berrett-Koehler, 1997.

Pascale, R. T. *Managing on the Edge*. New York: Simon & Schuster, 1990.

Peirce, N. R., and Johnson, C. *Boundary Crossers: Community Leadership for a Global Age*. College Park, Md.: Burns Academy of Leadership Press, 1997.

Peirce, N. R., with Johnson, C. W., and Hall, J. S. *Citistates: How Urban America Can Prosper in a Competitive World*. Washington, D.C.: Seven Locks Press, 1993.

Perlman, E. "Playing Together." *Governing*, Aug. 2001, pp. 40–48.

Peters, T. J., and Waterman, R. H., Jr. *In Search of Excellence: Lessons from America's Best-Run Companies*. New York: HarperCollins, 1982.

Pfeffer, J., and Sutton, R. I. *The Knowing-Doing Gap: How Smart Companies Turn Knowledge into Action*. Boston: Harvard Business School Press, 2000.

Pool, R. "When Failure Is Not an Option." *Technology Review*, July 1997, pp. 38–45.

Potapchuk, W. R., Crocker, J., and Schechter, W. H., Jr. *Systems Reform and Local Government: Improving Outcomes for Children, Families, and Neighborhoods*. Washington, D.C.: Program for Community Problem Solving, 1997.

Putnam, R. *Bowling Alone: The Collapse and Revival of American Community*. New York: Simon & Schuster, 2000.

Raley, G. A. *The New Community Collaboration Manual*. Washington, D.C.: National Assembly of National Voluntary Health and Social Welfare Organizations, 1997.

Schaffer, R., and Thomson, H. "Successful Change Programs Begin with Results." *Harvard Business Review*, Jan.-Feb. 1992, pp. 80–89.

Schein, E. H. *Organizational Culture and Leadership: A Dynamic View*. San Francisco: Jossey-Bass, 1985.

Schlesinger, A. M., Jr. *The Disuniting of America: Reflections on a Multicultural Society*. New York: Norton, 1991.

Scholtes, P. R., Joiner, B. L., and Streibel, B. J. *The Team Handbook*. (2nd ed.) Madison, Wis.: Oriel, 1996.

Schorr, L. *Common Purpose: Strengthening Families and Neighborhoods to Rebuild America*. New York: Anchor Books, 1997.

Schulte, B., and Keating, D. "Poverty Determines Pupils' Performance." *Washington Post*, Sept. 2, 2001, pp. A1, A12.

Schumacher, E. F. *Guide for the Perplexed*. London: Trinity Press, 1977.

Schwarz, R. M. *The Skilled Facilitator: Practical Wisdom for Developing Effective Groups*. San Francisco: Jossey-Bass, 1994.

Seifter, H. *Leadership Ensemble: Lessons in Collaborative Management from the World's Only Conductorless Orchestra*. New York: Times Books, 2001.

Shrage, M. *Shared Minds: The New Technologies of Collaboration*. New York: Random House, 1990.

Shore, B. *The Cathedral Within*. New York: Random House, 1999.

Simmons, A. *The Story Factor*. Cambridge, Mass.: Perseus, 2001.

Simpson, M. Interview on NPR's *Morning Edition*, Sept. 11, 2000.

*Smart Start Collaboration Network Analysis Report*. Chapter Hill: Frank Porter Graham Child Development Center, University of North Carolina, 2000.

Snow, D. "What Are We Talking About?" *Chronicle of Community*, 1999, 3(3), 33–37.

Spock, B. *Baby and Child Care*. New York: Meredith Press, 1945.

Stewart, T. A. "The Search for the Organization of Tomorrow." *Fortune*, May 18, 1992, pp. 92–98.

Stewart, T. A. "Mapping Corporate Brainpower." *Fortune*, Oct. 30, 1995, pp. 209–212.

Stewart, T. A. *Intellectual Capital: The New Wealth of Organizations*. New York: Doubleday, 1997.

Swope, C. "Restless for Results." *Governing*, Apr. 2001, pp. 20–23.

Tannen, D. *You Just Don't Understand: Women and Men in Conversation*. New York: Ballantine Books, 1990.

Tannen, D. *Talking from 9 to 5: Women and Men in the Workplace: Language, Sex and Power*. New York: Morrow, 1995.

Tischler, L. "Seven Strategies for Successful Alliances." In *Fast Company Electronic Newsletter*, Dec. 2001. [http://www.fastcompany.com].

Tocqueville, A. de. *Democracy in America*. (R. D. Heffner, ed.). New York: Mentor Books, 1956. (Originally published 1835.)

Trojanowicz, R., and Bucqueroux, B. *Community Policing: A Contemporary Perspective*. Cincinnati, Ohio: Anderson, 1990.

Tully, S. "The Modular Corporation." *Fortune*, Feb. 8, 1993, pp. 106–114.

U.S. Forest Service National Collaborative Stewardship Team. *Collaborative Stewardship Within the Forest Service*. Washington, D.C.: U.S. Forest Service, Apr. 2000.

Untermeyer, L. (ed.). *Modern American Poetry: An Introduction*. New York: Harcourt, 1919, 81–83.

Walker, C. *Partnership for Parks: Lessons from the Lila Wallace-Reader's Digest Urban Parks Program*. Washington, D.C.: Urban Institute, 1999.

Walters, J. "Save Us from the States!" *Governing*, June 2001, pp. 20–27.

Walton, M. *Deming Management at Work*. New York: Putnam, 1990.

Weber, R. C. "The Group: A Cycle from Birth to Death." In L. Porter and B. Mohr (eds.), *NTL Reading Book for Human Relations Training*. (7th ed.) Alexandria, Va.: National Institute for Applied Behavioral Science, 1982.

Weick, K., and Sutcliffe, K., with Obstfeld, D. "High Reliability: The Power of Mindfulness." *Leader to Leader*, 2000, *17*, 33–38.

Winer, M., and Ray, K. *Collaboration Handbook: Creating, Sustaining, and Enjoying the Journey*. St. Paul, Minn.: Amherst H. Wilder Foundation, 1997.

Wondolleck, J., and Yaffee, S. L. *Making Collaboration Work: Lessons from Innovation in Natural Resource Management*. Washington, D.C.: Island Press, 2000.

Zakaria, F. "Globalization: What's in It for You?" Talk delivered at the Chautauqua Institution, Chautauqua, New York, Aug. 9, 2001a.

Zakaria, F. "The Myth of the Super-CEO." *Newsweek*, Sept. 3, 2001b, p. 33.

# Index

Shared purpose: as element of basics, 74–76; identifying, 75–76; in JNET example, 70. *See also* Purpose

Shore, B., 95

Short, C., 146, 147, 149, 150, 151, 152, 153, 158, 161, 162, 203, 220

Shrage, M., 37

Shriver, M., 148

Simpson, M., 95

*The Skilled Facilitator* (Schwarz), 84

Slaughter, J., 191

Smart Growth program, University of Maryland, 280–281

Smart Start, 85–86, 148, 195, 281

Snow, D., 7

Social epidemics, 232–233

Society, characteristics of, obstructing collaboration, 48–52

Somerville, I., 11

Spock, B., 17

Stakeholders, involving, as strategy for creating constituencies, 139

Stettinius, W., 11–12

Stewart, T. A., 8

Stone, R., 100

Stories, as technique for forming and sustaining relationships, 100

Strategic thinking, 158–160

Strategies: for beginning organizational change, 225–230; for creating constituency for collaboration, 131–143; for creating line of sight, 116–117; for creating sense of high stakes, 113–125; for developing sense of urgency, 117–119; for forming and sustaining relationships, 95–105; for sustaining collaborative culture in organizations, 231–237

Streamlined Sales Tax Project, 5, 193

Strengths, taking advantage of, 189–192

Stripling, B., 91

Subin, M., 146, 162

Success, visible signs of, as strategy for creating constituency, 132–135

Sun, D., 200

Sutton, R. I., xvii, 165, 200

Sweeney, B., 158–160, 161, 162–163, 220

Symbols: for branding, 104; to create constituencies, 136–139

Systems level, hurdles to collaboration at, 52–55

**T**

Techniques. *See* Strategies

Technology, as reason for current interest in collaboration, 15

Tedco, 5

Termination, of collaboration alliance, 175–176

Thinking: political, as strategy for creating constituencies, 141–143, 264–266; strategic, by collaborative leaders, 158–160

Thomas, J. W., 137

Thomas, M. W., 133, 134, 141–142

Thompson, J., 223, 229

Thompson, T., 5

Thomson, H., 81

Time: pace of collaborative project, 258–259; scheduling, for forming and sustaining relationships, 101–102

*The Tipping Point* (Gladwell), 232

Tischler, L., 94

Tocqueville, A. de, 49

Transparency, as helping create open process, 84

Treasure Valley Partnership (ID), 153, 281

Trust: developing, in JNET example, 65–66; how to build, 261–262; lack of, as hurdle to collaboration, 41–42

Trusting relationships. *See* Relationships

Turf concerns, as hurdle to collaboration, 42–43

**U**

University of Maryland, Smart Growth program of, 280–281